FOOD LOVERS'
GUIDE TO
ORLANDO

FOOD LOVERS'
GUIDE TO
ORLANDO

The Best Restaurants, Markets & Local Culinary Offerings

1st Edition

Ricky Ly

Guilford, Connecticut

Copyright © 2013 Morris Book Publishing, LLC

Editor: Amy Lyons
Project Editor: Lauren Brancato
Layout Artist: Mary Ballachino
Text Design: Sheryl Kober
Illustrations by Jill Butler with additional art by Carleen Moira Powell and MaryAnn Dubé
Maps: Melissa Baker © Morris Book Publishing, LLC

ISBN 978-0-7627-8116-4

Printed in the United States of America
10 9 8 7 6 5 4 3 2 1

All the information in this guidebook is subject to change. We recommend that you call ahead to obtain current information before traveling.

Contents

Introduction: Orlando—The City Beautiful, 1

How to Use This Book, 3

Restaurant Price Key, 4

Keeping Up with Orlando Food News, 4

Local Food Bloggers, 6

Orlando Area Farmers' Markets, 9

The "Best of Orlando," 13

Orlando Downtown, 15

Best of the Neighborhood, 16

Foodie Faves, 20

Specialty Stores, Markets & Producers, 37

Winter Park, 41

Best of the Neighborhood, 42

Foodie Faves, 49

Specialty Stores, Markets & Producers, 75

Central Orlando, 80

    Greater Central Orlando, 80

    Mills 50 District, 87

    The Milk District, 105

    Ivanhoe Village, 108

    College Park, 111

    Audubon Park Garden District, 116

Universal/International Drive, 122

    Best of the Neighborhood, 123

    Foodie Faves, 126

    Specialty Stores, Markets & Producers, 142

Restaurant Row/Sand Lake Road, 143

    Best of the Neighborhood, 143

    Foodie Faves, 146

    Specialty Stores, Markets & Producers, 155

Disney/Lake Buena Vista, 156

    Best of the Neighborhood, 156

    Foodie Faves, 160

North Orlando, 168

      Best of the Neighborhood, 168

      Foodie Faves, 172

      Specialty Stores, Markets & Producers, 185

West Orlando, 188

      Best of the Neighborhood, 189

      Foodie Faves, 192

      Specialty Stores, Markets & Producers, 198

East Orlando, 200

      Best of the Neighborhood, 201

      Foodie Faves, 205

      Specialty Stores, Markets & Producers, 212

South Orlando, 214

      Best of the Neighborhood, 214

      Foodie Faves, 217

      Specialty Stores, Markets & Producers, 224

Food Trucks, 226

Recipes, 235

Le Coq au Vin's Coquille St. Jacques
(Chef Reimund Pitz of Le Coq au Vin), 238

Veal Sweetbreads (Chef James Petrakis of The Ravenous Pig), 240

Julie Petrakis's Crème Caramel
(Chef Julie Petrakis of The Ravenous Pig), 242

Honey Earl Grey Tuile Cookies
(Chef Julie Petrakis of The Ravenous Pig), 244

The Original Gin & Jam (Larry Foor of The Ravenous Pig), 245

Slow-Roasted Jerk-Spiced Local Pork
(Chef Hari Pulapaka of Cress Restaurant), 246

Glazed Duck (Chef Brandon McGlamery of Luma on Park), 248

Farro Salad with Corn, Tomato, Basil, and Goat Cheese Bruschetta
(Chef Brandon McGlamery of Prato), 250

The Rio Cocktail (Jeremy Crittenden of Luma), 251

The Cetriolo Cocktail (David Arnold of Prato), 252

Lake Meadow Green Goddess–Stuffed Eggs
(Chef Kathleen Blake of The Rusty Spoon and Pine Twenty2), 253

Waterkist Meets Lake Meadow Bloody Mary
(Chef Kathleen Blake of The Rusty Spoon and Pine Twenty2), 255

Tuna Tataki (Chef Chau Trinh of Sushi Pop Seafood and Chops), 256

Sautéed Garlic Edamame
(Chef Chau Trinh of Sushi Pop Seafood and Chops), 257

Quinoa Salad (Chef Collette Haw of Barnie's CoffeeKitchen), 258

Smoked Salmon Tartine
(Chef Collette Haw of Barnie's CoffeeKitchen), 259

4Rivers Bacon-Wrapped Jalapeños (Chef John Rivers of
4Rivers Smokehouse), 260

Cowboy Steak by Cowboy Kitchen (a new concept launched
by Chef John Rivers of 4Rivers Steakhouse), 261

Coca-Cola & Potato Chip Cupcake (The Sweet Shop at
4Rivers Smokehouse), 262

Honey Walnut Shrimp (Tony and Kathy Chen of Imperial Dynasty), 264

Grilled Blue Cheese–Crusted Filet (Executive Chef Michael Rumplik of
Rosen Center Hotels), 265

"A Short Rib by Any Other Name . . . Still Tastes Delicious"
(Chef Bryce Balluff of Fork in the Road Food Truck), 267

Crystallized Ginger Olive Oil Cupcakes with Lime Buttercream, Opal
Basil, Mint, and Lime Zest (Chef Hollis Wilder of Sweet! by Good
Golly Miss Holly), 270

Orange Cream Dream Cupcake (The Yum Yum Cupcake Truck), 272

Fresh Fruit 'n' Nut Salad with Citrus Goat Cheese Dressing
(Julie Fagan of PBFingers.com), 274

Blood Orange Tofu Cheesecake (Kiran and Tarun Srivastava of
KiranTarun.com), 276

Citrusy Champagne Sangria (Kiran and Tarun Srivastava of
KiranTarun.com), 278

Florida Seafood Pasta in a White Wine Sauce
(Julie Deily of TheLittleKitchen.net), 279

Strawberry Sangria (Aggie Goodman of AggiesKitchen.com), 281

Grandma's Potato Salad (Katie Jasiewicz of KatiesCucina.com), 282

Lump Crab–Stuffed Florida Avocado (Chef Tony Adams of
Big Wheel Food Truck), 283

Spinach Empanada (Chef Gabrielle Arnold of La Empanada
Food Truck), 285

Grilled Swordfish with Heirloom Tomatoes (Chef Dawn Viola), 287

Appendices

Appendix A: Orlando Eateries by Cuisine, 289

Appendix B: Food Events, 298

Index, 312

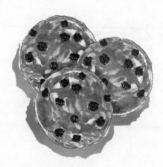

About the Author

Ricky Ly is the food writer for Tasty Chomps! (tastychomps.com), a food and restaurant website dedicated to finding culinary adventures throughout Orlando as well as journeys and foodie discoveries overseas.

Born and raised in West Palm Beach, Florida, he developed his passion for food and adventures very early on, instilled by his Vietnamese and Chinese immigrant parents. His first memories were of pork belly and hard-boiled egg dishes in the late afternoons and steaming dim sum plates of sweet and slurpy shrimp rice paste and dumplings on Saturday mornings. In 2003 he moved away to attend the University of Central Florida in Orlando, where among other things, he graduated with a bachelor's degree in civil engineering and wrote for the university's student newspaper, the *Central Florida Future*.

He currently resides in Orlando, working by day as a civil engineer and writing by night as he continues his lifelong quest to find great eats in all sorts of nooks and crannies of the world. TastyChomps .com recently received awards from the *Orlando Sentinel* and was featured on Zagat's *Fork and Tell*. You can follow him online on twitter at @tastychomps and on Facebook at facebook.com/tastychomps.

Acknowledgments

To my parents, Hung and Nga Ly, who taught me love and compassion for all things, and my sisters, Christina and Crystal, for inspiring me to be a better brother. To my best friend and the love of my life, May Wong, for being the foundation to my soul and for being there each step of the way. Thank you.

Thank you to my friends and family for their support through this process. A big thank-you to Pearleen and Al Buchala of Megayummo.com for their companionship along this journey. Thank you to all the wonderful chefs, bloggers, and food lovers everywhere for being a part of this book. Also, thank you to my editor, Amy Lyons, for believing in me.

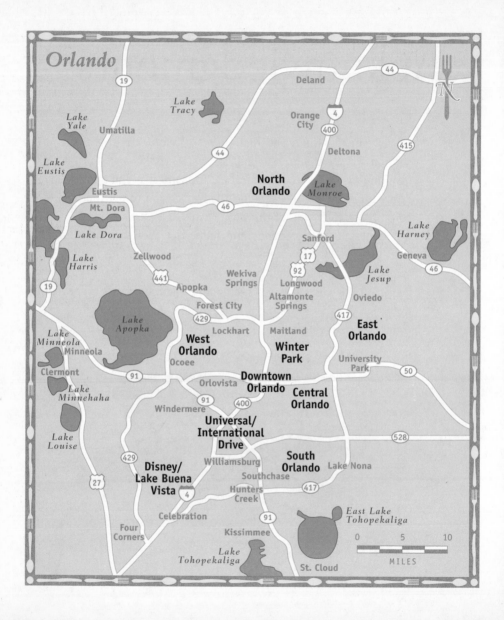

Orlando

19

Lake Tracy

Deland

44

Lake Yale

Umatilla

Orange City

4

400

Lake Eustis

44

Deltona

415

Eustis

North Orlando

Lake Monroe

Mt. Dora

46

Lake Dora

Sanford

Lake Harney

Zellwood

17

Geneva

46

Lake Harris

441

Wekiva Springs

92

Longwood

Lake Jesup

19

Apopka

Forest City

Altamonte Springs

Oviedo

Lake Apopka

429

Lockhart

Maitland

417

East Orlando

Lake Minneola

Minneola

West Orlando

Winter Park

Clermont

91

Ocoee

University Park

50

Lake Minnehaha

Orlovista

Downtown Orlando

91

91

400

Central Orlando

Windermere

Lake Louise

Universal/ International Drive

528

429

Williamsburg

South Orlando

Lake Nona

Disney/ Lake Buena Vista

Southchase

417

4

Hunters Creek

East Lake Tohopekaliga

27

Celebration

0   5   10

Four Corners

91

Kissimmee

MILES

Lake Tohopekaliga

St. Cloud

Introduction: Orlando—The City Beautiful

Orlando, the City Beautiful, was settled first by cattle ranchers in the 1800s and later became a hub for the growing Florida citrus industry. It wasn't until 1965, when a man named Walt Disney came secretly to the area and bought some nearby swampland for what would later become Walt Disney World, that Orlando began to grow into a true city. In addition to Walt Disney World Resort, other world-class tourism destinations have sprung up, including Universal Orlando Resort (which recently opened its Wizarding World of Harry Potter) and SeaWorld Orlando. Last year alone, Visit Orlando (Orlando's official convention and tourism bureau) reported over 55 million visitors to the region, vastly outnumbering the 1 million or so people who call greater Orlando their permanent home and making tourism one of the largest factors of the local economy.

Though its roots are humble, Orlando has great aspirations: a new multimillion-dollar structure, the Amway Arena, was just built to house the Orlando Magic basketball team; cutting-edge medical research facilities and hospitals are building up in the Lake Nona area, dubbed the new "Medical City"; and the University of Central Florida has grown to become the third-largest university in America, surrounded by a notable simulations and defense industry in the nearby Central Florida Research Park.

Because of its strong tourism industry, Orlando is often stereotyped as a place known for its many chain restaurants. I think chain restaurants have their place: when you are away from home you sometimes want the consistency and comfort of knowing what you're getting each time. Darden Restaurants is headquartered here; the company's portfolio includes not only everyday chains such as Olive Garden, Red Lobster, and LongHorn Steakhouse, but also more high-end chains, such as The Capital Grille and Seasons 52.

But this book isn't about the myriad usual suspects, the chains that dot the Orlando foodie landscape like the hundreds of lakes throughout central Florida. It's about the neighborhoods, the chef-owners, and the cooks and industry workers who come together to bring you a dish made from their hearts and minds.

The local food culture is growing each day in Orlando with groups such as Slow Food Orlando tirelessly promoting and encouraging the slow food movement, working to bring more food that's good for the people who eat it, good for the people who grow it, and good for the planet. Chefs are using more and more local, farm-fresh, and sustainable foods to make their dishes. From pockets of Vietnamese enclaves and a growing "Little Brazil" near International Drive, to growing farmers' markets that feature local, all-natural foods and a huge food-truck scene, Orlando is becoming more and more of a food lover's delight every day.

Food Lovers' Guide to Orlando is separated into neighborhood chapters, and within each you'll find these categories:

Best of the Neighborhood

Best of the Neighborhood represents the top choices in the area in terms of dining experience and cuisine, showcasing Orlando's finest restaurants.

Foodie Faves

This category is broad enough to include any restaurant we think you should check out and the ones favored by lovers of good food. That could be an old standby, or a new spot that's exciting even to locals.

Specialty Stores, Markets & Producers

Many types of food shops—from the well-edited locavore grocery store to butchers and bread makers—warrant a visit.

Recipes

At the end of the book, you'll find a whole chapter on recipes. Many of these are from the city's most famous artisan food entrepreneurs.

Restaurant Price Key

The prices and rates listed in this guidebook were confirmed at press time. We recommend, however, that you call establishments to obtain current information before traveling. Dollar signs are provided only for restaurants that offer full meals and some sort of seating (or operate out of a truck). All restaurant prices are based on the following general guidelines for an appetizer, entree, and dessert for one person (using the most common prices) before drinks, tax, and tip:

Price Code

$	Less than $10
$$	$10 to $15
$$$	$16 to $30
$$$$	More than $30

Keeping Up with Orlando Food News

The world of food in Orlando is constantly changing and evolving. To find out the latest news on food events and restaurant reviews, check out these local resources at their websites or in print.

Orlando News & Magazines

Heather McPherson is the food editor, restaurant reviewer, and a multimedia journalist for the *Orlando Sentinel*. She oversees the weekly Cooking & Eating section, writes four weekly columns (food and culture, restaurant recipes, and restaurant reviews), and provides daily content for orlandosentinel.com, her blog orlandosentinel.com/thedish, and Twitter @os_thedish.

Orlando Weekly food editor **Jessica Bryce Young** and food critics **Faiyaz Kara** and **Holly Kapher** bring local restaurant reviews each week in the local, quirky alternative news weekly (orlandoweekly.com).

Orlando magazine's respected restaurant critic, **Joseph Hayes,** writes the food review and columns monthly for the magazine (orlandomagazine.com).

Scott Joseph has been reviewing restaurants for more than 23 years, first as food critic at the *Orlando Sentinel* and now as publisher of the online Scott Joseph's Orlando Restaurant Guide. In addition to the website, he also publishes a paperback guide and recently released a smartphone app version. Joseph is a regional judge for the prestigious James Beard Foundation Awards and has been named to the "50 Most Powerful People" list in *Orlando* magazine (scottjosephorlando.com).

Edible Orlando magazine is one of 70 Edible Communities magazines that create editorially rich, community-based, local-foods publications throughout the US and Canada. Edibles connect consumers with family farmers, growers, chefs, and food artisans of all kinds and believe that every person has the right to affordable, fresh, healthful food on a daily basis and that knowing where our food comes from is a powerful thing (edibleorlando.com).

Orlando Business Journal brings late-breaking and top business news stories from all over Orlando, and online blogs, helmed by **Anjali Fluker,** have a particular eye on the Orlando restaurant scene (bizjournals.com/orlando).

Writer **Rona Gindin** keeps readers up to date on Orlando, national, and international restaurant and travel news. Check her blog for Orlando dining specials, travel deals, contests, promotions, and menu updates and her dining features in *Orlando Home & Leisure* magazine (ronagindin.com).

Local Food Bloggers

Food bloggers are tweeting, writing, and blogging pretty much daily about the foodie scene in Orlando. Stay up to date with these wonderful resources. Most of the local bloggers are alumni of the University of Central Florida in Orlando who spend their off-work hours scouring the central Florida landscape for foodie finds and news.

MegaYummo.com—Founded by Pearleen and Al Buchala, this food blog was one of the first in Orlando and features local Orlando restaurants, events, and craft beer. Their food photography is also first-rate and the blog provides insightful tidbits about Orlando's growing local food culture.

Droolius.com—Founded by Julius Mayo Jr., Droolius is a food blog with drool-worthy photography depicting food at some of the most delicious places to eat, in hopes of feeding your visual appetite. Currently based in Orlando, Mayo travels locally and around the nation to sample great food and take enticing food photos.

EatLocalOrlando.com—Founded by Chris Roberts, this local Orlando food blog focuses on finding new restaurants in the Orlando area and reviewing them. Roberts is also an avid fan of the local Orlando food-truck movement and has an Orlando food trucks guide on his blog.

Forkful.net—Founded by Marilyn Torres, Forkful is an Orlando-based resource to help locals and visitors alike navigate the Central Florida food scene, whether to satiate a craving, mark an occasion, or just share a pint. Torres is an alumna of the University of Central Florida with a bachelor of arts degree in creative writing.

TastyChomps.com—My food and restaurant blog is dedicated to finding culinary adventures throughout central Florida and around the world with news, reviews, events, and more. What started as a hobby to find and show off the local gems in Orlando has evolved into an award-winning resource featured in some of the best newspapers and magazines in Orlando today. It set the foundation for *Food Lovers' Guide to Orlando* and is one of my proudest personal achievements.

Community Resources

Slow Food Orlando is the local chapter of Slow Food USA, which seeks to bring food that is good, clean, and fair to central Florida. Their mission envisions a future food system based on the principles of high quality and taste, environmental sustainability, and social justice. The organization seeks to catalyze a broad cultural shift away from the destructive effects of an industrial food system and fast life—and toward the regenerative cultural, social, and economic benefits of a sustainable food system, regional food traditions, the pleasures of the table, and a slower and more harmonious rhythm of life. They host various events throughout the year, such as Eat Local Week in the fall and smaller events featuring local farms and producers. Visit slowfoodorlando.org and facebook.com/slowfoodorlando.

Online Resources

Chowhound.com has a wonderful and active Florida board composed of fellow foodies who often help others plan their culinary visits to Orlando as well as highlight some unique finds in the local food scene (chowhound.chow.com/boards/10).

Yelp.com has a huge online community with user reviews on everything from shops to restaurants. The site organizes and participates in events throughout the Orlando community offline as well. It's nice to use to gauge what your experience may be like from reading the various reviews on the establishment and making your own judgment.

Urbanspoon.com is a user-driven, dedicated restaurant review site featuring critics, bloggers, and reviewers. Menus, photos, addresses, directions, and pretty much everything you need to know to get to the restaurant can be found on Urbanspoon. The smartphone app is also particularly helpful when you are trying to find out about restaurants in your vicinity (urbanspoon.com/c/26/orlando-restaurants.html).

Orlando Area Farmers' Markets

Audubon Park Community Market, Stardust Coffee and Shag'd parking lot at 1842 E. Winter Park Rd., Orlando, FL; apmarket.wordpress.com; Mon 6 to 10 p.m. The Audubon Park Community Market is a family-friendly weekly gathering of growers, ranchers, fishermen, chefs, artists, handi-crafters, musicians, and neighbors. Since 2009 the Audubon Park Market has been central Florida's source for the best selection of local food, from freshly picked produce to fully prepared meals.

College Park Farmers' Market, Infusion Tea parking lot at 1600 Edgewater Dr., Orlando, FL; facebook.com/collegepark farmersmarket; Thurs 5 to 9 p.m. At the

College Park Farmers' Market the focus is all local, from produce and other farm goods to prepared foods, grocery items, and meals. The market brings you food that is grown, raised, caught, or carefully made right here in Florida, emphasizing freshness and encouraging sustainable practices.

Winter Garden Farmers' Market, W. Plant Street and S. Highland Avenue in Historic Winter Garden at the Winter Garden Pavillion, Winter Garden, FL; wintergardenfarmers market.com; Sat 9 a.m. to 2 p.m. Held beneath a large pavilion structure in the heart of Winter Garden, this popular farmers' market on the west side of Orlando brings together families and farmers each week with fresh, local produce, artisanal breads, honey, craft goods, and more.

Winter Park Farmers' Market, 200 W. New England Ave., Winter Park, FL; cityofwinterpark.org; Sat 7 a.m. to 1 p.m. Very popular farmers' market that provides fine produce, plants, baked goods, local honey, crepes, orchids, bagels, and much more.

City of Maitland Farmers' Market, Lake Lily in Maitland, FL; itsmymaitland.com; Sun 9 a.m. to 2 p.m. Located at beautiful Lake Lily, this farmers' market is fun for families and friends who like to stroll by the lake and pick up some local goods and produce.

Downtown Orlando Farmers' Market, Lake Eola Park, Orlando, FL; orlandofarmersmarket.com; Sun 10 a.m. to 4 p.m. This farmers' market, located at iconic Lake Eola, is the only one serving the downtown Orlando community and provides a pleasant place to stop by for a morning stroll or run while picking up pastries, breads, produce, and arts and crafts.

Homegrown Local Food Cooperative, 2310 N. Orange Ave., Orlando, FL; (407) 895-5559; homegrowncoop.org; daily 10 a.m. to 7 p.m. The Homegrown Local Food Cooperative operates as a biweekly buying club in partnership with small and medium Florida farmers and producers, and also sources from bakers and artisans of organic, healthy, vegan, and raw foods within Florida. They provide everything local and organic: vegetables, fruit, fresh-cut herbs, sprouts, freshly baked breads, honey, grass-fed beef, free-range chicken, yogurt and cheese from grass-fed cows and goats, many vegan options (vegan bakeries, local organic tempeh, prepared foods, etc.), free-range eggs, fair-traded teas and coffee, green home products, green garden supplies, bath and body products, and much more. There is also a special online ordering process, which you can find out more about on the website, making it even more convenient to buy local, organic farm-fresh produce and food.

PLACES TO PICK YOUR OWN PRODUCE

Orange County

Beck Brother's Blueberries, 12500 Overstreet Rd., Windermere, FL 34786; (407) 656-5344; facebook.com/pages/Beck-Brothers-blueberries-U-Pick/121170221296165. Pick your own blueberries.

Seminole County

Pappy's Patch U-Pick Strawberries, Florida Ave., Oviedo, FL 32765; (407) 366-8512; facebook.com/pages/Pappys-Patch-U-Pick-Strawberries-Official-Page/349267811756813. Pick your own strawberries in a strawberry patch and pay per pound.

Soggy Acres Pomelo Grove, 100 Tuskawilla Rd., Winter Springs, FL 32708; (407) 443-3808; mjsoileau@mail.ucf.edu.

Sundew Gardens, 2212 Red Ember Rd., Oviedo, FL 32765; (407) 430-2178; sundewgardens@gmail.com; sundewgardens .com; facebook.com/pages/sundew-gardens/300609518579. Sundew uses natural growing practices where you can pick up seasonal Florida garden fresh vegetables, herbs, fruit, and eggs.

U-Pick Blackberries, 500 Snowhill Rd., Geneva, FL 32732; (407) 883-9676. Pick your own fresh blackberries when in season.

The "Best of Orlando"

Best of Local Orlando
Big Wheel Food Truck
Cress Restaurant
K Restaurant
Luma on Park
Prato
Primo by Melissa Kelly
The Ravenous Pig

Best Burgers
The Crooked Spoon
Oblivion Tap Room
The Ravenous Pig
Tap Room at Dubsdread

Best Dim Sum
Chan's Chinese
Golden Lotus
Ming's Bistro
Trey Yuen

Best Latin
Guavate
Padrino's Cuban Bistro
Rice and Beans Latina Cocina

Best Sushi
Mikado Sushi
Nagoya Sushi
Shin Sushi
Sushi Pop

Best Pizza
Del Dio's Pizza
Goodfella's Pizza
Pizzeria Valdiano

Best Steaks
A Land Remembered
Bull & Bear
The Capital Grille
Shula's Steakhouse

Best Vietnamese
Lac Viet
Pho 88
Pho Hoa
Pho Vinh

Best Fine Dining
Chatham's Place

The Venetian Room
Victoria and Albert's

Best for Group/Business Gatherings
Chatham's Place
Hollerbach's Willow Tree Cafe
The Ravenous Pig
Texas De Brazil
Vines Grille and Wine Bar

Best for the Budget Foodie
Banh Mi Nha Trang
Border Grill
The Donut King
Mediterranean Deli
Pao Gostoso
Tako Cheena
Tasty Wok
Taverna Opa
YaYa's Cuban Cafe

Orlando Downtown

Downtown Orlando has seen an upswing since the recent opening of the multimillion-dollar Amway Center, home of the Orlando Magic NBA basketball team. Surrounding downtown Orlando's skyscrapers and city hall are local bars, lounges, and restaurants that cater to the quintessential city life. In addition to the Amway Center, the CityArts Factory, Saks Comedy Lab, and the Dr. Phillips Performing Arts Center all provide quality entertainment for the citizens and visitors of Orlando.

The Thornton Park neighborhood, located just east of the landmark Lake Eola in downtown Orlando, is home to some of the oldest houses in the area, built in the original Florida "cracker" style with wraparound front porches, shaded by oak trees and brick-lined streets. In the evenings, a short light show begins at Lake Eola's fountain with some prerecorded swing-band music playing in the background. It's not uncommon to see joggers, dog-walkers, men in business suits, and the homeless, all walking around Lake Eola side by side in the late afternoon. The neighborhood is bordered by Washington Street, Summerlin Avenue, and Central Boulevard, where visitors can survey nearby shops and restaurants.

The Boheme, 325 S. Orange Ave., Orlando, FL 32801; (407) 313-9000; theboheme.com; Valet and Parking Garage; Modern American; $$$$. One of only a few AAA Four-Diamond restaurants in town, The Boheme inside the Grand Bohemian hotel is one of the classiest venues in downtown Orlando to go all out on that business lunch, romantic dinner, or special occasion. When entering the Grand Bohemian, you walk by the Bösendorfer Lounge, one of Orlando's best hotel bars and best places to sip a martini, and the place where some of the area's hottest jazz musicians perform on weekend evenings. The namesake of the Imperial Grand Bösendorfer piano (one of only two in the world) features a round bar deco-rated in black marble, red stones, and mirror pieces that give the lounge a sultry, romantic feeling. The Boheme features eclectic cuisine, offering classic dishes with a modern twist, such as the cognac lobster bisque or the luscious roasted Chilean sea bass with pecorino crust, boulangerie potatoes, and rock crab minestrone topped with shellfish *anglaise*. Nearly two dozen sparkling wines and Champagnes are perfect starters or accompaniments to a solid catalog of old- and new-world vintages that round out the list. The Boheme also opens early for breakfast—try the poached eggs Boheme served with applewood-smoked bacon, citrus hollandaise, and toasted English muffin or cinnamon Grand Marnier french toast. The Bohemian Sunday Brunch is worthwhile not only for the many dishes featuring charcuterie, snow crab legs, smoked salmon, eggs

Benedict, crab cakes, prime rib at the chef's carving table, Belgian waffles, gourmet omelets, and a delectable dessert display, but also for the live jazz playing in the background.

Kres Chophouse, 17 W. Church St., Orlando, FL 32801; (407) 447-7950; kreschophouse.com; Valet and Parking Garage; Steak House; $$$. Located in the historic Kress building (once housing the five-and-dime retail department store), Kres Chophouse is a swanky, classy restaurant and one of the best in the downtown Orlando area. Inside, the lighting is dim and tall, red velvet–backed booths line the walls. The place is nice for a fancy date night out before hitting the clubs and lounges nearby. Try the featured Kres mixed grill, a huge plate of garlic shrimp, tender filet mignon, and double lamb chops, served with a side of asparagus and three-cheese au gratin.

Pine Twenty2, 22 E. Pine St., Orlando, FL 32801; (407) 574-2160; pine22.com; Parking Garage and Street Parking; Burgers; $$. This counter-service restaurant led by Chef Kathleen Blake (who also co-owns nearby downtown restaurant **The Rusty Spoon** [see p. 18]) features the ultimate create-your-own-burger experience with conscious-choice eating inside a modern, sleek setting. With over 300,000 ways to create your own mouthwatering meaty explosion, made from locally sourced, raised, grown, or produced products, the possibilities are virtually endless for what you can do to your burger to truly "have it your way." The ingredients, when possible, are locally sourced from Palmetto Creek Farm's Hereford pork, Waterkist Farm, Lake Meadow Naturals eggs and chicken, and Deep Creek Ranch beef. There is a decidedly gourmet touch to this atypical burger joint: your sauces include herb aiolis, mango chutney, roasted garlic aioli, or ginger soy glaze among others, and ingredients are listed with little symbols representing which items are house made or locally sourced. If you are indecisive or daunted by the task, as a few of us are, try some of the precreated list of Chef Blake's signature sandwiches and salad bowls. Try the 22 Burger, made with a half pound all-natural, grass-fed beef, sautéed mushrooms, smoked bacon, charred onions, and blue cheese, or the Big Boy BBQ, made with Palmetto Creek pulled pork, onion rings, slaw, and house-made 22 BBQ sauce. Vegetarians can enjoy the experience, too, with the Veggie, a house-made black bean burger with sprouts, avocado, thick-sliced tomato, cucumber, and smoked chipotle aioli sauce. See Chef Kathleen Blake's recipes for **Lake Meadow Green Goddess–Stuffed Eggs** on p. 253 and **Waterkist Meets Lake Meadow Bloody Mary** on p. 255.

The Rusty Spoon, 55 W. Church St.; Orlando, FL 32801; (407) 401-8811; therustyspoon.com; Parking Garage; Gastropub/Modern American; $$$. In the 55 West building in the heart of the Church Street district, The Rusty Spoon is at the forefront of the farm-to-table movement here in Orlando, using locally sourced ingredients from local area farms, such as Lake Meadow Naturals from Ocoee and Waterkist Farms in Winter Park. Rusty Spoon Chef-Owner Kathleen

Blake, formerly of **Primo** (see p. 216), heads the restaurant, changing the menu and ingredients depending on what's in season. The Dirty South is a must-try, made with local snapper from Cape Canaveral, local head-on shrimp, and Cedar Creek clams with tomato and peanuts, all on top of a bed of luscious, creamy Southern grits in a rich shrimp broth. See Chef Kathleen Blake's recipes for **Lake Meadow Green Goddess–Stuffed Eggs** on p. 253 and **Waterkist Meets Lake Meadow Bloody Mary** on p. 255.

Shìn Japanese Cuisine, 803 N. Orange Ave., Orlando, FL 32801; (407) 648-8000; shinsushi.com; Parking Garage and Street Parking; Japanese; $$$. The decor is decidedly modern with a large water fountain sculpture in front with the word *shin* in Japanese (translated as *heart*). The space is not large, maybe fitting 50 people comfortably, but it is intimate and definitely has an urban feel to it. Like works of art, the sushi here at Shin is delicious and fresh, probably some of the freshest in Orlando. Try the specialty *hotate* roll, made with asparagus wrapped with fresh raw scallops from Hokkaido and each individually topped with *yuzu tobiko,* spicy mayo, and shredded peppers, or the shin volcano roll, laid out flat on the plate and made with a California roll topped with a mixture of baked fresh scallops, shrimp, *kanikama, masago,* cream cheese, and spicy mayo. My favorite meals have been *omakase,* or chef's choice of the sashimi platter, where the chef surprises you with various cuts and pieces of the freshest catch of the day.

Amura, 55 W. Church St. Orlando, FL 32801; (407) 316-8500; amura.com; Parking Garage; Sushi/Japanese; $$$. A ridiculously popular sushi spot featuring fanciful *maki* rolls, Amura is nestled in a modern, upscale setting. Rolls can get pricey for what they're worth. Try out the Atom Bomb roll, made with spicy tuna and salmon; the Godzilla roll, made with imitation crab, eel, smoked salmon, avocado, and orange sauce; or the Unforgettable roll, made with spicy tuna, eel, and tempura crunch.

Bento Cafe, 151 S. Orange Ave.; Orlando, FL 32801; (407) 999-8989; bentocafesushi.com; Parking Garage; Asian/Japanese; $$. Originally founded in Gainesville, and a hot spot for students from the University of Florida, Bento Cafe offers an affordable option for those wishing to try good food downtown, featuring pan-Asian-inspired cuisine using traditional wok stir-fry or fire-grilled methods as well as sushi. The decor is a stylish modern blue with technologic, futuristic gray overtones. At Bento Cafe, you can either order at the counter or sit down for full service. A bento is a single-portion takeout or home-packed meal common in Japanese cuisine, having items placed in various segments in a box. At Bento Cafe, boxes come with the main dish, a side of rice, cold noodles, green beans, a small salad, and a tiny finger cake for dessert. One of my favorite entrees is the Korean spicy chicken—creamy, warm, and tenderly fried to perfection. Other tasty options include the teriyaki chicken noodle bowl, the spicy seafood noodle soup, and the chicken katsu bento box. Be sure to try the signature rolls: 151, Orange Avenue, Bali Hai, and Torch, all exclusively offered in Orlando.

Cafe Trastevere, 825 N. Magnolia Ave.; Orlando, FL 32803; (407) 839-0235; cafetrastevere.com; Street Parking; Italian; $$$. Cafe Trastevere is named for the charming medieval neighborhood on the outskirts of Rome, bringing that intimate, romantic setting to Orlando. Located just north of downtown, the restaurant is set in a quaint, old two-story house and features an outdoor patio dining area in the backyard with candlelit tables on terraces overlooking Magnolia Avenue, perfect for the cooler months in central Florida. The delightful menu is devoted to northern and southern Italian traditions, including pasta, gnocchi, fish, chicken, beef, and vegetarian dishes. The creamy crab and corn bisque is a popular starter. Saltimbocca alla Romana (which means "jumps in the mouth'" in Italian), a thinly pounded veal scaloppine with prosciutto, spinach, sage, and Marsala wine sauce, and the eggplant parmigiana are both excellent options for entrees. For dessert, don't miss the tiramisu, one of the best in town, made with ladyfingers dipped in espresso and liqueurs, then layered with mascarpone cheese and zabaglione sauce. Now, that's *amore.*

Suggested Date Night Itineraries!

Date Night Itinerary 1: Downtown Orlando

Grab a few drinks at The Rusty Spoon, walk over to Kres Chophouse for a nice romantic dinner, and then enjoy some wine at Eola Wine Company and dessert at The Dessert Lady. Maybe stroll around Lake Eola after dessert or head to one of the many nightclubs or lounges in downtown Orlando.

Date Night Itinerary 2: Winter Park

Take a stroll down Park Avenue and explore one of the many hidden courtyards along the Avenue. Have dinner at Prato, Bosphorous, or one of the many great restaurants in the area. Explore Rollins College and its unique Spanish missionary architecture or have a seat and charm the night away by chatting on a bench in Central Park.

Date Night Itinerary 3: International Drive

Start off the night with some minigolf at Pirate's Cove, go-karting at Fun Spot, or some video games at Dave and Buster's. Hop on the I-Drive Trolley and find some Shabu-shabu at Hanamizuki or belly dancing at Taverna Opa at Pointe Orlando. Then explore the many entertainment attractions and tourist traps while walking along International Drive.

Cevíche Tapas Bar & Restaurant, 125 W. Church St., Orlando, FL 32801; ceviche.com; (321) 281-8140; Parking Garage; Tapas/ Spanish; $$$. Cevíche, located in historic Church Street Station, serves up Spanish-style tapas, made of small plates perfect for group dining, in a dark and playful atmosphere that features old-world Spanish-Moroccan architecture with decorative mosaic-tiled walls. Live flamenco music emanates from the bar area on week-ends, complete with Spanish guitarists and flamenco dancers in full dress and waving fans. With over 100 dishes on the menu, there are sure to be a few hits and misses. Try the namesake Ceviche de la Casa, a great starter, made with fresh shrimp, scallops, squid, and fish marinated in lemon-lime juice and tossed with fresh tomatoes, onions, peppers, and cilantro. *Rabo de toro* is a dish sure to delight, consisting of oxtail slowly braised in a rich red wine reduction and served with potatoes. The paella *valenciana* is a popular dish big enough to share, made with lobster, scallops, shrimp, clams, squid, mussels, chicken, and mild chorizo sausage simmered with saffron rice. *Patatas bravas,* made of lightly fried potatoes and tossed in a spicy homemade red aioli sauce, is also a hit. For dessert, don't miss the *pudin de la pan,* a bread pudding served with dried fruits and ice cream, or the famous tres leches, a meringue cake with cream and nutmeg.

Citrus Restaurant, 821 N. Orange Ave., Orlando, FL 32801; (407) 373-0622; citrusorlando.com; Parking Garage and Street Parking; Modern American; $$$. This sleek, stylish uptown Orlando res-taurant from Urban Life Management (which also owns **Hue** [see

p. 31] and **Cityfish** [see below] downtown in Thornton Park) features regionally inspired and locally sourced New American cuisine. Set in appropriately dark and light orange and brown hues, Citrus features a beautiful, long bar where guests love to "eat, drink, and be local," with salads, flatbreads, fresh snapper, and chops on the menu. The menu items are creative and playful, such as the shrimp and lobster fritters, served with roasted sweet corn, pineapple mint chutney, and avocado *crema,* or the chimichurri skirt steak with caramelized onion, arugula salad, golden mash, and a side of chimichurri sauce. Citrus rounds out its offerings with a signature dessert: Orange Avenue cake, a sweet orange cake layered with cream cheese icing and topped with mini white chocolate chips.

Cityfish Restaurant, 617 E. Central Blvd., Orlando, FL 32801; (407) 849-9779; cityfishorlando.com; Parking Garage and Street Parking; Seafood; $$. Located just a little way from Lake Eola in Thornton Park, Cityfish brings some coastal fish-shack sensibilities to the neighborhood, brought to you by Urban Life Management group, which also owns **Hue** (see p. 31) a few doors down and **Citrus** (see p. 23) in uptown Orlando. The atmosphere is mostly casual and relaxed with both indoor seating with a full liquor bar and patio seating outdoors. The seafood gumbo is made in house with a certain Cajun-spiced kick to it, a nod from the New Orleans–trained chef. Crispy fried pickles and jalapeño hush puppies also make great starters. Cityfish serves up fresh fish daily done grilled, fried, or Cajun style with smoked bacon succotash, Bliss potatoes, and hush puppies. The lobster roll is made with sweet Maine lobster chilled, lightly dressed, and served on a grilled New England–style bun and served with Old Bay fries and coleslaw. Dozens of West Coast and East Coast oysters are featured on the wall, changing daily and including such great choices as Kumamoto, Blue Point, and Appalachicola. The panko-and-potato-chip-crusted broiled sea scallops entree, served with salt potatoes, hush puppies, and daily vegetable, is always a winner, and so is the fried Oreo sundae for dessert, served with deep-fried Oreos, Blue Bell vanilla ice cream, hot fudge, and whipped cream. On Sunday evenings, the restaurant features a popular all-you-can-eat crab leg special.

The Dessert Lady, 120 W. Church St., Orlando, FL 32801; (407) 999-5696; dessertlady.com; Parking Garage; Desserts; $$. Serving up scrumptious cake slices as big as your head, this dessert hot spot is located at the Cheyenne Saloon in the Church Street Station area of downtown Orlando. While bar hoppers stumble about outside on the brick-laid street and music thumps the night away from nearby clubs, The Dessert Lady is a welcome sanctuary to enjoy your late-night sweet cravings. Don't miss the decadent carrot cake, made with three chunky layers of moist carrot cake, laced with cream cheese icing, and served with creme anglaise and dark rum–soaked raisins, or the chocolate zuccotto cake, a rich mousse cake with a dark and milk chocolate mousse center soaked in amaretto. If you're with a group and can't decide, you can create your own sampler with 4 indulgent half portions of the desserts to share. Enjoy with a glass of ice-cold milk, a rich espresso latte, or if you like, a glass of wine, and savor the view.

Dexter's, 808 E. Washington St., Orlando, FL 32801; (407) 648-2777; dexwine.com; Street Parking; Brunch/American; $$. Dexter's serves up a fun, creative menu that changes monthly, with fresh food and very fair prices. This is a great place to meet up for brunch, lunch, or dinner, so don't flinch when you see the lines out the door. People know a good place to eat when they see it; the crowds are a good indicator, especially for weekend brunch with jazz. Live music plays on Thursday, Friday, and Saturday evenings and local artwork hangs on the walls. For brunch, opt for the Dexter's Benedict, made with poached eggs, spinach, tomatoes, and smoked turkey on toasted french bread, topped with lava mustard hollandaise sauce and served with potato pancakes and fresh sea-

sonal fruit salad. Other popular dishes include the corned beef hash with eggs, made fresh in house with two poached eggs and a side of brioche toast, and the pan-roasted mahimahi and Pepper Jack grits, topped with a Tabasco fried egg and roasted corn and poblano pepper succotash. Don't forget the Bloody Mary, spiced with house-infused vodka and a shrimp cocktail skewer, or one of the plentiful mimosas that come in cranberry, mango, orange, grapefruit, peach, strawberry, and pineapple flavors.

Downtown PourHouse, 20 S. Orange Ave., Orlando, FL 32801; (407) 425-7687; downtownpourhouse.com; Parking Garage and Street Parking; Pub Food; $$. This downtown pub is a wee bit intimate, as it gets wall-to-wall crowded in the evenings with patrons who come to the bar to celebrate after hours. The food here is a step above the typical pub fare, with a slight gourmet flair from Chef Steve Stempel, a graduate of Le Cordon Bleu Academy of Orlando. The menu has quite an impressive list of burgers, cooked to your desired temperature, with toppings including applewood-smoked bacon, portobello, and guava barbecue, among others. Try out the signature Black and Tan, a sweet and hearty burger on a brioche bun with a stout glaze enclosed by fried onion rings and topped with gruyère cheese. The decadent lobster mac 'n' cheese made with seashell pasta is also a perfect item to go with that beer at the bar.

Eola Wine Company, 500 E. Central Blvd., Orlando, FL 32801; (407) 481-9100; eolawinecompany.com; Wine Bar; $$. With over 70 wines by the glass, wine flights, over 30 craft bottled beers, flatbreads, appetizers, and desserts, the Eola Wine Company is one of the best places in town to enjoy some vino. In addition to traditional cheeses and charcuterie to go with your wines, you can also order up the duck confit flatbread topped with caramelized onion, dried fig, and brie, and drizzled with balsamic vinegar, or the local rock shrimp tacos. The establishment also serves brunch, with quiches and bagel sandwiches. Try the Elvis bagel, made with peanut butter, cream cheese, banana, and honey. Additional location: 136 S. Park Ave., Winter Park, FL 32789; (407) 647-9103.

Gino's Pizza & Brew, 120 S. Orange Ave., Orlando, FL 32801; (407) 999-7827; ginospizzaandbrew.com; Parking Garage; Pizza; $. This is a downtown after-clubbing-hours kind of Orlando hot spot. Open late, this pizza joint has hot pizza ready in minutes baked in Bakers Pride ovens—it's no wonder there are lines out the door, with a few other stores a few blocks away. This location is a hole-in-the-wall and a bit narrow. The pizza is decent, especially if you like a nice thick crust. They serve up Napolitano-style pizza and New York Sicilian style, as well as hot and cold subs. Don't miss the garlic knots that come with the pizza.

Graffiti Junktion, 900 E. Washington St., Orlando, FL 32801; (407) 426-9503; graffitijunktion.com; Parking Garage and Street Parking; Burgers; $$. This neighborhood bar and burger joint features a boisterously loud, dive-y atmosphere, as the name suggests, with graffiti-art decorating the walls, large flat-screen televisions showing live sports, and slightly sticky, artfully painted picnic tables inside and a nice patio area outside for seating. Self-styled as an "American Burger Bar," this is one of the better places in Orlando for a big ol' juicy burger. The specialty burgers run with a theme, named after cities around America: the Brotherly Love burger is made Philly style with peppers, onions, mushrooms, and provolone; for cheese lovers there's the Cheese Head burger, served with 4 slices of American cheese inside and out; and then there's the Green Mountain, made with Canadian bacon, fried egg, and cheddar, to name a few. Fried eggs on anything are just glorious. Try the zucchini fries, too, made with long, thin slices of fried zucchini and topped with shavings of Parmesan cheese.

Gringos Locos, 20 E. Washington St., Orlando, FL 32801; (407) 841-5626; eatgringos.com; Parking Garage; Tex-Mex; $. Open till 3 a.m. and later, Gringos Locos is perfect for grabbing fresh Tex-Mex grub after hitting up the bars downtown. Providing friendly counter service in a bit of a dive-y setting, Gringos Locos serves up some creative if inappropriately named dishes, to say the least, though they may be perfectly appropriate for the late-night clientele. Burritos, tacos, chips and queso and salsa, enchiladas—pretty much the standard fare you'd find at any of the fast-casual Tex-Mex iterations that have popped up over the years, but with better and tastier ingredients. Go for the Double D's, a double-decker taco made with queso spread on a soft tortilla wrapped around a crunchy hard shell and then filled with cheese, lettuce, tomato, sour cream, and your choice of protein. Go with the flavorful pork.

Hamburger Mary's Bar & Grille, 110 W. Church St., Orlando, FL 32801; (321) 319-0600; hamburgermarys.com; Parking Garage; Burgers; $. Located off of Church Street in downtown Orlando and only a few blocks away from the new Amway Center, this hamburger haven serves up some of the tastiest and juiciest burgers in the city. The inside of Hamburger Mary's is colored with purples and golds, kind of like visiting your eclectic aunt's living room, complete with soft purple carpeting on the floor. A popular spot in the late evenings downtown, Hamburger Mary's serves up fresh, all-natural half-pound Angus beef burgers along with a full-service bar. Try the Queen Mary burger, made with melted cheddar and Jack cheeses and grilled onions, bacon, and Mary's own special sauce. On some evenings you can check out a drag show here with celebrity female impersonators (check showtimes by calling in).

The Harp and Celt Restaurant and Irish Pub, 25 S. Magnolia Ave., Orlando, FL 32801; (407) 481-2928; harpandcelt.com; Parking Garage and Street Parking; Irish; $. In October 2011, during a visit to Orlando, President Barack Obama and Orlando Mayor Buddy Dyer chose a humble pub in downtown Orlando to share a pint of Guinness and nachos, a place where you could find the everyday working man. That humble pub was The Celt. Two sides of the same coin, The Harp is the more refined sit-down restaurant, while just next door, The Celt is the louder, classic Irish pub and the perfect place to go to watch a soccer match. The Harp, currently open only for lunch but available for special bookings in the evening, serves up authentic Irish dishes: cottage pies, steak and mushroom pies, Scotch eggs made with hard-boiled eggs encased in sausage, and the traditional Sunday Irish full breakfast, consisting of 2 fried eggs, 2 Irish breakfast sausages, 2 blood pudding, 2 white pudding, 2 rashers (Irish bacon), beans, sautéed mushrooms, and toast; you'll feel like you're back in the old country in no time. Wash it all down with a nice pint from the extensive draft beer list. During crawfish season, they are popular for the low-country crawfish boils made fresh in house.

Organic Craft Beers in Orlando

With over 20 taps, Orlando Brewing serves up the only certified organic beers in town. Two of the first beers they ever made, the Orlando Brewing Blonde Ale and Pale Ale, are still among their most popular and are sold throughout Orlando at various bars and restaurants. Orlando Brewing, located downtown, is Florida's only certified organic brewery and one of only a handful in the entire country. This means that all the ingredients are grown without the use of insecticides, bioengineering, or irradiation, and no fillers or adjuncts are used. All of their beers are made in accordance with the Reinheitsgebot, the German Purity Law of 1516, using only natural, organic ingredients. They have expanded to include a wide range of styles, including a red, porter, stout, Hefeweizen, IPA, and more, with a variety of seasonal beers available, such as a Maibock, Oktoberfest, Steamee Summer, and Doppelbock. 1301 Atlanta Ave., Orlando, FL 32806; (407) 872-1117; orlandobrewing.com; Parking Lot; $.

Hue Restaurant, 629 E. Central Blvd., Orlando, FL 32801; (407) 849-1800; huerestaurant.com; Parking Garage; Modern American; $$$$. Standing for "Hip, Urban Environment," Hue features modern American fare with a creative touch. Outdoor patio diners can see and be seen, and the brunch is popular at this Thornton Park neighborhood mainstay. Try the PB&J Turnover, a unique turn on the familiar sandwich—here instead it's a puff pastry stuffed with peanut butter and grape jam, topped with crème anglais and marshmallow fluff. For dinner the golden lobster bisque, fried oysters served with jicama slaw and a sweet chile aioli, and the duck breast served with a cranberry reduction, English peas, and a butternut squash and amaretto risotto are all popular choices.

Mediterranean Blue, 435 E. Michigan St., Orlando, FL 32806; (407) 422-2583; mediterraneanblue.net; Parking Lot; Mediterranean; $. Mediterranean Blue is the creation of siblings Bob and Gail Givoglu, who draw from their Greek heritage to bring this friendly neighborhood joint alive. The gyros (pronounced YEE-ros) are the way to go here at this family-owned Greek spot south of downtown. Specialties include the Gyro King, consisting of sliced beef and lamb seasoned and roasted, served on grilled pita with onion, tomato, and house-made tzatziki sauce topped with feta cheese, and the Provence hot sandwich, made with sliced ham, brie, herbes de Provence–infused butter, and Dijon mustard on artisan bread. Don't forget to add a side of their unique Greek cheese fries, finished with olive oil, seasoned with sea salt and oregano, and topped with feta cheese. For the vegetarians and vegans out there, there's plenty of tabbouleh, Greek salad, quinoa salad, and other healthy dishes to choose from. Everything here is served on eco-friendly, biodegradable ware, if that's your shtick. Baklava cheesecake for dessert? Don't mind if I do.

Napasorn Thai, 56 E. Pine St., Orlando, FL 32801; (407) 245-8088; thaidowntown.com; Parking Garage; Thai; $$. This downtown staple for Thai has been serving up the cuisine since 2003. The decor is elegant and classy, from remnants of the French restaurant that previously occupied the space. Most of the dishes, traditional Thai staples, are done well: the pad thai is made up of delicious rice noodles stir-fried with eggs, green onions, and bean sprouts in a sweet sauce, and the drunken noodles are full of broad rice noodles cooked with garlic, bell peppers, mushrooms, tomatoes, and onions in a Thai basil–spiced sauce. The waterfall beef salad is also a good choice: 12 ounces of rib eye steak grilled and thinly sliced and mixed with lime juice, Thai herbs, onions, scallions, cilantro, and flakes of roasted rice. Try the roast, boneless duck entrees as well, served in curry or Thai basil sauces.

Nick's Italian Kitchen, 100 S. Eola Dr., Orlando, FL 32801; (407) 781-0724; nicksitaliankitchen.com; Parking Garage and Street Parking; Italian; $$$. Part of the ever-growing Funky Monkey empire, also known as FMI Restaurant Group, Nick's Italian Kitchen was created by Owners Nick Olivieri and Eddie Nickell as a way to bring their spin on Italian-style cooking to Orlando with an "everything made from scratch" attitude. Family recipes including Nick's grandmother's meatballs, made in a slow-cooked marinara sauce and topped with shaved Parmesan, offer an authentic take on

Italian cuisine. The decor is not your typical mom-and-pop Italian eatery with red and white checkered tablecloths; rather it's more refined and modern, sophisticated like a place you would find in downtown Manhattan. The risotto is made fresh and changes daily, and the lamb rack here is grilled to perfection, served with butternut squash, mashed potatoes, and minted rosemary compound butter. Also the osso bucco, homemade stuffed lobster ravioli, fresh fish, prime steaks, and veal chops with a wine list featuring bottles from all over the world make Nick's Italian Kitchen a place you'd want to come to over and over again. Don't forget to save room for dessert: the Coppa Nick's, made with milky *fior di latte,* pistachio, and chocolate gelato served with brandied cherries and *panna montata,* is a must-try.

Prickly Pear Steakhouse, 100 S. Eola Dr., Orlando, FL 32801; (407) 781-2539; pricklypearorlando.com; Parking Garage and Street Parking; Tex-Mex; $$$. This offshoot of the FMI Restaurant Group's empire features modern American Southwestern fare, where "Orlando meets the American Frontier." Decor is upscale and modern with touches of cactus and cowboy themes. Try the smoked duck quesadilla, made with tender, hickory-smoked duck and Jack cheese in a buttered tortilla with cranberry and pear chutney and a large dollop of guacamole for dipping. For something different, try the black and white soup, a black bean and jalapeño Jack cheese soup beautifully decorated with a sweet red chile puree. For burger lovers, the list of unique burgers includes the All-American, an Angus patty with smoked cheddar cheese, bacon, serrano mayonnaise, Texas barbecue onions, and mixed lettuce, as well as tender, lean bison burgers, elk burgers, and fish burgers. Don't miss the Prickly Pear's signature baby-back ribs, slow braised with a house-made barbecue sauce and mashed potatoes.

Shari Sushi Lounge, 621 E. Central Blvd., Orlando, FL 32801; (407) 420-9420; sharisushilounge.com; Parking Garage and Street Parking; Sushi/Japanese; $$. This modern and chic sushi lounge brings to downtown a hip, sophisticated meet-up spot for sushi lovers. Shari, named after the Japanese word for the vinegar rice component of sushi, is distinguished among sushi joints in Orlando as a place with creative rolls executed with culinary flair. Not only is high-quality fish a sign of great sushi, but the *shari* sushi rice itself is as important or even more so when creating great sushi. Start off with the Japanese buffalo lobster, fresh lobster tail lightly fried tempura style, tossed in a spicy shichimi-pepper aioli and finished with cilantro oil, or the coconut sea bass, Chilean sea bass lightly breaded in shredded coconut, deep fried, and served atop raspberry-dressed watercress and lemon pepper aioli. Then try the *tai* ceviche, made with seasonal whitefish sliced sashimi style, with *yuzu* citrus, seasoned with Hawaiian pink salt and Thai Sriracha hot sauce and topped with micro cilantro, or the jalapeño pepper hamachi, imported Japanese hamachi with fresh wasabi lime sauce, cracked black pepper, lime zest, and diced serrano pepper and sprinkled with micro cilantro. For a special dinner, sit by the bar and experience the sushi chef's specialties with the multicourse *omakase* dinner, leaving all the choices up to the chef for the best items of the day. Don't forget to order one of the signature mixed drinks, such as the Shari-tini, Chopin vodka shaken and served chilly with shichimi pepper cream cheese–stuffed olives, or the saketini, Sho Chiku Bai Junmai sake, shaken with your choice of flavors: raspberry, strawberry, or mango.

310 Lakeside, 301 E. Pine St., Orlando, FL 32801; (407) 373-0310; 310restaurant.com; American; $$$. A gorgeous restaurant and bar with high ceilings and an upscale atmosphere (and popular for special parties and corporate outings), 310 Lakeside features New American cuisine just across the street from Lake Eola. Though it's not exactly lakeside dining, the food is decent and so are the prices, with a menu including salads, sandwiches, burgers, steak and seafood entrees, and more. Try the Steak 310, a sandwich served on an artisan roll made with grilled rib eye steak topped with roasted red pepper, portabello mushroom, and melted provolone cheese. Save room for the desserts, made in house, such as the hard chocolate shell filled with chocolate whipped cream and fresh berries and the chocolate trifle, a chocolate lover's dream made with chocolates topped with Heath bar bits and whipped cream. If you're at the bar, go for the famous sangria, the 310 Pomegranate Punch, or the Hangar One Velvet Cosmo before going out on the town.

Italian Beefstro, 705 W. Colonial Dr., Orlando, FL 32804; (407) 601-7444; italianbeefstro.com. Italian Beefstro sits in on busy Colonial Drive just a few blocks west of the I-4 exit in a small, nondescript building with a little fountain in front. Inside you get in line to order your food at the counter. The people who work here are all very nice and hospitable, which is greatly appreciated. Italian Beefstro's staff pride themselves on serving Italian beef sandwiches, a specialty from the windy city of Chicago. The Italian beef sandwich has slices of juicy roast beef and sautéed green peppers in a hoagie roll. For 30 cents extra, they add hot *giardiniera* (pickled veggies) and the sandwich is dunked in the flavor-filled juice that runs off the beef (I call it beefy juices). It's a dripping, juicy, delightful mess of an Italian roast beef sandwich. Italian Beefstro also serves up classic Vienna Beef Chicago hot dogs topped with tomato, pickles, sport peppers, celery salt, and relish. Overall, I thought the sandwiches were pretty good and worth a try, especially for all those displaced Chicago residents.

Virgin Olive Market, 807 N. Orange Ave., Orlando, FL 32801; (407) 601-7848; virginolivemarket.com; Street Parking and Parking Garage. This neighborhood noshery just north of downtown Orlando features friendly service with fresh and healthy fare, from soups, salads, and sandwiches to breakfast items as well as espresso, beer, and wine. For morning munchies you can build your own bagel or enjoy hearty oatmeal, breakfast tacos, quiche, and fresh baked goods. For lunch or dinner, lasagna, salads, and sandwiches become more prominent, with two different homemade soups each day (one is vegetarian). Start off with some of the hummus platter, homemade with fresh baby greens, kalamata olives, cucumber slices, and sweet grape tomatoes served with warm pita points, or one of the signature soups, such as tomato basil or red pepper bisque (when available). For sandwiches, try one of the many creatively named offerings, such as the Brute, a rare roast beef sandwich with Havarti cheese on ciabatta, with organic baby lettuce, tomato, onion, house dressing, and horseradish mayo, or the Laughing Ucello, roasted turkey breast, provolone cheese, fresh basil, tomato, and onion with a sun-dried tomato aioli on focaccia bread. The Big Cheese is the ultimate grilled cheese sandwich made with buffalo mozzarella, roasted red peppers, and fresh basil with pesto mayo, served on focaccia bread. For heartier fare, try the Grateful Loafer, a homemade turkey meat loaf made with oats and fresh veggies, topped with provolone cheese, tomato, onion, arugula, and sweet chile aioli served on herbed focaccia bread with a side of mushroom gravy. The signature Olive Oyl salad, with baby spinach leaves topped with turkey breast, Gorgonzola crumbles, walnuts, fresh strawberries, and pears, is a crowd favorite and is served with homemade Dijon vinaigrette. For dinner service, they offer a variety of artisan flatbread pizzas.

Yalaha Bakery, 1213 N. Orange Ave., Orlando, FL 32804; (321) 800-5212; yalahabakery.com; Street Parking. If you've ever been out to Lake County on scenic CR 48, you probably have heard of this authentic little German bakery, housed in a quaint country village building off the road, straight out of a scene from *The Sound of Music*. Known for the hearty multigrain and rye breads and mouthwatering pastries, Yalaha Bakery has been a culinary staple in Lake County for over 17 years now, with many a foodie venturing out to the shop to sample the authentic goods. In August 2011, co-owners Juergen and Anne Marie Klumb opened a charming little neighborhood outpost near downtown Orlando off of Orange Avenue just across from Lake Ivanhoe (in the Ivanhoe Village District, just a few shops south of **Ethos Vegan Kitchen** [see p. 62]). Anne Marie Klumb manages this location, staffed by friendly and helpful workers who are eager to help out with suggestions. The local Yalaha Bakery in Orlando has breads and pastries shipped in from the home-base bakery in Lake County fresh each morning. An impressive wall of freshly baked German-style bread loaves and rolls lines one side of the bakery, ranging from pretzel breads to rye to pumpernickel and more. The bread here is of high quality and made with fresh, natural ingredients—free of preservatives and chemical additives. A case of traditional German deli meats, bratwursts, and sandwiches sits on one side of the shop, and an espresso machine stands nearby ready to serve up some great cappuccino and coffee for the early risers. But to me, the main attraction is the beautiful display of colorful, sweet pastries and cakes at the center. German apple pies, peach and apple strudels, Black Forest cake, apple Normandy, lemon ginger cookies, frangipane butter cookies filled with raspberries, and more line the display, beckoning your sweet tooth to bite in through the glass case. So many choices—it can be a bit overwhelming when you want to try them all. I would recommend the Bee Sting cake, a unique, moist cake filled with Bavarian cream and topped with almonds and orange blossom honey, a truly delightful treat. It comes as a huge square, big enough to share, but you won't because you'll want to savor it later, thinking of those rolling hills and country village houses, the place where Yalaha bakes magic into pastries and breads.

Winter Park

The charming city of Winter Park, lying just to the north of Orlando, was founded in 1885 as a winter resort for vacationing New Englanders. Today it is home to some of the best restaurants in town as well as a plethora of quaint shops, boutiques, museums, and art galleries, and a park that hosts concerts and art festivals year-round. Notably, the Winter Park Sidewalk Art Festival attracts thousands of artists, families, and patrons each year, and each fall the Winter Park Harvest Festival brings together local farmers and producers and chefs in celebration of local food and the farm-to-table movement.

On Park Avenue in beautiful historic downtown Winter Park, one can easily imagine spending a romantic night out or a lovely weekend morning walking along the city's winding brick roads and side streets, underneath the camphor and Southern live oak trees draped in Spanish moss. Visitors can discover some fantastic restaurants in the hidden gardens along the side streets and alleys surrounding Park Avenue. The lively and often crowded Winter Park Farmers' Market takes place weekly in downtown Winter Park on

Saturday. There you can shop around for some of the best local honey, vegetables, fruits, French pastries, and much more. At the east end of Morse Boulevard you can take an hourlong tour with the Winter Park Scenic Boat company through the chain of lakes—with a nice backyard view of some of the lovely homes—in Winter Park and learn about some of its history and wildlife.

Best of the Neighborhood

Bosphorous Turkish Cuisine, 108 S. Park Ave., Winter Park, FL 32789; (407) 644-8609; bosphorousrestaurant.com; Street Parking and Parking Lot; Turkish; $$. Named after a strait in the heart of Istanbul, Turkey (once known as Constantinople to the Western world), this authentic restaurant features some of the best Turkish cuisine in Orlando. The atmosphere is beautifully refined, hinting of the faraway world of Turkey, walls painted in gold and dark lavender, with shelves displaying narghile water pipes (also known as hookahs), with service that matches the ambience—both attentive and knowledgeable. Start off with the always impressive lavas, the huge balloon-shaped hollow, unleavened bread served with your choice of many mezes, appetizers to enjoy the bread with including hummus or dill cucumber yogurt dip. Or you could order the mixed appetizer (Karisik Meze) and try all of them: the combination of hummus, baba ghanoush, sautéed eggplant, tabbouleh, *ezme* salad, *tarama* (red caviar with oil and lemon juice), *haydari* yogurt, and stuffed grape leaves is ample to share. I highly recommend the chicken *adana* kebab (spelled *kebap* here, a local variant of the skewered roasted meat dish), the Bosphorous house specialty and favorite consisting of grilled aromatic morsels of chicken seasoned with fresh garlic, light hot peppers, red bell peppers, parsley, and Turkish spices. Another popular entree is the beef tenderloin shish kebab, tender cubes of beef tenderloin delicately marinated, then charcoal-grilled, filling and succulent. Entree dishes are also served with fragrant, fluffy jasmine rice pilaf, pickled red cabbage, sliced onion, and carrots. Try the *doner* kebab, similar to the Greek gyro or Arabic shawarma meat, cut from a vertically rotating lamb meat mixture, but do ask if they are nearing the end of the stick, as it can get dry. In addition to kebabs, Bosphorous also serves up a whole list of seafood, sautéed dishes, and traditional Turkish pizza-like pocket pies stuffed with ingredients called *pides*. Enjoy with some of the world-renowned Turkish coffee (*Turk kahvesi*) made with roasted coffee beans crushed with a mortar and pestle, served hot from a special coffee pot, called *cezve,* with your desired amount of *sekerli,* or sugar. End with a nice slice of baklava dessert, sweet flaky layers of phyllo dough and nuts that melt in your mouth like honey.

4Rivers Smokehouse, 2103 W. Fairbanks Ave., Winter Park, FL 32789; (407) 474-8377; 4rsmokehouse.com; Street Parking; Barbecue; $$. The wildly popular 4Rivers Smokehouse is one of

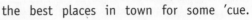

the best places in town for some 'cue. Already with 3 locations in central Florida (with one in Longwood and another in Winter Garden), this one is set to move to a larger building and is poised for even greater success. Founded by John Rivers (who has been invited in the past to cook at the acclaimed James Beard House in New York), 4Rivers has been something of a phenomenon here in central Florida, with constant lines out the door for the St. Louis–style ribs, smoked chicken wings, or burnt-end sandwiches made with half Angus beef brisket and half pulled pork smoked in signature 4Rivers sauce. What's not to love? They also serve up some premium items, such as leg of lamb and beef short ribs. Leave with a Happy Trail, one of the many dessert items, such as the signature cupcakes, bread puddings, or fried Oreos made in-house at The Sweet Shop. Interestingly, the 4Rivers family has been experimenting with a pop-up kitchen for a new upscale restaurant concept called Cowboy Kitchen. See John Rivers's recipe for **Cowboy Steak** on p. 261.

Hillstone, 215 S. Orlando Ave., Winter Park, FL 32789; (407) 740-4005; hillstone.com; Valet and Parking Lot; Modern American; $$$. This national chain restaurant, formerly Houston's, is best known for its breathtakingly beautiful view on Lake Killarney from tall windows facing the lake and a nice-sized outdoor dining area with a pier leading out to a covered dining area on the dock. The view is rather stunning, especially on those cool central Florida afternoons. Their Hawaiian rib eye, with flavors reminiscent of Korean *kalbi* barbecue short ribs, is marinated for 48 hours in a pineapple juice–soy sauce blend and is hardwood grilled, served with a baked potato. Also try the wood-grilled artichokes, tasty little morsels that you dip with their remoulade sauce, but do remember not to eat the brittle exterior.

Luma on Park, 290 S. Park Ave., Winter Park, FL 32789; (407) 599-4111; lumaonpark.com; Parking Lot and Valet; Modern American; $$$. The upscale and trendy Luma on bustling Park Avenue prides itself on its original, locally inspired American cuisine helmed at the front lines by Executive Chef Brandon McGlamery. Locally sourced ingredients are all the rage nowadays, but Chef McGlamery (trained at Thomas Keller's French Laundry and also a former chef de cuisine at Bacchanalia in Atlanta, Georgia) was one of the first in the Orlando area to truly emphasize this trend in his dishes and offerings at Luma. The decor at Luma is beautifully modern and upscale, with shades of beige and impressive brown wood, marble, and metal, all encasing a very busy, high-paced dining room like a scene from a night in New York City. The menu changes with the seasons and availability of ingredients from local farms like Rabbit Run Farms and Lake Meadows Naturals, but some of the favorites include the truffle popcorn with grated Parmesan, the cauliflower-onion tart, and the signature snapper ceviche dish, made with fresh snapper and zest of oranges and limes, basil, jicama, mango, radish, and brunoise. See Luma's recipe for **Glazed Duck** on p. 248 and Jeremy Crittenden's recipe for the **Rio** cocktail on p. 251.

Prato, 124 N. Park Ave., Winter Park, FL 32789; (407) 262-0050; prato-wp.com; Street Parking and Parking Lot; Italian; $$$. The team from **Luma on Park** (see p. 45), helmed by Executive Chef Brandon McGlamery and Chef de Cuisine Matt Cargo, has brought to life Prato, the new Park Avenue hot spot. The menu here, changing seasonally, celebrates cuisine from Italy's rich culinary landscape, blending Italian classics with modern techniques and seasonal ingredients. The ambience is one of a rustic farmhouse blended with a modern, communal lounge feel, a long U-shaped bar, high ceilings, and large window-paned doors. The place is all anchored around 2 imported Acunto wood-burning ovens from Naples, Italy, lightly touching each baked dish with a signature, smoky finish. Fresh, creative salads, pizzas, and pastas utilizing locally sourced produce, responsibly farmed meats, and sustainable seafood dominate. Start with the red snapper crudo, a refreshing plate of exquisitely cut slices of raw red snapper, drizzled with a pistachio-currant vinaigrette and served with sliced radishes. Squash blossoms stuffed with ricotta, roasted chiles, and almonds or roasted butternut squash salads with burrata mozzarella and field greens are all fantastic when in season. The Widowmaker pizza, consisting of fennel sausage, arugula, toscano, romesco sauce, and a local farm egg, over easy, baked in the center, is just perfect for dipping and sharing. The signature Prato meatballs, available only at dinner, are made and ground in house with veal, pork, beef, and a host of other wonderful ingredients and served in a roasted tomato sauce with cipollini onions *agrodolce*—perfecto. The pastas, also handmade in house, are delightful: ranging from the duck ragout Bolognese rigatoni to the Laughing Bird shrimp ravioli. Entree items include favorites like the chicken leg candito served with apricot *mostarda* and marble potato and the short rib *brasato,* served with *soffritto* on garlic crostini and topped with a poached farm egg. Save room for dessert: the chocolate sea salt hazelnut budino pudding and the luscious tiramisu in a jar are surely worth the few extra calories. An extensive bar menu is also available with wines from Spain and Italy, craft beers from Cigar City Brewing, and delicious cocktails, such as the Amalfi sunset, made with limoncello, house grenadine, fresh orange juice, and cherries. See Prato's recipe for **Farro Salad with Corn, Tomato, Basil, and Goat Cheese Bruschetta** on p. 250 and David Arnold's recipe for the **Cetriolo** cocktail on p. 252.

The Ravenous Pig, 1234 N. Orange Ave., Winter Park, FL 32789; (407) 628-2333; theravenouspig.com; Valet and Parking Lot; Modern American/Gastropub; $$$. James Beard Award nominees and Chef-Owners James and Julie Petrakis, trained at the prestigious Culinary Institute of America, brought the art of the American gastropub to

Orlando with much success. Subtle browns and brick walls adorn the walls of The Ravenous Pig, with a trendy and modern, yet also homey ambience. This is one of the best restaurants in Orlando and you can tell by the dedication that the chefs and staff put into the food. Be sure to make a reservation if you intend to dine here, or you can try your luck first-come, first-serve in the bar area, replete with an impressive list of microbrew and craft beers on tap. The restaurant is renowned for the house-made charcuterie and use of natural, seasonal ingredients with an ever-changing and creative menu. The steak frites, porcini-marinated prime Niman Ranch flat-iron steak, served with thin-cut truffle fries in a pint glass and a house-made sauce, is a favorite. Also popular is the Pub Burger, one of the very best burgers in Orlando, made with a juicy, flavorful Angus beef patty cooked to your liking and topped with caramelized onions and buttermilk blue cheese on a fresh brioche bun. The Ravenous Pig also serves house-made ice creams and sorbets. For dessert, try the Pig Tails, warm cinnamon-sugar-tossed fritters with a bittersweet dark chocolate espresso sauce. The Chef-Owners of The Ravenous Pig also operate the Cask and Larder restaurant up the street on Fairbanks Avenue at the location of the former Harper's Tavern, complete with smoked oysters and a table for whole roast animals. See The Ravenous Pig's recipe for **Veal Sweetbreads** on p. 240, Chef Julie Petrakis's recipe for **Crème Caramel** on p. 242, and Larry Foor's recipe for the **Original Gin & Jam** on p. 245.

Anna's Polish Restaurant, 3586 Aloma Ave., Suite 7, Winter Park, FL 32792; (407) 657-0020; annaspolishrestaurant.com; Parking Lot; Polish; $$. This comfortable little restaurant serves up traditional Polish classics like the ones your Polish grandma made. Run by Anna, the kitchen is where they churn out delicious pierogies and kielbasa sausages imported from the Midwest, and homemade stuffed cabbage, filled with rice, pork, beef, and spices and served with tomato or mushroom sauce. The pierogies, a Polish specialty, come in potato and cheese, seasoned meat, or sauerkraut and mushroom varieties and are boiled and served with caramelized onions and sour cream. If you have a hard time choosing appetizers, get the Polish Trio appetizer, made of 2 pierogies, 2 potato pancakes, and fresh Polish sausage. The red borscht, a traditional soup made with shredded beets, fava beans, and vegetables and topped with sour cream, is sure to please, as is the more obscure white borscht, a hearty, filling soup made from fermented rye flour with smoked sausage and egg. Gypsy potato pancake, a plate-size potato pancake filled with chunks of beef, onions, and bell pepper in a rich gravy, topped with sour cream and parsley, and the Silesian dumplings (*pyzy*), round potato dumplings stuffed with ground pork served with bacon pieces or homemade mushroom sauce, will surely fill you up and have you ready to thank Anna for the lovely, authentic Polish meal. Before you go, save room for the walnut delight (*pychotka*), a crunchy walnut cake delight divided by yummy vanilla cream and topped with walnuts.

Antonio's La Fiamma Ristorante and Antonio's Market and Cafe, 611 S. Orlando Ave., Maitland, FL 32751; (407) 645-1035; antoniosonline.com; Parking Lot; Italian; $$$. With a fine-dining atmosphere and good service, this central Florida landmark serves up classic, authentic Italian fare with an expert hand. Antonio's La Fiamma serves up a fantastic list of pastas, pizzas, salads, and other staples, but try something from the wood-burning ovens, assembled by Italian oven makers on location. The eggplant *involtini*, baked in the wood-burning oven, is made with eggplant dipped in a light batter and filled with ricotta, mozzarella, Parmesan, and sun-dried tomatoes, served with a fresh tomato sauce. The wood-grilled salmon here is divine, lightly brushed with olive oil and fresh herbs, then grilled over the wood fire. Lobster ravioli are stuffed with lobster meat and Italian flat-leaf parsley, tossed with sautéed escarole in an arrabbiata sauce. Beef short ribs are done here very well, too, with a balsamic barbecue sauce and served over cheddar polenta. For meat lovers, try the pan-seared filet mignon served with a wild mushroom ragout, served with the chef's accompaniments. Don't miss the list of Italian desserts, such as the tiramisu cake. Downstairs from the more refined, sit-down Antonio's La Fiamma, the intimate and more relaxed Antonio's Market and Cafe has everything you need for your Italian kitchen. For those dining in, the cafe serves up house-made pizzas, antipasti, salad, and pastas, and has the same items ready for to-go. Don't miss the signature *pollo carciofi,* moist chicken breast sautéed with artichoke hearts, garlic, and basil in a white wine, zesty lemon sauce and served with fresh vegetables and roasted potatoes. If you are in the mood for some down-home Italian-style cooking and feel extra hungry, try the savory lasagna Bolognese, which layers fresh homemade meat sauce with pasta, ricotta, and mozzarella, all topped with *pomodoro* sauce. The seating area is small and is surrounded by the market's wines and olive oils, which could get awkward when shoppers get a little too close for comfort while you're dining. The market has a huge wine selection, chocolates, tomato sauce, cuts of deli meats, such as capocollo, pancetta, and prosciutto, cheeses, fresh vegetables, and fresh pastries, such as cannolis and Italian rum cake. It's all you could ever dream of for an Italian meal at home.

Armando's Cucina Italiana & Pizzeria, 463 W. New England Ave., Winter Park, FL 32789; (407) 951-8930; facebook.com/pages/Armandos-Cucina-Italiana-Pizzeria/268037553234090; Street Parking and Parking Lot; Pizza; $$$. This lively, new Italian place in the now gentrified Hannibal Square just west of Park Avenue on New England Avenue features outdoor seating and live music in addition to its authentic Italian menu mainstays. The place is spacious and airy, with a nice-sized bar area, stylish white walls, and sophisticated digs, making it a popular hangout spot with the adults. They serve a nice list of salads, antipasti, pastas, and panini sandwiches, but the stars of Armando's are the hand-crafted, slightly charred thin-crust pizzas made in the 1,000-degree ovens. Start with the carpaccio *di carne* and *pere,* a dish made with thinly sliced raw beef topped with sweet pear slivers and shaved Parmesan cheese, and drizzled with Gorgonzola sauce. Honor Italy with the Margherita pizza, made with fresh mozzarella, plum tomato sauce, and green basil (they all make up the colors of the Italian flag), or the San Giovanni, a devilishly good pizza made with sautéed mushrooms, mozzarella, and fried eggs drizzled with truffle oil. For meat lovers, you can't go wrong with the Carne, a sausage, chicken, prosciutto ham, and pancetta pizza with mozarrella and fresh tomato sauce.

Austin's Coffee, 929 W. Fairbanks Ave., Winter Park, FL 32789; (407) 975-3364; austinscoffee.com; Parking Lot; Coffeehouse; $. This comfy, 24-hour, locally owned and indie coffeehouse serves as a relaxing, hipster hangout spot with a nice selection of salads, gourmet sandwiches, hot pressed panini, tea, beer, wine, and of course, organic fair-traded coffee roasted in house. The Chunkey Monkey, a frozen coffee with chocolate and banana, is sure to delight during those hot central Florida summer days. For veggie lovers, try the soy ginger marinated tempeh panini on whole wheat, served with black olives, red onion, vegan American cheese, romaine lettuce, stone-ground mustard, and "vegannaise." There also are open-mic nights with live poetry, comedy, and hip-hop acts.

Barnie's CoffeeKitchen, 118 S. Park Ave., Winter Park; (407) 629-0042; barniescoffeekitchen.com; Parking Lot and Street Parking; Coffeehouse; $. Founded in Orlando in 1980 as Barnie's

Coffee & Tea Company right on Park Avenue in Winter Park, the coffee shop has changed vastly over the years from being a major chain to scaling back and remodeling with Barnie's CoffeeKitchen, the first of many more to come, focused on chef-inspired gourmet foods in addition to coffee staples. Skeptics can rest assured, the team is led by President/CEO Jonathan Smiga, a former director of education for the Culinary Institute of America in Hyde Park. The new design feels very West Coast, like an old friend's kitchen dining room with shelves of their coffees, small, handmade wooden tables, and a few larger communal tables that allow for strangers and old friends to share a space. Watercolor paintings using coffee as a medium from local artist Steve Mikel hang along the walls. The CoffeeKitchen also features a giant coffee roaster and an extensive list of over 50 hand-selected coffees, many of which are single origin, fair traded, organic, or Rainforest Alliance certified. From the music that plays in the background to the lovely little chocolates and handcrafted jewelry sold here, all are made from coffee-producing regions. The coffee here is wonderful, with daily special brews and baristas showcasing the pour-over brew style, which allows for a more flavorful, smooth coffee. The baristas here are also deft at latte art, featuring designs of rosettas, falling leaves, and even phoenixes carefully drawn on the surface of the latte. The dining menu is an unexpected surprise, with many local, organic ingredients. Breakfast menu items include French pastries, the breakfast panini made with local Lake Meadows organic eggs, applewood-smoked bacon, spinach, aged cheddar, and tomato jam on country white bread, and Israeli *shakshuka,* made with two poached organic eggs on tomato ragout, feta cheese, and thyme. For lunch, heartier fare such as coffee-rubbed Wagyu beef carpaccio tartine and Tanglewood Farms chicken panini are sure to please. Don't miss the *affogato*— made with smooth, sweet, salted caramel gelato with a shot of espresso. See Chef Collette Haw's recipes for **Quinoa Salad** on p. 258 and **Smoked Salmon Tartine** on p. 259.

The Bistro on Park Avenue, 348 Park Ave. North, Winter Park, FL 32789; (407) 539-6520; bistroonparkavenue.com; Parking Lot and Street Parking; French/Cajun; $$$. Tucked away off of north Park Avenue in a lovely little hidden courtyard, this quaint restaurant with a glass-encased garden room is one of the examples of why this area is known as Winter Park's "Little Europe." They serve up a wonderful brunch menu till 11 a.m. featuring the traditional crab cakes, omelets, eggs Benedict, and pancakes. Serving up American, French, and Cajun dishes, they have everything you want if you are hankering for a taste of the old French Quarter, with the New Orleans– style grilled oysters topped with garlic butter and melted Parmesan cheese, oyster and shrimp po' boy sandwiches, and favorites like the perfectly flavored, rich crawfish étoufée and savory jambalaya.

Black Bean Deli, 325 South Orlando Ave., Suite 1-1, Winter Park, FL 32789; (407) 628-0294; 1835 E. Colonial Dr., Orlando, FL 32803; (407) 628-0294; blackbeandeli.com; Parking Lot; Cuban/ Sandwiches; $. The quirky, teeny-tiny Black Bean Deli is a staple of the Winter Park area, sitting in a small strip mall in an even smaller shack just north of Fairbanks Avenue on Orlando Avenue (US 17/92). You would probably be best advised to try to get their goods for takeout or grab one of the few stools by the window. Black Bean Deli is renowned for its Cuban sandwiches, plentiful, juicy slices of sweet ham, roast pork, swiss cheese, and pickles all pressed inside a wonderful Cuban bread. The bread is what makes these sandwiches stand out, I believe, as they are fresh and soft, and you can tell they were made with careful attention. *Excellente.* The *medianoche* sandwich, made with sweet ham, roast pork, and swiss cheese on sweet bread, is also popular. If you want more substantial non-sandwich fare, they also serve platters with Spanish baked chicken, *picadillo,* and other Cuban favorites with rice, black beans, sweet plantains, and green salad.

Briarpatch Restaurant and Ice Cream Parlor, 252 N. Park Ave., Winter Park, FL 32789; (407) 628-8651; Street Parking and Parking Lot; American; $$. Located near the northern end of posh Park Avenue, Briarpatch is a quaint and very popular restaurant with wooden floors and country-home feeling serving up wonderful breakfast and brunch items. The staff here, mostly composed of students from nearby Rollins College, can be a bit aloof, but the menu, which includes eggs Benedict, omelets, pancakes, and Belgian waffles, is spot-on. The chunky chicken salad is also a favorite, as is the homemade zucchini bread, cheese grits, and thick slices of Southern-style fried green tomatoes. The brie and raspberry french toast is a bit overwhelming for one, so try to share it with a friend. Outdoor seating, under bright yellow umbrellas, is popular when the often fickle central Florida weather allows. For dessert, try some homemade ice cream from the ice cream parlor area or one of their huge slices of homemade cakes, such as the red velvet cake and carrot cake, from the rotating glass display cabinet.

Cafe 118 Degrees Living Cuisine Cafe & Juice Bar, 153 E. Morse Blvd., Winter Park, FL 32789; (407) 389-2233; cafe118.com; Parking Lot; Vegetarian; $$$. Cafe 118 Degrees has a unique theme: Not only is the entire menu organic and vegetarian, but all of their food is also prepared completely raw. The restaurant is named after the optimal temperature at which foods are "cooked" here, with the belief that food cooked above 118 degrees begins to break down its enzymes and minerals, resulting in diminished nutritional value. Cafe 118 rotates items in and out seasonally to ensure freshness. The dishes here are truly creative, creating truly unique textures and tastes out of natural ingredients without any meat. The spiced macadamia hummus with sun-dried tomato flax crackers appetizer is light and soft on the palate, almost airy and creamy. The pad thai is made with zucchini and carrot noodles, and pad thai sauce, drizzled with a sesame cashew glaze, and the lasagna is made with sun-dried tomatoes, herb pesto, and macadamia ricotta. All in all I enjoyed my meal and thought it was quite ingenious to create such inventive dishes made entirely with vegetables and fruits and non-meat products, entirely without cooking it above 118 degrees.

Chez Vincent, 533 W. New England Ave., Winter Park, FL 32789; (407) 599-2929; chezvincent.com; Street Parking and Parking Lot; French; $$$. This charming, intimate restaurant with white linen tablecloths in Hannibal Square is often featured as one of the best French restaurants in Orlando. Greeted by the French-accented maître d' and waiters, you'll find dishes that represent traditional French cuisine. Start with the *feuillettè* d´escargots, sauté of escargot stuffed in a puff pastry with a port wine sauce or some of the crème de *champignon,* a wonderful, savory cream of mushroom soup. Seafood and meats make up the menu ranging from the coquilles St. Jacques, made with sautéed sea scallops in a tarragon sauce, to the *carré d'agneau au bleu,* pan-seared rack of lamb in blue cheese sauce. Save room for the tarte tatin, an upside-down warm apple pie dessert with vanilla ice cream. At the end of the night, Chef/Co-Owner Vincent Gagliano can be seen walking around saying hello to guests and passing around glasses of port wine to share. It's a lovely way to end an evening, imagining yourself transported to a quaint little place in France. Hannibal's on the Square lounge, adjacent to Chez Vincent and sharing a doorway, provides live music on the weekends and a full bar for predinner cocktails and specialty wines in an upscale, modern setting.

Cocina 214 Restaurant & Bar, 151 E. Welbourne Ave., Winter Park, FL 32789; (407) 790-7997; cocina214.com; Street Parking and Parking Lot; Tex-Mex/Mexican; $$$. The owners of Cocina 214 missed the Tex-Mex food of their native state of Texas so much that they created this restaurant on Park Avenue to bring the flavors that they missed so much to Winter Park. *Cocina* in Spanish means kitchen and the 214 stems from their home city Dallas's area code, bringing together a contemporary Mexican and Tex-Mex kitchen concept in its dishes with fresh, local ingredients and bold flavors. The 214 salsas are all made in house and come as mild (fire-roasted salsa), medium (verde and pineapple habañero), and hot (habenero and coconut habañero). Start with the 214 seviche, made with fresh seasonal fish, jalapeño, and chunks of cucumber, tomato, and avocado with citrus. Try the truffle and mushroom quesadilla, sautéed mushrooms with truffle oil served with sour cream and guacamole. The taqueria menu features a multitude of tacos made in different ways, such as the brisket tacos, with beef brisket, pico de gallo, and cheese served on flour tortillas, or the Don Carlos, blackened fish tacos with slaw, avocado, and jalapeño vinaigrette salsa. There is also an exhaustive selection of margaritas, mojitos, tequilas, and specialty cocktails for enjoyment with your Tex-Mex dishes. The 214 Skinny Margarita on the rocks is made with Tierras Organic Tequila, a slice of lime, organic agave nectar, and orange juice.

Croissant Gourmet, 120 E. Morse Blvd., Winter Park, FL 32789; (407) 622-7533; croissantgourmet.com; Lot and Street Parking; French/Bakery $. **Off of Park Avenue on Morse Boulevard, Croissant Gourmet** is one of the many joys I think of when wandering around Winter Park's popular shopping and restaurant area. In addition to creating some of the most gorgeous pastries in town, this little French bakery also serves up delectable sandwiches, quiche, crepes, and salads for lunch. Two display cases hold the wonders of Croissant Gourmet: fruit tarts topped with raspberries and blueberries, éclairs, napoleons, assorted croissants, apple turnovers, macarons, and many more all made fresh and locally. Try the almond croissant, a flaky, buttery, and fluffy croissant with a nice, sweet, creamy filling of almond paste. Or try the rectangular jalousie pastry; similar to a strudel and a play on jalousie-style windows, it's filled with almond cream and raspberries. The *croque madame* sandwich, a variation of the *croque monsieur,* is deftly made with ham and gruyère cheese, hand-dipped in egg, then pan-fried in butter to a nice crisp. Finally, the croque is topped with a luscious sunny-side-up egg. The golden-yellow yolk oozes down the sandwich when you cut into it, preferably with fork and knife, making the Croissant Gourmet's *croque madame* a truly transcendent experience. The shop is a bit small and narrow, with only a few tables inside and a bar stool area near the glass case for the bakery items. It can get a bit awkward for patrons who want to sit and enjoy their meal along the bar area without getting bumped into by others browsing the pastries or lined up to order by the register. Sit outside and enjoy the nice Florida weather with your pastries and people-watch on the avenue. Pass me another croissant, *s'il vous plaît*.

Dexter's, 558 W. New England Ave., Winter Park, FL 32789; (407) 629-1150; dexwine.com; Street Parking and Parking Lot; Brunch/ American; $$. See listing description under the Thornton Park entry, p. 308.

Dylan's Deli, 1198 Orange Ave., Winter Park, FL 32789; (407) 622-7578; dylansdeli.net; Parking Lot; Sandwiches; $. More cafe than deli, not unlike one you might find in Paris, this quaint little place features such French classics as crepes and *croque madame* sandwiches (called croque ma'ams here, for all our Southern friends). The homemade soups, such as creamed mushroom and tomato, are wonderful and there is a certain playfulness with the globally themed menu. Sandwiches, salads, and panini are all named after various cities across the world with their signature ingredients and breads, such as the Berlin sandwich, made with corned beef, black ham, sauerkraut, mushrooms, and Manchego cheese on wheat or oatmeal bread; the Oslo, a sandwich of smoked salmon with sweet onions, fresh dill, and herb cheese on dill ciabatta; and the spicy Tijuana with roast beef, bell peppers, pico, and cheddar on jalapeño and cheddar ciabatta. The Dylan panini, named after the owner's son, is made with pastrami, prosciutto, Gorgonzola, spicy pear, and a house sauce. For dinner, the sandwiches and soups are left off the menu in favor of *montaditos* (small open-face sandwiches with ingredients on top, or "mounted" on bread) with toppings such as brisket, swiss, and bacon-wrapped scallops. Also added for dinner are tapas plates, including stuffed artichokes, prunes wrapped in prosciutto, and orange glacé duck, as well as trays of cheese, cured meats, homemade quiches, salads, and delightful desserts, such as their profiterolles and chantilly and berries cake. Try a glass from the extensive list of French and Spanish wines and cognacs to go with the above.

El Bodegon, 400 S. Orlando Ave., Winter Park, FL 32789; (407) 628-1078; bodegonrestaurant.com; Parking Lot; Tapas/Spanish; $$$. El Bodegon is one of the few places in Orlando where you can get authentic Spanish-style tapas. At the entrance stands a statue of a bullfighter in his regalia, welcoming you into the large wooden doors. Inside, the feeling is like that of a restaurant in Spain, small and quaint, intimate with the music of flamenco guitar in the background. Service here is good, though a bit spotty at times. This is forgiven after a few drinks of the delicious, fruity red wine sangria accompanied by some fantastic tapas dishes. The *tortilla espanola,* a large fluffy Spanish-style quiche made with delicious potatoes, is a favorite here. So are the *patatas a la brava,* boiled red bit potatoes sautéed in Louisiana red hot sauce and aioli sauce. The *tapas de la casa* is a tad pricey, coming with a few slices of ham and chorizo, Manchego cheese, and a few pieces of olives. I really enjoyed the clams in tomato sauce though as well as the *croquetas de jamon,* Spanish ham croquettes with aioli sauce and the *pimientos del piquillo rellenos,* Spanish baby peppers stuffed with crab meat in romesco sauce. Go with a group and enjoy all the bites together with good friends and good wine.

Ethos Vegan Kitchen, 601-B New York Ave., Winter Park, FL 32789; (407) 228-3898; ethosvegankitchen.com; Parking Lot; Vegetarian; $$. Featuring healthy, fresh, and hearty fare since 2007, Ethos Vegan Kitchen is one of central Florida's few fully vegan restaurants, with a large variety of 100 percent vegan dishes, a small selection of vegan beer and wine, as well as vegan bakery items made from scratch on site daily. The kitchen also uses mostly organic ingredients and is a gluten-friendly establishment, with daily specials every day of the week and a menu changing with seasonal fruits and vegetables. For lovers of hearty fare, try the oven-baked Sheep's Pie, a meat-free version of shepherd's pie made with sautéed broccoli, carrots, peas, and onions in a veggie gravy and topped with mashed potatoes, or the five-layered Yo Mama's Lasagna, made with hearty vegetables, marinara sauce, mozzarella, and lasagna noodles and served with garlic bread. The grilled black bean Samson burger and the coconut curry tofu wrap are also popular here, as are the custom hand-tossed pizzas.

Fiddler's Green Irish Pub and Eatery, 544 W. Fairbanks Ave., Winter Park, FL 32789; (407) 645-2050; fiddlersgreenorlando.com; Valet and Parking Lot; Irish; $$. The wood-framed walls of Fiddler's Green are the color of melted milk chocolate, a dark brown blending to black with dim lights scattered throughout the restaurant, revealing the dark-wood booths and chairs. One can easily imagine oneself in some quaint old-world pub off a brick-laid side street easily found in Ireland. It gets crowded here quickly, especially when live bands play on the weekend, and with a wonderful Irish beer selection on tap. Some favorite dishes at Fiddler's Green are the Wexford wings, 10 large wings "blimey" style: fried once, then dipped in hot sauce and fried again. The shepherd's pie here is the best in Orlando, made with fresh ground sirloin in a rich brown gravy topped with champ and veggies. Champ is a northern Irish dish, made by combining mashed potatoes and chopped spring onions with butter and milk. Also popular is the famous Ballymaloe Chicken and the bangers and mash.

Green Lemon Cafe, 1945 Aloma Ave., Winter Park, FL 32792; (407) 673-0225; greenlemoncafe.com; Parking Lot; Sandwiches; $. This cozy little cafe features an array of sweet and savory crepes, panini pressed sandwiches, flatbreads, and salads, specializing in Boar's Head deli meats. The menu features varieties of crepes, including chicken florentine, turkey brie, and a Norwegian crepe filled with salmon, capers, and red onions. The Cuban panini and turkey bacon panini are also popular.

Keller's Real Smoked Bar-B-Q, Multiple Locations, 7756 University Blvd., Winter Park, FL 32792; (407) 388-1222; kellersbbq .com/index.html; Parking Lot; Barbecue; $$. Although the state does not rank high among the greats of barbecue renown, here in central Florida we are lucky to have a few places that have stepped up to the plate and brought us some delicious barbecue. From old family traditional recipes and cooking techniques, the folks at Keller's start off every morning trimming fresh beef, pork, chicken, ribs, and turkey. It's all slowly smoked and basted (with a secret sauce recipe handed down over generations) over aged Blackjack oak. Keller's is a popular spot for locals to go for lunch, known for their superb barbecue. The pork ribs and chicken are very popular, but the Sloppy Pork sandwich (Keller's delicious rendition of the Sloppy Joe) is a creation of pure porky pleasure. It's made of slowly smoked, savory, and tender pulled pork in a sweet and tangy sauce all tucked inside a sesame seed bun. Not only is it absolutely tasty but it's also quite a large and filling sandwich, scoring high on the value and taste charts.

Le Macaron, 216 N. Park Ave., Winter Park, FL 32789; (321) 295-7958; lemacaron-us.com; Parking Lot; Bakery; $. Off of Park Avenue, just north of Morse Boulevard, you can walk down an alleyway corridor with a beautiful koi fish pond and stumble upon a small French confectionary shop called Le Macaron. The purveyors of this bakery shop, an offshoot of the original store in Sarasota, are a charming Frenchman and his wife, who take pride in their assortment of chocolates, macarons, and house-made gelatos. The decor reminds me of a small boutique shop, minimalist and modern. Some seating is available outside. Their flavors include Belgian chocolate, gingerbread, Sicilian pistachio, crème brûlée, caramel salted butter, candied ginger chocolate, black vanilla from Madagascar, lemon, fresh mint, raspberry, passion fruit black chocolate, basil white chocolate, chestnut, walnut, crunchy praline, black currant (cassis), and Colombian coffee. Le Macaron also features award-winning, beautifully adorned Norman Love chocolates and truffles. Of particular note, their luscious, unique purple violet flower–flavored gelato is probably one of the best-kept secrets in Orlando.

Mediterranean Deli, 981 W. Fairbanks Ave., Orlando, FL 32804; (407) 539-2650; Parking Lot; Mediterranean; $. Mediterranean Deli is the definition of a hole-in-the-wall. Inside, the restaurant is tiny, with only about 10 seats, and the counter takes up about half the space. The soundtrack is provided by a small CD player that bellows out Middle Eastern music in stereo sound. Scenes of ancient ruins in Lebanon are plastered on the walls of this strip-mall deli. The owner is one of the friendliest and most gracious people in the restaurant business and gives service with a smile. Two rotisserie sticks of *shawarma* meat rotate around a heat source waiting to be carved for consumption. Trays of various salads and sides, from hummus and grape leaves to Greek salad, shirazi, and tabbouleh, line the counter. The most popular item at Mediterranean Deli is the gyro sandwich, prepared in a wonderfully fluffy pita bread with fresh lettuce and tomatoes and a delicious tzatziki cream along with a generous heaping of freshly grilled gyro meat. The gyro here really is among the best in town.

mi Tomatina Paella Bar, 433 W. New England Ave., Winter Park, FL 32789; (321) 972-4881; mitomatina.com; Street Parking and Parking Lot; Tapas/Spanish; $$. Winter Park's mi Tomatina Paella Bar is named for Spain's famous La Tomatina festival, where participants engage in an all-out tomato fight in the streets, splashing the streets in red. Luckily, this intimate little restaurant located in historic Hannibal Square won't have you throwing tomatoes anywhere anytime soon. The tomatoes here are sprinkled throughout the menu of paellas and tapas, starting with the tomato dipping sauce with the complimentary house bread. The decor at mi Tomatina is inspired by the Spanish artist Joan Miró, recognizable for the use of bold reds, blues, and yellows, and simple shapes, with a set of paintings on the wall and colorful mosaic tiles on the tiny tables. If you go for the paella, be ready for a wait—it takes 20 to 30 minutes to make these dishes. It's worth the wait, though, especially to achieve that cherished fragrant, dark brown caramelized crust on the bottom layer of rice, called *socarrat* by the Spanish. Try the paella *fabulosa,* paella rice cooked with squid, octopus, mussels, clams, shrimp, and chicken, but make sure to go with a group to share the feast, as it comfortably feeds two or more.

While you're waiting, mi Tomatina also features a substantive menu of both hot and cold tapas dishes to go with your red or white sangria, made from Spanish wines. Start off with the *plato chico,* served with Manchego cheese, Serrano ham imported from Spain, *morcilla* (a black pudding sausage), and cuts of *lomo* tenderloin over olive oil. The *papas bravas* here are a gourmet version of the more familiar home fries—roasted chunks of potatoes tossed in imported truffle oil, fresh parsley, and shaved Manchego cheese and served with a house-made tomato and pepper red dipping sauce. Try the hearty tortilla con chorizo, a traditional Spanish egg, potato, and onion dish topped with chorizo sausage and accompanied by chive aioli, or the rather American classic macaroni and cheese with a Spanish spin, made with orecchiette pasta and Manchego cheese, oven baked for a gratin finish. Probably my favorite item on the menu is the divine *pato con peras,* succulent pan-roasted duck layered with slices of white wine–poached pear and topped with a sweet pear glaze—perfection! Also try the slow-braised oxtail in a Spanish wine sauce accompanied by a delicate potato mousse and Pedro Ximenez sherry reduction, sweet and savory. After paella, you'll be ready for dessert. Helmed by the talented Chef José Baranenko, mi Tomatina also features a delectable dessert menu with twists on traditional dishes, such as the sweet Tarta Santiago, a crispy puff pastry with Marcona almond filling, served with almond amaretto cream reduction and an almond Florentine cookie. On Thursday through Saturday, join them for a festive evening of flamenco guitar and entertainment.

Nelore Churrascaria, 115 E. Lyman Ave., Winter Park, FL 32789; (407) 645-1112; neloreorlando.com; Street Parking and Parking Lot; Brazilian/Steakhouse; $$$$. This upscale Brazilian steak house is an all-you-can-eat buffet featuring an endless array of grilled meats, seasoned Brazilian style with coarse salt crystals, and served tableside by gauchos (Brazilian cowboys) who walk around the restaurant with skewers of beef and knives. There is a salad bar with over 40 items to start the meal, including tabbouleh, asparagus spears, salmon, shrimp, grilled portobello mushrooms, hearts of palm, red beets, artichokes, black beans and rice, yucca, and more. When you are ready for the meat to arrive, flip the disc on your table from red to green, signaling the gauchos to start heading your way with their meats. You use the small tongs on the table to help grab the meat from the skewers as the gauchos slice them off. As stated previously, the predominant flavor and ingredient of the Brazilian-style meats is salt, so make sure to pick up some green chimichurri sauce to adjust flavors to your liking. There are 15 meats available, including sirloin, leg of lamb, beef ribs, *picanha* house special roast, flank steak, filet mignon, filet mignon wrapped in bacon, chicken breast wrapped in bacon, Parmesan pork, chicken drumstick, sausage, and rib eye. Brazilian cheese bread accompanies the steak, and make sure to try the national drink of Brazil, the Caipirinha, while you are there. For dessert, the house specialty, creme de papaia, or papaya cream, is served with a cassis liquor.

Paris Bistro, 216 N. Park Ave., Winter Park, FL 32789; (407) 671-4424; parisbistroparkavenue.com; Parking Lot and Street Parking;

French; $$$. This beautiful little bistro hidden in an alleyway on the north end of Park Avenue will make you feel like you're in Paris, "La Ville-Lumière," with its romantic lighting, plush red velvet banquette seats, and large mirrors above, and a large tree lit up outside its glass doors. Sounds of Edith Piaf's "La Vie en Rose" and other French classics float on and caress the room's air. Start off with the tender frog legs sautéed in garlic herb butter, or escargots de Bourgogne, luscious little snails cooked with earthy garlic and parsley herb butter. *Boeuf bourguignon,* beef slowly cooked and stewed with vegetables and pinot noir red wine, is done expertly by Executive Chef Sebastian Colce, as is the *canard,* exquisitely sautéed duck breast served with a creamy butter peach sauce or cherry sauce. For dessert, don't miss the crème brûlée or the profiteroles, delightfully light puff pastries filled with ice cream, drizzled with warm chocolate syrup, and topped with whipped cream. *Bon appétit.* Some seating is available by the Avenue's sidewalks for those who wish to dine outside.

Pizzeria Valdiano, 510 N. Orlando Ave., Winter Park, FL 32789; (407) 628-5333; pizzeriavaldiano.com; Parking Lot; Pizza; $. The pizza here, with its crunchy, flavorful crust and delicious toppings and cheese, is simple yet great. They showcase their goods inside a glass case: specials of the day, resplendent pizza pies and strombolis, Sicilian-style rectangular grandma pizza slices, and more. The pizza Valdian is made with sausage, pepperoni, meatballs, green peppers, mushrooms, and onions over exquisitely melted mozzarella and a crust with just enough olive oil to dance with the dough, creating a perfect balance. The crust is particularly crispy yet fluffy, making it incredibly delicious. The smell of the pizza is absolutely intoxicating. The tortellini primavera here is filled with mozzarella and served in a light creamy Alfredo sauce ripe with plum tomatoes, red, green, and orange peppers, red onions, minced garlic, fresh sliced mushrooms, and chopped spinach topped with grated Parmesan, along with 2 garlic rolls brushed with olive oil. A satisfying meal for the palate and the heart.

Rincon Cubano Cafeteria, 3327 Forsyth Rd., Winter Park, FL 32792; (407) 679-5600; Parking Lot; Italian; $. This small, slightly hidden, mom-and-pop Cuban spot is known for its lunch specials and Cuban roast pork. You order at the counter here and can choose from a variety of dishes and specials depending on the day of the week: *pollo guisado, picadillo, pollo con papas,* and others. The Cuban roast rork comes with two sides, such as chickpeas with chorizo sausage, boiled yucca, or rice and beans. Similarly, the *pan con lechon,* a roast pork sandwich, is among the best in town. Enjoy it with a nice cup of *cortadito* espresso with milk and sugar and some guava pastries or *quesitos*. Empanadas are also popular here but can go quickly if you aren't there early enough.

Shipyard Brew Pub, 200 W. Fairbanks Ave., Winter Park, FL 32789; (321) 274-4045; shipyardemporium.com; Parking Lot; Pub Food; $. Founded by the folks from Shipyard Brewing Company, based in Maine, this brewpub features not only a 28-gallon microbrewery but also handcrafted breads baked in house and a market/deli area featuring wines, imported cheeses, and deli meats. Their jalapeño-cheddar loaves are some of the best locally baked bread—all baked each morning—in Winter Park. In addition to a nice list of draft beers, including seasonal Shipyard specials, stouts, IPAs, and Sea Dog Blueberry Wheat ale, they also have their house-made Capt'n Eli root beer on tap for the nonalcoholic drinkers out there. Try them with a beer flight, featuring 4 different 4-ounce samples of any of the draft beers, or join their mug club for special rates and goodies. The menu is mostly salads, sandwiches, and flatbreads with a nod to its New England roots—lobster rolls, clam chowder, and the like are also featured here. Try the Shipyard pot roast sandwich, with satisfying pulled pot roast, yellow cheddar, thinly sliced red onion, sweet banana peppers, and horseradish mayo on a ciabatta roll, or the Fork and Knife Meatball Melt, a big crispy baguette sandwich hollowed out, filled with tender meatballs and zesty red sauce, and baked with provolone. The chicken and shrimp étouffée is a faithful rendering of the Cajun dish made with white-meat chicken chunks, large shrimp sautéed in Cajun spices, peppers, tomatoes, and onions, then tossed in étouffée sauce and served over dirty rice.

Tibby's New Orleans Kitchen, 2203 Aloma Ave., Winter Park, FL 32792; tibbysneworleanskitchen.com; (407) 672-5753; Parking Lot; Cajun; $$. Created by the folks who brought together the local chain Tijuana Flats, Tibby's New Orleans Kitchen is their take on New Orleans–style Cajun cuisine. The decor inside is a raucous, vibrant affair with deep purple and light green walls and an eclectic mix of New Orleans paraphernalia decking the walls, creating a festive and fun atmosphere. This popular neighborhood joint serves up Cajun fare, such as oysters remoulade, andouille sausage jambalaya, seafood gumbo, 12-napkin roast beef po' boy sandwiches, Muffulettas, and more. Beer is served up in giant ice-cold chalices, so you'll feel like the king of the Mardi Gras parade when it's all done. Don't forget the bread pudding and fried beignets for dessert.

Winter Park Fish Company, 761 Orange Ave., Winter Park, FL 32789; (407) 622-6112; thewinterparkfishco.com; Parking Lot; Seafood; $$$. Helmed by Chef George Vogelbacher, who is an Orlando institution in himself, and with fish provided through Gary's Seafood, you know that the quality of the fish here is above par. As their motto goes, "Cheap fish isn't good, and good fish isn't cheap." The place has the rustic, dive-y feeling of a well-kept New England fish shack, with a nice display case of all the fresh fish cuts available, such as Alaskan salmon, tuna, grouper, and more—you can even buy some to take home if you like. You order at the counter here and the dishes are sent out to the patio deck seating outside or inside at one of the picnic table booths. For stew lovers, they have a wonderfully hearty cioppino seafood stew made with shrimp, mussels, clams, lobster tail, and fish in a rich tomato broth served with or without pasta, and a seafood bouillabaisse made in a fennel, leek, and saffron–infused broth. Try one of their many fresh fish plates prepared grilled, blackened, pan seared, fried, Cajun spiced, lemon pepper, or jerked with 2 sides. I particularly liked their blackened grilled yellowtail snapper with coconut rice. Fish Company favorites are also available, such as the grouper cheeks wrapped in parchment with red and green peppers, onions, and herb garlic butter, or the Florida cobia, pan seared and topped with basil truffle butter. Don't miss their sandwiches, such as the award-winning lobster roll made with lobster, celery, and mayo on a brioche roll.

The Wine Room on Park Avenue, 270 S. Park Ave., Winter Park, FL 32789; (407) 696-9463; thewineroomonline.com; Street Parking and Parking Lot; Wine Bar; $$. This cavernous, intimate wine bar and shop features a warm, relaxing atmosphere, welcoming wine novices and experts alike to sip and try one of the many different wines. Enomatic machines designed in Italy allow consumers to sample wines in various amounts, using cards that can be loaded periodically to pay. The Wine Room offers 148 wines by the 1-ounce pour and 100 wines by the half glass and full glass, so guests can sample many different wines without breaking the bank. Wines come from all over the globe, from Australia to South America, and feature interesting whites to sweet reds and even a critic's choice and rare wines room. In addition to wine, there is also a Champagne and beer bar as well as an extensive collection of artisanal and farmstead cheeses to pair with your wine, Champagne, or beer. At any given time, the Wine Room carries approximately 50 cheeses that can be enjoyed either alone or in one of the available cheese flights. The charcuterie sampler is also a popular treat, featuring a single serving of pepper salami, dry salami, and herbed salami, served with a French baguette and mustard. The *foie gras* mousse and mousse truffle, a luxurious black truffle mousse flavored with sherry wine, are also popular. For more substantial fare, try out the wild mushroom and blue cheese bruschetta with truffle oil or the melted brie, with baked pears, pancetta, and honey flatbread pizza, or one of the many salads, sandwiches, and desserts available. The orange caramel panna cotta, traditional Italian custard served with a dollop of orange marmalade, caramel sauce, and orange zest, is sure to go well with that dessert wine you may be sipping at the end of the night. Monthly wine classes are also available, as well as a chateau-style walk-in vault for private parties.

Specialty Stores, Markets & Producers

The Ancient Olive, 324 N. Park Ave., Winter Park, FL 32789; (321) 972-1899; theancientolive.com. This specialty tasting room features ultra-premium extra-virgin olive oils imported from around the world. Their oils come from Australia, Tunisia, Greece, Spain, Portugal, Argentina, and Italy, and each is provided with information regarding its origin, such as the crush date and the chemical profile, including polyphenol and oleic acid levels. The Ancient Olive also features fused olive oils *agrumato,* where the olive is crushed with whole citrus fruits, such as lemons or blood oranges. The balsamic vinegars here range from an 18-year-old traditional aged balsamic from Modena, Italy, to balsamic vinegars infused with such flavors as lavender, honey and ginger, fig, and espresso.

Eat More Produce, 1111 S. Orlando Ave., Winter Park, FL 32789; (407) 647-5292; eatmoreproduce.com; Parking Lot. Eat More Produce is like having a year-round farmers' market at your leisure. Plenty of produce is in season, including hydroponic tomatoes, as well as local artisan bread from Old Hearth Bakery, local Winter Park honey, gluten-free products, local eggs, and a whole section for wine. The deli section has a sizable selection of Boar's Head meats, and they serve up a few pretty good sandwiches as well. Try their Reuben or the Cuban. Recently a food truck was added, serving up fresh barbecue meats for lunch. Sign up for their online newsletter for the latest specials at the market, too.

Lacomka Russian Bakery & Deli, 2050 N. Semoran Blvd. #140, Winter Park, FL 32792; (407) 677-1101; lacomka-orlando .com; Parking Lot. This bakery and deli not only bakes some of the local Russian community's designer wedding cakes, but it also serves up delicious Russian cuisine favorites and pastries. Lacomka, which also has a well-stocked grocery area and deli section, serves up some savory *blinchiki*, Russian pancakes rolled with meat and mushrooms or cottage cheese, and hearty Ukrainian borscht soup, made with beets, cabbage, carrots, potatoes, onions, and meat. The Russian *pelmeni* and *vareniki*-style dumplings and *golubtsy* (stuffed cabbage) are also favorites here. The bakery section offers European wrapped chocolates, cookies, and homemade cakes, such as dark chocolate raspberry cake and a traditional Karina 5-layer Russian cake with buttercream and honey.

Lombardi's Seafood Market, 1152 Harmon Ave., Winter Park, FL 32789; (407) 628-3474; lombardis.com. One of the best seafood markets in Orlando—though we are only 30 minutes from the ocean, we are seriously lacking in seafood markets at the moment—Lombardi's has some of the freshest and best-priced seafood in

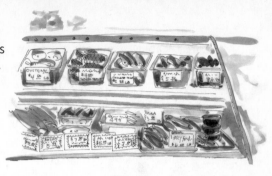

town. Their glass cases hold Atlantic salmon fillets, snow crab clusters, jumbo shrimp, grouper fillets, oysters, clams, blue crabs, and more. They also sell seasonings, spices, and fry batter for your fish if you like. Not many people know this, but there is a part of the market that serves as a seafood cafe. There you will find some great po' boy sandwich selections and chowders, as well as a fish of the day prepared blackened, grilled, or fried.

The Meat House Neighborhood Butcher & Grocer, 669 Orange Ave., Winter Park, FL 32789; (407) 629-6328; themeathouse .com. A "modern revival of your neighborhood butcher and grocer," the Meat House is a fancy, clean market featuring marinated and dry-aged steaks, chicken, beef, lamb, pork, veal, and more. They also sell local bread made by **Shipyard Brew Pub** (see p. 71) up the street, as well as spices and other grocery items.

Penzey's Spice, 102 N. Park Ave., Winter Park, FL 32789; (407) 788-7777; penzeys.com. Penzey's offers more than 250 gourmet spices and blends for your culinary needs.

Peterbrooke Chocolatier, 300 S. Park Ave., Winter Park, FL 32789; (407) 644-3200; peterbrookewp.com; Parking Garage and

Lot. Located in historic downtown Winter Park on Park Avenue, Peterbrooke Chocolatier was first established here in 2001. In 2009 the store underwent a change of ownership when Jami Wray and her husband, Kevin Wray, realized their dream of owning a chocolate store. Some of their more famous items include the Jami Shoos chocolate shoes, chocolate-covered bacon, and chocolate-covered pretzel Cat Tails. All are amazing. They also create special-order chocolate items and host demonstrations throughout the year.

The Spice & Tea Exchange, 309 N. Park Ave., Winter Park, FL 32789; (407) 647-7423; spiceandtea.com. With very knowledgeable and helpful owners and customer service, you'll be able to find gourmet seasonings and spices, cooking herbs, gourmet teas, sugars, sea salts, and signature blends and rubs for your dish or drink. There is a huge selection of gourmet spices: chile powders, cheese powders, smoked powders, and more. Try some of their best sellers, such as the Tuscany blend, butcher's rub, or the black truffle salt.

Whole Foods Market, 1989 Aloma Ave., Winter Park, FL 32792; (407) 673-8788; wholefoodsmarket.com/stores/winterpark. Whole Foods Market provides one of the largest selections of natural and organic foods in central Florida, featuring more than 75 locally grown fruits and vegetables every day, as well as fresh-cut, ready-to-use or ready-to-eat fruits and vegetables. If you're hungry and don't want to cook, check out the prepared foods section, containing more than 100 items from both a full-service and a self-service hot bar, salad bar, juice bar, soup bar, and dessert bar. There is also an extensive seafood department with an in-house seafood smoker, as well as a full-service butcher-style meat department featuring dry-aged beef, a bakery, and a cheese and wine corner. Check their calendar online for special events featuring local and national chefs and guests.

Central Orlando

Greater Central Orlando

 Best of the Neighborhood

Le Coq au Vin, 4800 S. Orange Ave., Orlando, FL 32806; (407) 851-6980; lecoqauvinrestaurant.com; Parking Lot; French; $$$. Since opening in 1976, Le Coq au Vin has continued to provide new-world flavors to classic French cuisine. Today the restaurant is owned and operated by Chef Reimund Pitz and his wife, Sandy, in partnership with original owners Chef Louis and Magdalena Perrotte. The farm-to-table philosophy is very much present, with many ingredients sourced here in Florida, and a few herbs are even grown in the garden on the premises. Set in a charming little country house just south of downtown Orlando, Le Coq au Vin provides a warm, classy interior atmosphere without being too stuffy—each evening you can see Sandy walking around to greet and welcome guests. Start off with a rich cup of *soupe a l'oignon,* a traditional onion soup with apple cider, cream, gratinée with gruyère and Emmental Swiss cheeses, or the very fresh Florida frog legs, lightly seasoned and sautéed, topped with tomatoes and cheese, and finished with beurre blanc. The namesake coq au vin is a delectable braised chicken with rich red wine, mushrooms, bacon, onions, rosemary, herbs, and carrots, served with egg noodles. For meat lovers, try the *tournedos,* beef tenderloin steak on shredded short ribs, with a blue cheese crust, forest mushrooms, set in a sweet port wine sauce, and served with classic carrots with thyme and au gratin potatoes. End the night with the luscious Grand Marnier soufflé, a fluffy, sweet delight. See Le Coq au Vin's recipe for **Coquilles St. Jacques** on p. 238.

Linda's La Cantina, 4721 E. Colonial Dr., Orlando, FL 32803; (407) 894-4491; lindaslacantinasteakhouse.com; Parking Lot; Steak House; $$$. One of the oldest establishments left standing in Orlando, Linda's La Cantina has been serving up USDA choice steaks cut on site to central Florida since 1947. Set against classic black and white-checked tablecloths, the menu features juicy, succulent, and tender seared steaks, such as filet mignon wrapped in bacon, top sirloin strip, rib eye, and New York strip, as well as a few Italian items harkening back to La Cantina's founding days as an Italian restaurant.

Charlie's Gourmet Pastries, 3213 Curry Ford Rd., Orlando, FL 32806; (407) 898-9561; charliesgourmetpastries.com; Bakery/ Desserts; $$. Charlie Hawks had been a baker at Wolfie's on the Beach in Miami for 20 years when he left the town to follow his dreams and opened Charlie's Gourmet Pastries in Orlando in 1971. Since then the bakery has doubled in size in the same location. Charlie's son is a fourth-generation baker, carrying on his father's dream. The bakery continues to bake all sorts of pastries, such as cakes, pies, cookies, cannolis, danishes, cheesecakes, turnovers, cupcakes, and more. Don't miss the checkerboard cake, apple raisin streudel, Boston cream pie, and black forest cakes.

Hot Dog Heaven, 5355 E. Colonial Dr., Orlando, FL 32807; (407) 282-5746; hotdogheaven.com; Parking Lot; Hot Dogs; $. Serving up authentic Chicago hot dogs since 1987, the local, family-run Hot Dog Heaven specializes in dishing out Vienna beef products to happy central Floridians. Step up to the counter to order and enjoy your dog inside or outside at one of the picnic tables facing the traffic on Colonial Drive. Try the authentic Chicago dog, a 100 percent pure beef Vienna natural-casing hot dog on a steamed poppy-seed bun, topped with mustard, relish, onion, tomato, pickle, and hot peppers with a side of hot slivers of crinkle-cut french fries.

Il Pescatore, 651 N. Primrose Dr., Orlando, FL 32803; (407) 896-6763; ilpescatoreonline.com; Parking Lot; Italian; $$. This small, family-owned Italian restaurant serves up made-from-scratch Italian classics. The Tortellini Di Stefano is served with a creamy meat sauce with a touch of prosciutto, baked, and topped with provolone cheese, while the *salsiccia con pepperoni* is made with sausage sautéed with onions and peppers in a light tomato sauce. Don't miss the gnocchi Piemontese, or the meat and cheese–filled canneloni, and penne *alla romana* pasta.

Johnny's Fillin' Station and Johnny's Other Side, 2631 S. Fern Creek Ave., Orlando, FL 32806; (407) 894-6900; johnnysfillin station.com; Parking Lot; Burgers; $. Johnny's Fillin' Station and Johnny's Other Side are rowdy little adjacent neighborhood restaurants in the setting of a former biker bar with the most popular item on the menu being the half-pound hamburgers. They boast of having the best burgers in Orlando, though some other places may make the same claim. Go for some cheesy tots and the Fillin' Station Full Service burger, a juicy, succulent beef patty topped with ham, mushrooms, and your choice of cheese with lettuce, tomato, and onion. If you are feeling more adventurous, try the Roy burger, topped with sour cream and jalapeños, or the Texas Toast Melt burger, topped with Thousand Island dressing and choice of cheese on thick slices of Texas toast. Freddy's Feed the Big Fella burger, a bacon cheeseburger with slivers of avocado and topped with a fried egg, may give you heartache later, but for the moment, it's worth it.

Oblivion Taproom, 5101 E. Colonial Dr., Orlando, FL 32803; (407) 802-4800; obliviontaproom.com; Parking Lot; Burgers/Pub Food; $. From the skull-and-bones motif to the creative menu items, Oblivion Taproom is not your everyday run-of-the-mill bar and grill. With over 40 rotating craft beers on tap and a large array of ciders, as well as a playful menu of comfort bar food, Oblivion Taproom is quickly becoming one of the more popular bars for beer lovers. Prepared by Culinary Institute of America–trained Chef Jim "Goody" Goodman, the menu contains smoked chicken wings, seasoned with a house barbecue dry rub, slow-smoked, "crisped," and served with house ranch, and daily specials like poutine burger, crispy tater bowls, and seasoned, deep-fried black-eyed peas. The burger list includes some fantastic, creative burgers, such as the Jalapineo, a teriyaki-marinated beef burger with jalapeño cream cheese, grilled pineapple, applewood-smoked bacon, and passion fruit aioli on a brioche bun, and the pretzel burger, using a warm pretzel bun slathered with caraway beer mustard and served with a side of cheese sauce.

Pizzeria Del-Dio, 3210 E. Colonial Dr., Orlando, FL 32803; (407) 898-1115; pizzeriadel-dio.com; Parking Lot; Pizza; $. Del-Dio's originated in Brooklyn, New York, and was a favorite neighborhood eatery in Carnasie for over 20 years. Family owned and operated, Pizzeria Del-Dio serves up traditional Italian pastas, soups, and New York–style pizza. The pizzas here use made-from-scratch tomato sauce and are hand tossed, probably some of the best in town, baked with a light airy crust and high-quality cheese and sauce ingredients. Try the *pasta e fagioli* soup or the homemade meatballs as well.

Yaya's Cuban Cafe and Bakery, 632 Hewett Dr., Orlando, FL 32807; (407) 275-7555; yayascubancafe.com; Cuban/Latin; $. This little neighborhood Cuban cafe is a bit hidden and definitely a hole-in-the-wall, though one with a lot of *sabor*. The first things you'll notice are the trays of *quesitos,* pastries filled with cream cheese and honey glaze, and *pasteles de queso* and guava. These pastries are all quite delectable. Breakfast at Yaya's includes 2 eggs, bacon, sausage, or ham on Cuban toast, and a small *cafe con leche* to jump-start your day. With any respectable Cuban establishment are the customary *frijoles negros* (black bean soup over rice) and Cuban sandwiches, pressed and filled with roasted pork, ham, swiss cheese, mustard, mayo, and pickles. The beef *frita* (*vaca frita*) is my favorite entree here, an ample portion of stewed beef seared to a crispy outer finish with onions and spices.

Specialty Stores, Markets & Producers

Freshfields Farm, 400 E. Compton St., Orlando, FL 32806; (407) 423-3309; freshfieldsfarm.com. This Orlando landmark provides some of the freshest produce and meats in town, with many of the products coming directly from farmers, growers, and packing plants. There are two parts to this market: the meat area featuring USDA choice beef and a variety of fresh seafood, and a produce section featuring an expansive list of daily specials and peak-season fruits and vegetables. Don't forget to pick up a cone of vanilla ice cream on the way out from the treat shop outside.

903 Mills Market, 903 S. Mills Ave., Orlando, FL 32806; (407) 898-4392; 903millsmarket.com; Parking Lot and Street Parking. Set in a quiet residential neighborhood, 903 Mills Market is the perfect place for some sandwich, flatbread, or salad noshing. The deli cafe serves up creative sandwiches, such as the Grateful Bread, composed of roasted turkey, cranberry mayo, blue cheese, stuffing, and red onion on your choice of bread. Try also the Magic Three Pointer, a meaty sandwich made of roast beef, ham, turkey, bacon, and swiss cheese with lettuce, tomato, onion, mayo, and mustard on rye bread, or the signature 903 Market chicken wrap, consisting of grilled chicken, mango, papaya, pineapple, walnuts, blue cheese crumbles, and poppy seeds on a spring mix with mango vinaigrette dressing. The hearty Rodger Dodger, a roast beef and corned beef sandwich topped with melted swiss on swirled rye with lettuce, tomato, and Thousand Island dressing, is sure to please as well.

Mills 50 District

Named after the intersection of Mills Avenue and SR 50 (aka Colonial Drive), the Mills 50 District is an eclectic neighborhood known for being a mix both of the arts and of cultural diversity. Throughout the neighborhood, local artists have painted various scenes on traffic-light boxes to express the area's quirky personality and uniqueness. On one side of the coin, businesses in the area cover a broad range with an independent bent: tattoo parlors, alternative medicine practices, visual art studios, design studios, photography, hair salons, and more, as well as popular bars and restaurants. The Mills 50 District also prides itself on being gay-friendly and open, and embracing all cultures and backgrounds. After 1975, when the Vietnam War ended, countless Vietnamese refugees fled persecution to America, with quite a few settling in central Florida. With any large immigrant population, markets and restaurants appear and grow to cater to their needs, and today Orlando's Mills 50 District is home to the largest concentration of Asian American–owned businesses in Florida. There are many Asian markets offering fresh produce and goods as well as restaurants serving Vietnamese, Chinese, Korean, Thai, and Japanese cuisine in the area. Each weekend hundreds of Vietnamese American families from around Florida travel to the district on their day off from work to enjoy some *pho* and to pick up nail salon supplies, groceries for the week, and a bag of *banh mi* sandwiches for the road.

Ánh Hông, 1124 E. Colonial Dr., Orlando, FL 32803; (407) 999-2656; Parking Lot; Vietnamese; $. This little Vietnamese shop on the corner of Mills Avenue and Colonial Drive features some great flavors. Standard Vietnamese fare is served here with a menu of over 150 items. Start with some *goi* (papaya salad) with Vietnamese beef jerky or pork and shrimp, or the raw beef with tripe and rice chips. Fresh summer rolls, rice platters with grilled pork, tomato, lettuce, and sunny-side-up eggs, and more are all good choices. The Pho Xe Lô Ánh Hông, a special combination with an extra-large bowl of beef rice noodle soup topped with brisket, beef navel, flank, omasa, tendon, eye of round, and beef balls, is sure to satisfy any hungry appetite.

Bananas Modern American Diner, 924 N. Mills Ave., Orlando, FL 32803; (407) 480-2200; bananasdiner.com; American; $$. This eclectic diner features some of the best food available late night in town, with reimaginings of traditional diner cuisine with a creative, culinary twist. Open 24 hours on Friday and Saturday, the diner features milk shakes, breakfast, eggs Benedict, ever-changing seasonal mac 'n' cheese, salads, burgers, and more. For the really hungry folks, try the classic chicken 'n' waffles, composed of deep-fried buttermilk chicken with a Belgian waffle and topped with country gravy, or the Garbage Plate, made of grilled chicken, hot dogs, or burgers, layered with hash browns and mac salad, and covered with sauce. For breakfast, there's the stuffed French toast and the buffalo Benedict, made with 2 poached eggs served atop toasted English muffin halves, melted blue cheese, hollandaise sauce, and a drizzle of buffalo sauce. Join them on Sunday for the gospel brunch show, led by female impersonators in drag.

Banh Mi Nha Trang, 1216 E. Colonial Dr., Orlando, FL 32803; (407) 585-6998; nhatrangsub.com; Parking Lot; Vietnamese/Sandwiches; $. It is a bit hard to find Banh Mi Nha Trang, as it is tucked away in a courtyard on Colonial Drive just to the east of the intersection with Mills Avenue. This unassuming hole-in-the-wall is a mom-and-pop shop, run by a lovable, friendly, and always smiling Vietnamese lady and her husband. Their English may not be the greatest, but their food transcends language boundaries. The mainstay is their *banh mi,* sandwiches made with Vietnamese deli meats, pickled carrots and daikon, herbs, and pâté all inside a sub roll. The owners make their own meats here and also sell homemade *nem chua* pickled meat and *cha lua* pork roll meats. They specialize in Banh Mi Nha Trang, a *banh mi* from the south-central coastal region of Vietnam and topped with a special garlic fish sauce and peppery goodness. Cash only.

Boston Bakery & Cafe, 1525 E. Colonial Dr., Orlando, FL 32803; (407) 228-1219; Parking Lot; Vietnamese/Sandwiches; $. Located just west of Bumby Avenue off of Colonial Drive, Boston Bakery & Cafe probably has some of the best *banh mi* in Orlando, if they have them available on your visit. This place neither has much to do with Boston nor is it a bakery in the traditional sense of the term. They sell *banh mi,* those lovely Vietnamese sub sandwiches filled with carrots and daikon, cucumbers, veggies, and deli meats or meatballs or pâté, all for $3. What makes the *banh mi* at Boston bakery good is their homemade French baguette bread that they bake in-house, fresh, tasty, and crunchy. Try their *banh mi dac biet,* a special combo with various cuts of Vietnamese deli meats. At this hole-in-the-wall, the service ranges from minimal to nil, and they don't take credit cards. But *banh mi* is a street-food item anyway, where travelers order, pick up, and head on their way. Make sure you give them a call first, as they sometimes run out of bread.

Dandelion Communitea Cafe, 618 N. Thornton Ave., Orlando, FL 32803; (407) 362-1864; dandelioncommunitea.com; Parking Lot; Vegetarian/Sandwiches; $. Serving up healthy vegetarian fare and loose-leaf teas since 2006, Dandelion Communitea Cafe has become a homey community cafe with a popular following among those seeking a healthier lifestyle. The cafe supports local, organic,

vegetarian, and eco-friendly initiatives and the menu reflects its philosophy. Try the Native Mama mix, made of highly nutritious quinoa, or the Fluffer Nutter sandwich, made with almond butter, bananas, and rice-mallow fluff. The Giddyup, one of the most popular wraps here,

is composed of fresh spring greens, crumbled blue corn chips, the house chili, and fresh diced tomatoes and scallions, and served with vegan queso or organic dairy cheddar.

Funky Monkey Wine Company, 912 N. Mills Ave., Orlando, FL 32803; (407) 427-1447; funkymonkeywine.com; Modern American/ Sushi; $$$. Serving up sushi, steak, and seafood as well as functioning as a classic wine bar, Funky Monkey Wine Company brings together creative and classic dishes. For starters, try the panko-almond-crusted fried goat cheese served with sun-dried tomato jam, fruit salsa, and crostini, or the Monkey Balls, made with seasoned rice, soy, green onions, cream cheese, sesame oil, and herbs. For sushi, try the signature Funky Monkey roll, made with spicy ahi tuna, avocado, cucumber, cream cheese, and sesame seeds. For those looking for more substantial fare, try the Jumbo Scallops Drunken, made with Maine lobster mashed potatoes and microbrew bacon sauce, and served with a side of vegetables. Reservations are recommended Friday evenings at Point Orlando when there is a Las Vegas–style female impersonator show. Additional location: 9101 International Dr., Orlando, FL 32819; (407) 418-9463.

Garden Cafe, 810 W. Colonial Dr., Orlando, FL 32804; (407) 999-9799; Parking Lot; Vegetarian/Chinese; $. Garden Cafe is a local vegetarian and vegan restaurant specializing in Chinese dishes

BUBBLE TEA

Boba, or bubble tea, was brought over to the States via Taiwan and popularized in little trendy bubble tea shops in college towns and Chinatowns throughout America. Chewy Boba Company is the place to find the tea in Orlando. The *bobas* in the drink are made of small tapioca starch balls that sink to the bottom of the drink, and you sip them up using oversize straws. Try the sweet Thai tea, or for something different, the iced taro milk tea with *boba,* a creamy purple drink deriving its flavors from the starchy, sweet taro root. For those wanting something cooler, try the sweet strawberry lychee slush with lychee jelly, made with crushed ice. 1212 E. Colonial Dr., Orlando, FL 32803; (407) 897-1377; Parking Lot; $.

using "mock" meats made with soy-based products, tofu, and flavorings. The crispy orange "beef," "pork chop" in Peking sauce, satay squid, "beef" and broccoli, and spring rolls are all popular favorites. The flavors all mimic the taste and texture of meat but are entirely meatless, so don't feel too guilty ordering these dishes.

Hawkers Asian Street Fare, 1103 N. Mills Ave., Orlando, FL 32803; (407) 237-0606; hawkersstreetfare.com; Parking Lot; Asian/ Malaysian; $. Although you won't see anyone yelling about here, the cuisine is heavily influenced by the food peddled by street hawkers in Asia, particularly in Malaysia. Many of the curry dishes, skewered beef, noodles, and more show the owner's family influence. The decor at Hawkers is similar to the urban warehouse feel of Chipotle, with walls accented by corrugated metal sheets and high bar-top stools. Photos of street-food scenes from Vietnam to Malaysia decorate the walls. Chinese newspapers are laminated into the tabletops, reminiscent of street stalls in Asia. Many of the dishes here are portioned tapas style to share. I recommend getting a few of each and also a noodle soup bowl for yourself. For an appetizer, the *roti canai* is one of the signature dishes from Southeast Asia; here it is served with a crispy pan-fried flat roti bread that you dip in the rich, tangy curry sauce. One of my favorite dishes is the *char kwa teo* noodles, a Malaysian dish from the Teochiu people who immigrated from China, reminiscent of a Chinese-influenced pad thai with touches of soy sauce. The very spicy prawn *mee* noodle soup is a satisfying bowl made with a shrimp- and pork-based soup, topped with slices of hard-boiled egg, Chinese vegetables, and shrimp. Try the curry *laksa* noodle soup as well. Hawkers has an impressive beer selection, including some beers that come from local Orlando Brewing Company downtown. Go with a group of friends, share, and enjoy, imagining yourself eating and drinking away the night in a street-stall restaurant in Asia.

King Cajun Crawfish, 914 N. Mills Ave., Orlando, FL 32803; (407) 704-8863; kingcajuncrawfish.com; Parking Lot; Cajun/Seafood; $.

This hole-in-the-wall located off of Mills Avenue just north of Colonial Drive serves up some very flavorful and tasty crawfish. Save yourself the mess of having a crawfish boil at home by coming to King Cajun Crawfish. You can order the crawfish in a variety of flavors including garlic, hot, and shabang! The owners are a family of Vietnamese immigrants who spent time in the Cajun bayous of Louisiana before transplanting to Orlando. In addition to crawfish, King Cajun Crawfish serves up some wonderful po' boy sandwiches of oyster, shrimp, fish, and chicken in soft baguette rolls, and a great bowl of gumbo soup with rice.

Lac Viêt Bistro, 2021 E. Colonial Dr., Orlando, FL 32803; (407) 228-4000; lacvietbistro.com; Parking Lot; Vietnamese; $$. The decor inside is subtle, with light, earthy tones and slightly dim lighting; paintings of Vietnamese women hang on the walls, historically renowned for their beauty, elegance, and veracity. The ambience is beautifully delicate and peaceful, much like the dishes found here. The *bo tai me,* thinly sliced tamarind-cured beef carpaccio with herbs, basil, and crushed peanuts, served with shrimp crackers, is a playful, tangy, delightful dish to start. The dishes here are more influenced by the northern Vietnamese cuisine style, featuring *bun cha ha noi,* a Hanoi-style grilled pork platter with rice vermicelli noodles, and *banh cuon lac viet,* a rice crepe with a combination of ground pork, grilled pork, and ground shrimp rice crepes served with black pepper seasoned pork casserole. The *canh bun,* a northern Vietnamese–style noodle soup, is made with a light broth, seasoned ground shrimp, crab meat, tomato, and water spinach.

COOKING CLASSES AT
TRUFFLES AND TRIFLES

Started by Marci Arthur over two decades ago, Truffles and Trifles is Orlando's local cooking school, which can be a fun social event. Couples, singles, families, coworkers, and children alike are invited. For lessons in techniques from summer grilling, to Italian dishes, to baking sweet desserts, you can pick the course you want to learn from the most. Classes get booked quickly, as only 25 seats are available, so make sure to register early. Don't forget to visit the gourmet shop, with Belgian chocolates, cocoas, vanillas, and kitchen equipment to aid in your cooking journey. Or pick up some custom gourmet cookies, cakes, cupcakes, breads, and desserts to go. 11 Smith St., Orlando, FL 32804; (407) 648-0838; trufflesandtrifles.com.

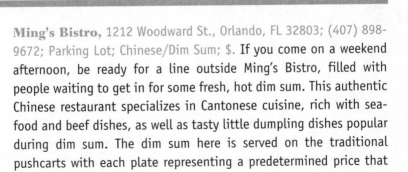

Ming's Bistro, 1212 Woodward St., Orlando, FL 32803; (407) 898-9672; Parking Lot; Chinese/Dim Sum; $. If you come on a weekend afternoon, be ready for a line outside Ming's Bistro, filled with people waiting to get in for some fresh, hot dim sum. This authentic Chinese restaurant specializes in Cantonese cuisine, rich with seafood and beef dishes, as well as tasty little dumpling dishes popular during dim sum. The dim sum here is served on the traditional pushcarts with each plate representing a predetermined price that the push cart ladies mark down on your ticket as you go, running the gamut from steamed chicken feet and pork spare ribs to shrimp dumplings and pork-stuffed bean curd skin. For heartier fare, ask for the beef chow fun noodles, sweet and sour Peking-style pork chop, or ginger scallion fish fillets. Don't be afraid to follow local custom and call out to your waitresses here if you need something.

Pho 88, 730 N. Mills Ave., Orlando, FL 32803; (407) 897-3488; pho88orlando.com/index.htm; Parking Lot; Vietnamese; $. If you are looking for a casual, comfortable place for an introduction to Vietnamese cuisine, Pho 88 is where to begin. It's no wonder why, with large glass windows facing busy Mills Avenue and plenty of seating for large parties, this place is packed with people every day of the week. The popular and delectable *pho* (beef noodle soup) is a must-try. Get the *pho dac biet,* the beef rice noodle soup topped with eye round steak, well-done flank, fat brisket, soft tendon, book tripe, and beef balls, and help yourself to the assortment of bean sprouts, basil, mint, and herbs to add to your soup as you like. For chicken lovers, the *pho ga* is a tasty alternative; the noodle soup is made with chicken broth and chicken meats instead of beef. There are over 178 items on the menu, including a whole list of *banh mi* sub sandwiches, rice platters with grilled tofu, pork, chicken, or beef, stir-fry dishes, rice vermicelli noodle bowls, and vegetarian dishes. Savor it all with a glass of *cafe sua da*, Vietnamese iced coffee with condensed milk, or *da chanh,* Vietnamese limeade. The avocado and jackfruit smoothies are creamy, sweet, and decadent drinks meant to be enjoyed on hot summer days. Take some time to check out the ever-changing local graffiti art on their south wall, too.

Pho Hoa Noodle Soup Restaurant, 649 N. Primrose Dr., Orlando, FL 32803; (407) 895-6098; phohoa.com; Parking Lot; Vietnamese; $. Pho Hoa specializes in *pho,* the Vietnamese national dish, a beef rice noodle soup. The *pho* here is rich and flavorful and is among the best in town. *Bo la lot,* a grilled betel leaf–wrapped beef, is a popular starter, as are the *chim cut chien,* crispy fried quail served with salt, pepper, and lime. For those looking for more authentic dishes, try the *bo kho,* a hearty Vietnamese-style beef stew made with beef, carrots, and a mixture of cinnamon, star anise, curry, and Chinese 5-spices and served with either french bread or rice noodles. Though this is a chain, it is locally owned by a Vietnamese family and each item has this location's own little personal touch.

Pho Vinh Restaurant, 657 N. Primrose Dr., Orlando, FL 32803; (407) 228-0043; phovinhorlando.com; Parking Lot; Vietnamese; $. One of the best Vietnamese restaurants in town, Pho Vinh provides some of the most authentic and delicious Vietnamese dishes. The decor is elegant and warm, and the service here is better than many of the other Vietnamese places in town. *Pho,* the national dish of Vietnam, is a specialty here with a rich, beefy broth and fresh rice noodles. Start out with an order of *cha giò,* fresh and tasty fried spring rolls, and wrap them in the accompanying lettuce, dip into the *nuoc cham* fish sauce, and enjoy. For beginners, try the *pho bo vien,* the beef rice noodle soup served with beef balls. For the more advanced, get the *pho dac biet,* a special combo beef rice noodle soup with slices of medium-rare steak, brisket, flank, tendon, and tripe. Try also the *ech chien bo,* butter-fried frog legs with lettuce and tomatoes, a relic of Vietnam's French colonial past.

Pom Pom's Teahouse and Sandwicheria, 67 N. Bumby Ave., Orlando, FL 32803; (407) 894-0865; pompomsteahouse.com; Parking Lot; Sandwiches; $. Here at this indie, homey sandwich shop—with walls bedecked in local artwork—there are over 20 types of sandwiches to order, with each 'wich set to a playful yet delicious gourmet theme. Like the Mama Ling Ling's Thanksgiving, a monstrous sandwich of turkey, ginger cranberry chutney, gouda, stuffing, mashed potato, and cream cheese served with a side of gravy, so now you can have that after-Thanksgiving-dinner-meal feeling all year round. Or try the villainous Fu Man Chu, made with a sweet hoisin barbecue sauce–based Asian pulled pork, watercress, goat cheese, ginger cranberry chutney, and spicy red onions, a perfect lunch for all those deviants out there. It's got sweetness from the barbecue and cranberry chutney, a little tart from the red onions, savory from the pulled pork, and creamy from the goat cheese. It sounds like quite the mess, but it's strangely satisfying and fulfilling. Pace yourself; these sandwiches are large and can easily be shared between two people. There is also a wide variety of diverse salads to tantalize your taste buds. The place is pretty small and can get quite busy, so sit back, relax, and enjoy one of the many house blend or specialty teas, such as the Rooibos Love tea. End the meal with one of their fabulous desserts, such as the red velvet cupcake imported from nearby **Blue Bird Bake Shop** (see p. 117). One thing I love about Pom Pom's, despite the very hip ambience, is the eclectic clientele: from trendy hipsters, to twenty-something working ladies in heels, to college students on a first date, everyone is here together under one roof enjoying good food. Sometimes on the weekends they are open 24 hours, when interesting late-night conversations over tea and sandwiches are sure to ensue. A tiny teahouse with a big heart in the City Beautiful.

Raphsodic Bakery Urban Pastry Art House, 710 N. Mills Ave., Orlando, FL 32803; (407) 704-8615; raphsodic.com; Street Parking; Vegetarian/Bakery; $. Located in the heart of Orlando, in a refurbished old building, Raphsodic dedicates itself to organic, vegetarian baked goods. At Raphsodic, they sell homemade hummus, gluten-free cupcakes, organic cookies, and more, all 100 percent vegan and 100 percent free from animal testing and made without any milk. They also do not use trans fats, hydrogenated oils, or synthetic flavors in their food. My favorite is the lemon ginger cupcake (contains gluten), which is a moist, deliciously sweet cupcake with a hint of ginger on top of the icing.

SEA Thai Restaurant, 3812 E. Colonial Dr., Orlando, FL 32803; (407) 895-0985; seaorlando.com; Parking Lot; Thai; $$. Five fundamental flavors—spicy, sour, sweet, salty, and bitter—make up the balanced meal for Thai cuisine. Touches of turmeric spice, coconut milk, and lime juice span the various styles from northern to southern regions of Thailand. The *mee grob* is a great starting dish, composed of delicate, crispy rice noodles and shrimp tossed in a sweet and sour tamarind sauce, topped with roasted cashew nuts, Kaffir lime leaves, scallions, cilantro, and bean sprouts. For beef lovers, try the Water Fall Beef dish, made with slices of grilled steak, tossed red onions, roasted rice powder, scallions, cilantro, and hot pepper in a northeastern Thai country-style lime juice dressing. For those who want a taste of the sea, try the delectable Triple Flavor sauce fish, made with golden fried snapper, tilapia, or salmon topped with sautéed chopped onions and bell peppers in a spicy and sweet tangy sauce. My favorite is the pineapple duck curry, crispy boneless duck with pineapple and tomato in a red curry cream sauce. Get the mango with sticky rice when in season for dessert.

Shin Jung Korean Restaurant, 1638 E. Colonial Dr., Orlando, FL 32803; (407) 895-7345; Parking Lot; Korean; $$. Inside a tiny house on Colonial Drive, Korean-style marinated barbecue meats sizzle on iron plates as smoke rises into the vents above. The beef *bulgogi* and *kalbi*-marinated short ribs hiss and crackle as flames flicker below the grills. The smell of Korean barbecue is intoxicating, especially if you are eating at Shin Jung. The dining area is tiny; maybe 40 people can fit in here at one time. Try the *soon* tofu, a spicy silk tofu–based soup, or the *kimchijigae,* a spicy kimchee-based soup, seafood pancake, *bulgogi*-flavored chicken, pork, or beef, and *kalbi* beef short ribs. The meal is served with *ban chan,* tiny dishes of pickled cucumbers, cabbage, bean sprouts, anchovies, mashed potato, kimchee, and other small appetizers, changing daily.

Tako Cheena by Pom Pom, 932 N. Mills Ave., Orlando, FL 32803; (321) 236-7457; takocheena.com; Parking Lot and Street Parking; Asian/Mexican; $. Pom Moongauklang, founder of **Pom Pom's Teahouse and Sandwicheria** (see p. 98), and partner Edgardo Guzman created Tako Cheena with a fusion concept of Asian and Latin American flavors (hence the name). This eatery is small and set up probably best for a bite to go or at the bar by the kitchen. Takos can come filled with Thai peanut chicken, Korean beef, yellow curry tofu, panko-crusted codfish, or Asian braised beef, and are made to order in the open kitchen. There are also Japadogs, Asian hot dogs made with Chinese sausage, African-inspired beef burritos stuffed with beef and quinoa, and savory Korean-style burritos filled with *bulgogi* beef and fried rice. The empanadas here are a treat, filled with chicken, beef, or vegetables and flavored differently every week. Don't forget to try the various house-made sauces found here, such as the tomatillo and Kaffir lime, sweet chile and smoked ghost pepper, or roasted Guajillo tomato.

Tasty Wok BBQ & Noodle House, 1246 E. Colonial Dr., Orlando, FL 32803; (407) 896-8988; Parking Lot; Chinese; $. With reasonable prices and great portions of authentic Chinese food,

Tasty Wok serves up some delicious Cantonese-style barbecue and noodle soups. Roast ducks, roast pork, and soy sauce–marinated chicken hang from the window display in this hole-in-the-wall. The thickly sliced beef chow fun noodles and the beef crispy pan-fried noodles are both excellent. For a sampler of the various barbecue dishes available, order the 3-meat rice combination plate, where you can order any 3 barbecue meats on top of rice with a side of *gai lan,* or Chinese broccoli. You can choose from roast duck, roast pork, crispy-skin roast pork, soy sauce chicken, or barbecued squid. For noodle soup lovers, try the amply stuffed shrimp wonton noodle soup or the noodle soup with braised stew beef.

Tony's Deli, 1323 N. Mills Ave., Orlando, FL 32803; (407) 898-6689; Parking Lot; Mediterranean; $. Since 1977, this little family-owned Lebanese deli and market has served up some great Middle Eastern fare for lunch. There are dish trays filled with the standard items: yellow rice and lentils, hummus, tabbouleh, beet roots, salads, and more. Try some of the gyro sandwiches; baba ghanoush, made with roasted eggplant, tahini sauce, garlic, and lemon juice; or the kibbe, made with ground beef and wheat stuffed with pine nuts and onion. Pick up some spices or noodles from the market area or some of the meat-and-spinach pies at the counter.

Yum-Mì Sandwiches, 1227 N. Mills Ave., Orlando, FL 32803; (407) 894-1808; yummisandwiches.com; Parking Lot; Vietnamese/

Sandwiches; $. **Yum-Mì Sandwiches,** where the bread is baked fresh daily, focuses on bringing a modern twist to the traditional Vietnamese *banh mi* submarine sandwich and is a passion project of the Phans (sisters Linda and Rosa, and brother David), who are a part of the family of the popular **Pho 88** (see p. 96) restaurant down the street. With upbringings in a Vietnamese family, the Phans' inspiration came from the traditional flavors acquired growing up and with an open mind for the cultural diversity surrounding the Orlando area. Most of the prices range from $2.75 to $7.95. Try the VP sandwich, which stands for "Vietnamese Philly," made with 2 fried eggs and *thit nuong* (grilled beef) inside. The eggs over easy ooze fresh yolk onto your *banh mi,* making for a divine lunch. For vegetarians, try the Lost Tofu (made with lemongrass-spiced tofu) and the made-to-order fresh fruit *boba* tea freezers. There are also other Vietnamese street-food staples, such as steamed pork buns and pâté-a-choux meat pastries. Try them all.

Specialty Stores, Markets & Producers

Dong A Supermarket, 816 N. Mills Ave., Orlando FL 32803; (407) 898-9227; dongacorporation.com; Parking Lot. Dong A Supermarket has a wide range of Asian foods, spices, noodles, teas, and other exotic ingredients needed to fulfill that Chinese recipe you've been dying to try out. The products come from all parts of Asia, including China, Japan, Thailand, the Philippines, Vietnam, and Malaysia.

Phuoc Loc Tho Market, 2100 E. Colonial Dr., Orlando, FL 32803; (407) 898-6858; Parking Lot. Probably the largest Asian super-market in the Mills 50 district, this place has all your Asian kitchen needs. Stock up on rice noodles, Asian vegetables such as *gai lan*, canned fruits, snacks, drinks, meats, and more. There is also a small section that sells Chinese barbecued meats, such as roast pork and roast duck, as well as Vietnamese *banh mi* sub sandwiches to go.

Saigon Market, 1232 E. Colonial Dr., Orlando, FL 32803; (407) 898-6899; Parking Lot. Come early on weekend mornings to pick up some of the freshest Chinese bakery items and pastries in town, still hot and fluffy from the ovens. The egg tarts are very popular here and can run out quickly, but there's still Chinese barbecue buns, hot dog buns, coconut cream buns, and even durian buns aplenty. The supermarket side has aisles and aisles of Asian spices, frozen goods, prepared street foods to go, exotic vegetables and fruits, teas, and snacks available. The ladies who work at the registers always seem to be smiling and try their best to help customers.

Tien Hung Complete Oriental Foods & Gifts, 1110 E. Colonial Dr., Orlando, FL 32803; (407) 422-0067. One of the first Asian markets in the area, Tien Hung has one of the most extensive selections of seafood and meat cuts available. In addition to the regular lineup of Asian vegetables, rice noodles, spices, and teas, you have pretty much all you need to make your own homemade *pho* beef rice noodle soup. There is also an area that sells Vietnamese *banh mi* sandwiches, ranging from regular cold cuts to sardines, tofu, and grilled pork varieties, a popular to-go item for those on long road trips. Also try their smoothies made in house, from taro- to durian-flavored smoothies with *boba,* the black tapioca pearls. There are also a few to-go prepared-food items by the registers that you might find at local Vietnamese restaurants, such as *goi cuon,* summer rolls wrapped in clear rice paper and filled with rice noodles, shrimp, and veggies.

The Milk District

The T.G. Lee milk factory looms over this new and growing district of popular bars and unique boutique shops, as well as a few restaurants that have a vibrant, local vibe with an independent streak. The popular Tasty Tuesdays at the Milk District bring together local gourmet food trucks with the signature Milk District bars along Robinson Street so that families and friends can grab a bite, a drink, and a place to sit and dine, all in one convenient place, saving patrons that awkward moment of scarfing down chicken and waffles while squatting over a parking lot curb.

Beefy King, 424 N. Bumby Ave., Orlando, FL 32803; (407) 894-2241; beefyking.com; Parking Lot; Sandwiches; $. Beefy King is an Orlando institution, home of the famous steamed Beefy King roast beef sandwiches and Beefy Spuds (tater tots) sides. The large sign out front with a crowned bull, the Beefy King himself, snorting out steam from his nostrils, is an Orlando icon. Lunchtime is always busy here, filled to the brim with Orlando natives and transplants. From businessmen to students out for the summer, all are united under this 1960s-era relic for a nostalgic taste of the high school cafeteria-style, crispy fried tater tots. The chairs and booths and diner-style stools all look the same as they were in 1968 when Beefy King first opened. For a city with so many openings and closings each year, the staying power of Beefy King is uncanny and shows that Orlando's love for the roast beef sandwich here is timeless. This sandwich is juicier and more natural tasting due to the steaming process that traps the juices from the roast beef, going perfectly with the horseradish sauce or barbecue sauce. They also serve up ham, turkey, pastrami, corned beef, barbecue beef, and barbecue pork sandwiches.

Drunken Monkey Coffee Bar, 444 N. Bumby Ave., Orlando, FL 32803; (407) 893-4994; drunkenmonkeycoffee.com; Parking Lot; Coffeehouse; $. This cozy little coffee shop in the Milk District serves up some great coffee and chai, as well as quiches, panini, soups, and sandwiches, with a healthy heaping of vegan and vegetarian options and baked goods. The indie, artsy vibe is augmented by the local art and paintings on sale inside the shop. The coffee is fair traded, organic, and Rainforest Alliance, and is roasted in house. Try the Mojo Jojo, a Vietnamese-style beverage with sweetened condensed milk, cinnamon, and vanilla flavoring.

Maxine's on Shine, 337 N. Shine Ave., Orlando, FL 32803; (407) 674-6841; maxinesonshine.com; Asian/Mediterranean; $$. Nestled in an old neighborhood house, Maxine's on Shine serves up Italian and Mediterranean fare with an eclectic twist. Start off with some stuffed grape leaves or share one of the many flatbreads. Try the signature dish: curry-crusted barramundi, a luscious, pan-seared mild curry-crusted Australian sea bass served over a bed of spinach, roasted red bell peppers, shallots, and black beans, topped with grilled asparagus.

Spooky's Black Cat Cafe and Milk District Marketplace, 207 N. Primrose Dr., Orlando, FL 32803; (407) 896-2377; themilk districtmarketplace.com; Parking Lot; American; $. The atmosphere here is a lot like a witch's den: mystic symbols and local paintings with a rather dark yet playful theme. Though it's not much of a marketplace, Spooky's Black Cat Cafe serves up quite the delightfully eclectic menu, with influences from India and East Asia plus American comfort food. Start off with some Dragon Eggs, 3 wasabi and Sriracha deviled eggs over a sweet chile soy sauce, or the Naan Bread Nosh, toasted seasoned Indian bread served with your

choice of roasted garlic olive oil dip, pesto, baba ghanoush, *baingan bharta, pav bhaji,* black bean hummus, or traditional hummus. For more American fare, try the pulled pork on waffles, cooked in milk stout beer and topped with cilantro chimichurri sauce, or one of their famous meat loaf subs. The tour of India, a trio of *baingan bharta*–style eggplant curried dip, *pav bhaji*–style vegetable curry dip, and *patra* rolls of aloo leaf, curry, and tamarind, will surely transport you on a passage to south Asia. There is also a large selection of over 100 beers and wines to enjoy at Spooky's.

Ivanhoe Village

There's always something unique going on in this historic area known as the Antique District, for its many antiques shops and Bohemian-artist feel with an eclectic mix of small businesses, restaurants, and lakeside views. Arts and science lovers rejoice: the Orlando Ballet, Theatre Downtown, Orlando Science Center, Orlando Repertory Theatre, Mennello Museum, Orlando Museum of Art, Shakespeare Theatre, Orlando Fire Museum, and the Garden Club are all located within the Ivanhoe Village district.

Foodie Faves

Artichoke Red Vegan Market, 1813 N. Orange Ave., Orlando, FL 32804; (407) 898-3353; artichokered.com; Street Parking;

Vegetarian/Market; $. This tiny market provides all your basic vegan needs, showing the way to a cruelty-free lifestyle. From vegan vitamins and supplements to vegan cosmetics and body care, this shop has pretty much all the bases covered. Pick up some fair-traded organic coffees, teas, cheeses, breads, or pastas, or something vegan for your pets at home.

The Greek Corner, 1600 N. Orange Ave., Orlando, FL 32804; (407) 228-0303; thegreekcorner.net; Parking Lot; Greek; $. This simple Greek restaurant sitting on beautiful Lake Ivanhoe serves up great authentic Greek dishes in a casual setting. Start off with some *dolmathakia,* grape leaves stuffed with rice, herbs, and spices, or *spanakopita,* spinach and feta cheese pie in phyllo dough. If you don't know what to try, get the hot or cold meze platter, where you get a combination of Greek appetizers. For traditionalists, try the gyro sandwich, made here with a mixture of ground beef and lamb, combined with herbs accompanied by fresh tomatoes, onions, and tzatziki sauce, wrapped in grilled pita bread. For seafood lovers, don't miss the Greek salmon, grilled over an open flame and marinated with lemon and olive oil, and served over rice. For meat lovers, sample the tender chunks of braised lamb, simmered in a traditional tomato sauce with cinnamon spice and served on rice pilaf. Leave some room, though, for the baklava or *galaktoboureko,* a sweet Greek-style milk, egg, and custard–filled pastry.

Tim's Wine Market, 1223 N. Orange Ave., Orlando, FL 32804; (407) 895-9463; timswine.com; Street Parking; Wine Market; $. Tim Varan and Brock Magruder opened Tim's Wine Market in October 1995 with a focus on service, selection, and value. Throughout the years, their staff has educated thousands of people in central Florida on the merits of artisan-made wines. Their newsletter, *Wine of the Month,* features hundreds of hand-selected wines chosen by Tim to display a sense of place, varietal correctness, balance, and above all value. Sign up to be a member of one or all of the many clubs for Tim's Wine Market, where members enjoy benefits on pricing and other perks.

White Wolf Cafe, 1829 N. Orange Ave., Orlando, FL 32804; (407) 895-9911; whitewolfcafe.com; Parking Lot and Street Parking; Brunch/American; $$. An eclectic array of stained-glass chandeliers hang inside the cafe, with vintage antiques (most for sale) and thick granite-slab tables. The menu here is just as eclectic, with pleasurable entrees to enjoy before catching a show at one of the nearby theaters, as well as a little drink at the bar. Breakfast is also popular here, with quiches and Bloody Marys among the top items. Try the White Wolf Wake Up, consisting of 2 pancakes or French toast, 2 eggs any style, bacon or turkey bacon, patty or link sausage, turkey sausage, or ham, and your choice of hash browns, home fries, or grits, sure to fill up the empty tank after a long night out. The crab cake eggs Benedict consists of poached farm fresh eggs, crab cakes and avocado piled high on an English muffin, topped with creamy hollandaise sauce, served with your choice of hash browns, home fries or grits. For lunch, the menu features a popular Moroccan chicken salad, a blend of grilled chicken breast, bananas, raisins, and almonds mixed with a honey curry dressing over romaine lettuce. Rachael Ray, who once filmed here for an episode of *$40 a Day* on the Food Network, has a flatbread pizza named after her, made with prosciutto, fresh spinach, provolone cheese, extra-virgin olive oil, and a homemade balsamic glaze.

College Park

This quiet, sleepy neighborhood just minutes northwest of downtown Orlando derives its name from the many streets within its boundaries named after universities, such as Princeton, Dartmouth, Harvard, and Yale. Edgewater Drive is the main thoroughfare for College Park, filled on both sides with teahouses, diners, restaurants, cafes, salons, boutique shops, parks, and the historic Dubsdread Golf Course. Jack Kerouac, the bard of the Beatnik generation, lived in the area when he wrote *The Dharma Burns* at the time *On the Road* made him a national sensation. A foundation was created to buy his house, known as the Kerouac House, and it is now used for a writer-in-residence program.

K Restaurant, 1710 Edgewater Dr., Orlando, FL 32804; (407) 872-2332; krestaurant.net; Parking Lot and Street Parking; Modern American; $$$. James Beard Award nominee and Chef-Owner of K Restaurant Kevin Fonzo uses rustic, locally sourced ingredients—including K's own backyard herb and vegetable garden—to create masterful interpretations of classic dishes. A graduate of the Culinary Institute of America, and formerly a part of the culinary team for the Peabody Orlando, Chef Fonzo opened K Restaurant in 2001, working almost exclusively with ethically and sustainably operated local farms, such as Waterkist Farms, Palmetto Creek Farm, 3 Boys Farm, Lake Meadow Naturals, and others. Highlights of the seasonally changing menu include bone marrow from Deep Creek Ranch with a roasted onion marmalade and red wine sauce, served with crostini, and the K Stack salad, made with tomato, herbed goat cheese, and 3 Boys Farm greens, with citrus dressing. For those looking for a great rendition of steak, don't miss the tender, rich filet mignon served with a red Cabernet Sauvignon sauce, dusted with wild mushroom and truffle, and with a healthy dose of potato gratin.

Les Petits Pleasures, 2120 Edgewater Dr., Orlando, FL 32804; (407) 422-4702; lespetitspleasures.com; Street Parking; French/Bakery; $. Ooh la la! This French bakery is truly a delight. The little patisserie with light lavender walls on Edgewater Drive features many sweet pleasures, such as flaky, buttery chocolate almond croissants, fruit tarts topped with strawberries and blackberries, little morsels of macarons, decadent slices of vanilla flan, *rochers coco,* moist apple sponge cakes, chocolate éclairs, napoleons, and more. The bakery, open for breakfast, lunch, and dinner, also serves up some scrumptious hot sandwiches, quiches, and crepes for those wanting something savory to go with the sweets. Try their *vol-au-vent,* which means "windblown" in French, a flaky, delectable puff pastry stuffed with chicken, mushroom, swiss cheese, and a creamy, rich béchamel sauce. The Hawaii *croque monsieur* is a playful twist on the traditional grilled ham, swiss cheese, and béchamel sandwich, topped with pineapple. The savory royal crepe is luscious, stuffed with *noix de St. Jacques* scallops, crème fraîche sour cream, Parmesan cheese, and mushroom. You will fall in love with everything here, *mes amis.* It's all about the little things in life.

Tap Room at Dubsdread, 549 W. Par St., Orlando, FL 32804; (407) 650-0100; taproomatdubsdread.com; Parking Lot; Burgers/American; $$$. Located on the scenic, historic Dubsdread Golf Course, the Tap Room offers classic American fare with a sophisticated touch. The Tap Room classic cheeseburger is fantastic, a half-pound burger with Tillamook cheddar cheese, lettuce, tomato, and onion. There are also jumbo lump crab cakes, flatbreads, steak, seafood, and pasta dishes. Sit on the outdoor patio for a late-morning brunch and enjoy the beautiful view of the golf course, a truly Floridian experience.

Foodie Faves

Christo's Cafe, 1815 Edgewater Dr., Orlando, FL 32804; (407) 425-8136; christoscafe.com; Parking Lot; Breakfast/American; $. This small neighborhood diner has been serving up hearty breakfast, brunch, and burger items in College Park for over 40 years. The menu is classic diner fare with a touch of Greek influence. Pancakes, deep-fried French toast, and Greek omelets stuffed with lamb and feta cheese are all available for diners to nosh on inside or outside on the patio seating. Try the Hungry Man breakfast combo, with 3 eggs, 2 strips of bacon, ham, a sausage patty, and your choice of home fries, hash browns, or grits, and a biscuit or toast. It's sure to fill you up and get you ready to go for the day.

Juliana's, 2306 Edgewater Dr., Orlando, FL 32804; (407) 425-1801; julianascollegepark.com; Parking Lot; Italian; $$. Serving up fine Tuscan cuisine, this intimate little eatery on College Park's Edgewater Drive serves up some delicious Italian fare. Start off with some of the house special bruschetta *toscana,* topped with capers, olives, tomatoes, and pecorino cheese, or the crispy calamari with zucchini and tomato *brodetto.* The earthy, tender braised lamb shank with saffron risotto and mushroom Cabernet sauce is an excellent entree choice.

Paxia Alta Cocina Mexicana, 2611 Edgewater Dr., Orlando, FL 32804; (407) 420-1144; paxiarestaurant.com; Parking Lot; Mexican; $$. Paxia takes deep-rooted, traditional Mexican dishes and uses modern cooking techniques to present them in a contemporary way. Start off with some house-made guacamole *fresco,* made from ripe avocados, onions, tomato, and cilantro. Sample some of the house tacos *al pastor* style, with juicy, achiote-spiced pork, sweet pineapple pico sauce, and a touch of cilantro, and served with an avocado-tomatillo salsa. For meatier fare, try the grilled skirt steak with red chimichurri or the chicken *enmoladas* with poblano mole, Mexican rice, and *queso fresco* in a corn tortilla. *Buen provecho!*

Specialty Stores, Markets & Producers

Woo Sung Oriental Food Mart, 5065 Edgewater Dr., Orlando, FL 32810; (407) 295-4077. Have a hankering to make your own Korean-style beef short rib *kalbi* barbecue at home? Woo Sung, an Asian market with not only Japanese, Chinese, Vietnamese, and Filipino products, but also an extensive selection of Korean cuisine ingredients, is the perfect place to start. Choose from stacks of kimchee jars and pepper pastes to an entire row of various types of seaweeds and rice to whole sections of different types of frozen mandoo dumplings, pork bacon, squid, and beef cuts. They have all the vegetables and ingredients you'll need to make your own bowl of Korean bibimbap mixed rice at home. Pick up some of the house-made pickled vegetables, anchovies, bean sprouts, and tofu, usually found accompanying Korean side dishes in tiny plates known as *banchan*. Try some of their prepared *soon* tofu or *kimchijigae* stews for an easy dinner.

Audubon Park Garden District

This neighborhood, located at the intersection of Winter Park Road and Corrine Drive, is named partly for its proximity to the nearby Leu Gardens, a popular 50-acre garden featuring one of the largest rose gardens in Florida. Audubon Park Garden District is an eclectic mix of local Orlando businesses—bike shops, restaurants and coffee shops, bakeries, diners, a community garden—and it even hosts a funky annual Zombietoberfest (neighborhood zombie crawl) in October. The area has a hipster feel to it, probably stemming from the Stardust Video & Coffee shop, a popular place to grab coffee or a sandwich while finishing some work on your MacBook. It's also the location of the weekly Audubon Park Community Market, where vendors provide local goods, foodstuffs, produce, and handmade crafts made right here in Florida.

Bikes, Beans & Bordeaux, 3022 Corrine Dr., Orlando, FL 32803; (407) 427-1440; b3cafe.com; Parking Lot; Sandwiches; $. Bikes, Beans & Bordeaux is a casual neighborhood cafe serving up savory soups, sandwiches, and salads as well as wines, with a cycling flair. Bikes, Beans & Bordeaux boasts a delectable menu of organic, vegetarian, and low-fat items with cycling-themed names. The Rasmussen, a homemade fresh chicken salad sandwich, is made with nonfat plain yogurt, a dab of light mayonnaise, celery, red onion, walnuts, grapes, and special seasonings. Try the Lance-wich, named after Lance Armstrong: the turkey and ham are piled high on a double deck of multigrain bread with your choice of toppings.

Blue Bird Bake Shop, 3122 Corrine Dr., Orlando, FL 32803; (407) 228-3822; bluebirdbakeshop.com; Parking Lot; Bakery/Desserts; $. Specializing in cupcakes, Blue Bird Bake Shop is a quaint and cozy little shop serving up more than 30 flavors ranging from red velvet to Sweet Cakes, Ch-chocolate to peanut butter and jelly, rotating on a daily basis. They also offer brownies, cookies, scones, muffins, and other bakery fare. My favorite is the Neapolitan cup-cake, made with layers of chocolate, strawberry, and vanilla cake topped with a strawberry buttercream icing. Other popular cupcakes include the

Downside Up, made with vanilla cake and topped with a chocolate buttercream icing sprinkled with vanilla jimmies. The cupcakes are moist, luxurious, and overall wonderful.

Junior's Diner, 2920 Corrine Dr., Orlando, FL 32803; (407) 894-8871; Parking Lot; Breakfast/American; $. This Audubon Park neighborhood eatery serves up classic diner fare. From pancakes to omelets, eggs, and sausage, Junior's Diner has been a popular place to meet up for locals looking for some good down-home cooking for breakfast. Try some of the specials, such as the homemade biscuits and gravy or the skillet with home fries, eggs, sausage, and everything but the kitchen sink. The country-fried steak and burgers provide some strong Southern comfort as well.

Rainbow Sno-Cones, 3116 Corrine Dr., Orlando, FL 32803; (407) 896-9105; Parking Lot; Desserts; $. For those looking for a little cool respite, Rainbow Sno-Cones features delicious little dessert treats known as snowballs that will be sure to cool you down. Made popular in New Orleans, these balls of shaved ice are finer and more silky smooth, like fresh snow, than their coarser, less refined cousin, the snowcone. The desserts here are made using an old-fashioned shaved-ice machine just like the ones they use in New Orleans to get that fine consistency. Owner Bob Homer and his family have owned and operated this small walk-up storefront for over 17 years

REDLIGHT REDLIGHT CRAFT BEER PARLOUR

Named by *Draft Magazine* as one of America's 100 best beer bars for 2011, this popular place set in a bit of a run-down old building has a loyal following for its extensive list of craft beer. At Redlight Redlight, 23 beers are on draft, and roughly 200 bottles are ready at all times as well as a number of ciders, meads fermented with honey, sakes, wines, beer cocktails, sodas, and vintage bottles of beer. 2810 Corrine Dr., Orlando, FL 32803; (407) 893-9832; redlightredlightbeerparlour.com; Parking Lot; $.

and it remains a popular place for central Floridians for the many flavors (over 35) and tasty snowballs. The syrupy flavors are made of sugar rather than fructose-based corn syrups and include flavors like strawberry, mango, coconut, grape, root beer, piña colada, and more. There are flavor combinations, too, like the Rainbow, Fuzzy Navel, and the White Russian, which is a combination of coffee, chocolate, and sweet cream. My favorites include the Tiger's Blood (it was here first, years before Charlie Sheen popularized the term), made with strawberry and coconut flavors. I requested some condensed milk on top to make it extra sweet. Prices are very cheap, with most items under $2. Cash only.

Seito Sushi, 4898 New Broad St., Orlando, FL 32814; (407) 898-8901; seitosushi.com; Parking Lot; Sushi; Japanese; $$. The decor at Seito Sushi is ultra-sleek, ultra-modern. It's just a beautiful place to be. Sushi is the main attraction here, and the chefs are expertly trained in the art. Highlights include the Popeye roll, wrapped in rice paper and made with baby spinach, spicy mayonnaise, shrimp, snow crab salad, rice, and avocado, as well as the Torchamaki, a spicy crawfish with asparagus roll wrapped with whitefish, drizzled with Cajun mayonnaise, and then set ablaze with a small torch. For a luxurious experience, order the sashimi grand selection, containing 16 pieces of chef's choice sashimi. Though the menu is composed of mostly Japanese items, some wonderful Korean-inspired dishes are hidden in the menu. The spicy Korean *chirashi* bowl, a rice bowl topped with various cuts of fresh sashimi, has pickled vegetables and a sweet and spicy chile vinegar dressing added for a nice Korean kimchee-flavored kick. *Kalbi,* sweet soy-ginger-garlic blend marinated with chargrilled beef ribs and sautéed onions, is also a great entree stemming from Korea. Additional location: 8031 Turkey Lake Rd., Orlando, FL 32819; (407) 248-8888.

Stardust Video & Coffee, 1842 E. Winter Park Rd., Orlando, FL 32803; (407) 623-3393; stardustie.com; Parking Lot; Coffeehouse; $. Founded in 1970, this hipster haven is headquarters for many artists and creative types in town. Featuring baked goods, sandwiches, coffee, and craft beer on tap, Stardust has all you need to keep those creative juices flowing throughout the day. Try the Grinderman sandwich, made with chicken, pesto, goat cheese, and hot sauce, or the Rob Reiner, a pressed meat loaf sandwich with barbecue sauce and provolone cheese. Vegan scones, whoopie pies, cupcakes, shortbread cookies, and more are also available for noshing. The Stardust parking lot is home to the **Audubon Park Community Market** (see p. 9) on Monday evening.

(see p. 9)

Sushi Lola's, 2806 Corrine Dr., Orlando, FL 32803; (407) 898-5652; sushilolas.com; Parking Lot; Sushi/Japanese; $. Previously a sandwich shop, the latest incarnation of this space is a Japanese-Korean sushi restaurant with a creative, whimsical flair. The space is intimate yet comfortable. Sushi is probably the most popular thing here, though there are a few Korean dishes, such as *kalbi* and *bulgogi* bento boxes, to try as well. If you're in the mood for something different than the traditional sushi roll, try the Dirty Old Man roll, a California roll topped with chopped tuna, *masago,* spicy sauce, salmon, whitefish, yellowtail, and imitation crab meat, or the Playboy roll, made with shrimp tempura, cream cheese, imitation crab, and avocado, topped with tuna, black and red *tobiko,* scal-

lion, tempura flakes, eel sauce, and spicy mayo. A little-known but very good item here is the miso ramen noodle soup, made in house, with chopped *negi, narutomaki,* boiled egg, roast beef, *wakame, menma,* and *moyachi*.

Universal/ International Drive

Just off of I-4, a few exits south of downtown, you will find Universal Orlando Resort, a mega complex of entertainment that includes theme parks Universal Studios Florida and Universal's Islands of Adventure, as well as Universal CityWalk, a shopping and dining district, and three resort hotels. The Wizarding World of Harry Potter at Universal's Islands of Adventure not only helped bring to life the storied (and nonalcoholic) butterbeer, but also enchanted the millions of tourists and Harry Potter lovers to visit since its opening, helping the Orlando area break a record 54 million visitors in 2011.

International Drive (also known as I-Drive) is the family-friendly, tourist-happy district of Orlando, anchored by the Orange County Convention Center and SeaWorld theme parks to the south and the popular Orlando Premium Outlets at I-Drive on the north end, filling a stretch, as its name suggests, with an international flair. If you look past all the kitschy tourist shops, you will find quite a few overlooked gems. The ever-growing number of Brazilian tourists—with their bright yellow and green backpacks to boot—in Orlando has resulted in a small offshoot known as Little Brazil along International Drive complete with a bakery, churrascaria steak house, and grocery shops catered for visiting Brasileiros as well as for the immigrants who have decided to stay here. Not only that, but you also can find some of the best Indian and Japanese food around town here as well as one of the few places for authentic Ethiopian. Closer to the convention center is Pointe Orlando, a destination shopping and dining center with its own IMAX-equipped (the real IMAX) movie theater and the Orlando Improv Comedy Club.

Best of the Neighborhood

A Land Remembered, 9939 Universal Blvd., Orlando, FL 32819; (407) 996-3663; landrememberedrestaurant.com; Valet and Parking Lot; Steak House; $$$$. A Land Remembered, a classic Florida-style steak house in Rosen Shingle Creek resort, is named after Patrick Smith's rich novel featuring Florida's historic moments and landscapes. Decked in dark woods, palm tree–esque lamp shades, and old-Florida themes, A Land Remembered can be seen as a throwback to the days of central Florida's cattle-raising history. The steaks here are truly superb, featuring Harris Ranch Black Angus Five Diamond Prime Beef, the same beef that's served at the famed Bern's Steakhouse in Tampa, Florida. Try the bone-in rib eye steak, a juicy, slightly charred cut served perfectly at the desired medium rare. The meat is tender and flavorful—and altogether one of the best steaks I have had in Orlando. For dessert you are treated with the creations of award-winning Executive Pastry Chef David Ramirez, with choices ranging from chocolate flourless cake to Warm Pioneer Bread Pudding to A Land Remembered Key Lime Pie. Try their chocolate mousse cake, a 12-ounce chocolate mousse cake layered with pecan nougatine and milk chocolate cream filling and topped with raspberry ganache and fresh fruit.

Hanamizuki Japanese, 8255 International Dr., Orlando, FL 32819; (407) 363-7200; hanamizuki.us; Parking Lot; Sushi/Japanese; $$$. I find quiet comfort in the nostalgic, down-home feeling of Hanamizuki, a restaurant reknowned for its Kyoto-style cuisine and some of the best authentic Japanese food this side of the Pacific. The decor of Hanamizuki is simple: shades of light green walls framed by terraced roofs, silhouetting the image of a Japanese temple. With the sounds of the *shamisen* playing in the background, the ambience is serene and tranquil. The chef at Hanamizuki prides himself on the quality and taste of his offerings, from the fresh sashimi to the delicious noodle bowls and more. Try the Hanamizuki roll, made with cooked salmon, eel, egg, and flying fish roe topped with baked sesame seeds. If you have the opportunity to visit during lunch, I recommend ordering the Shio butter ramen noodle soup, made with a deeply flavorful broth, and topped with boiled egg, bamboo shoots, *chashu* pork slices, and scallions. Order with it a half portion of the fried rice, cooked fresh with slivers of scallions and eggs and topped with slices of red ginger—among the best fried rice dishes I have ever tasted. For dinner the *nabeyaki udon*, Shabu-shabu, and *negima* (Japanese beef rolls with scallions) are all popular choices, or you can try one of the many daily chef specials.

Napa at The Peabody, 9801 International Dr., Orlando, FL 32819; (407) 345-4570; peabodyorlando.com; Parking Garage; Modern American; $$$$. Though named for California's wine country, the dining menu is "seasonal, local, organic, sustainable, whenever possible" and is a prime exhibit of the farm-to-table movement, which also has strong roots in the Napa Valley. Many of the items and ingredients on the menu come from within an hour's drive of Orlando. The decor is modern and filled with dark woods, offering a sophisticated dining experience amid the busy traffic and convention world nearby on International Drive. Start off with some of the creamy bisque made with roasted sweet corn and Florida rock shrimp, or the butternut squash soup with decadent white truffle oil and cinnamon marshmallows. For steak lovers, try the Meyer Ranch natural beef fillet, accompanied by fingerling potatoes and vegetable hash in a Barolo wine sauce. Also exceptional are the braised beef short-rib ravioli and the line-caught grouper with red miso, bok choy vegetables, and a ginger green bean relish.

Texas De Brazil, 5259 International Dr., Orlando, FL 32819, (407) 355-0355; texasdebrazil.com; Parking Lot; Brazilian/Steak House; $$$$. This very popular Brazilian steak house is a churrascaria, a kind of meat buffet orchestrated by gauchos (Brazilian cowboys) who galavant from table to table with their cuts of meat until you signal them to stop with a bicolored red and green disc. A sizable salad and antipasti bar is filled with over 50 types of appetizing dishes, such as tomatoes, spring greens, olives, slices of salami and chorizo, pasta, lobster bisque, and even sushi, but the focus remains on the skewers of beef when you return to your table. The gauchos, surly men in blue button-up shirts, arrive one by one, rotating through the room in rapid succession wielding metal skewers of fire-roasted meaty delights. Crispy shanks of lamb, tender garlic roasted chicken, bacon-wrapped filet mignon, flank steak, top sirloin, Parmesan-encrusted pork and chicken, chorizo sausage, and more cuts of beef are on the list. Wash the palate with the garlic mashed potato and sweet cinnamony fried banana sides.

Foodie Faves

Aashirwad Indian Cuisine, 5748 International Dr., Orlando, FL 32819; (407) 370-9830; aashirwadrestaurant.com; Parking Lot; Indian; $$$. Serving fine Indian cuisine near International Drive, Aashirwad cooks its curries and tandoori meats with tender care. Set in a dimly lit dining room, accented by dark-wood touches,

Aashirwad's traditional Indian offerings (and a few Indo-Chinese dishes as well) are a delight. The traditional Samosas, lentil- and potato-stuffed fried puffs, are a good starter. Dip some of the airy, lightly burnt garlic naan bread into some creamy chicken tikka masala, boneless pieces of tender chicken breast cooked in a spiced onion, ginger, and tomato sauce. The tandoori chicken is exceptional, tender chicken legs and thighs marinated in yogurt and spices, and roasted in the tandoor, the traditional Indian clay oven, and still sizzling when it arrives at the table. Try the lunch buffet, with trays and trays of Indian veggies, curries, and meat dishes for a reasonable price.

Agave Azul, 4750 S. Kirkman Rd., Orlando, FL 32811; (407) 704-6930; agaveazulorlando.com; Parking Lot; Mexican; $$. One of the best Mexican establishments in Orlando, Agave Azul serves up some delicious, authentic Mexican fare. Begin with some sopa Maya, a Mexican-style chicken soup with rice, vegetables, and slivers of avocado. Try some of the *al pastor* street tacos, made with marinated pineapple adobo pork inside 3 masa corn shells and topped with cilantro and onions just like they do in Mexico City. The luscious goat cheese rellenos, hearty enchiladas *rancheras,* corn masa pockets of *gorditas de carne,* and shrimp *camarones al mojo de ajo* are all popular items here at Agave Azul.

Border Grill, 5695 Vineland Rd., Orlando, FL 32819; (407) 352-0101; bordergrillorlando.weebly.com; Parking Lot; Mexican, $. This hole-in-the-wall provides some of the most authentic Mexican fare outside of Mexico City. The tacos here are the stars, with various styles written on the chalkboard. Try one of the many taco styles, such as the braised *carnitas* pork tacos, tacos *al pastor* made with marinated and grilled pork, *carne asade* with grilled steak, *pollo asado* (grilled chicken), chorizo, *lengua* (beef tongue), and *pibil*-style tacos made with Yucatan-style pork marinated in orange juice and baked in banana leaves. The tacos come in corn tortillas with cilantro and onions, and a variety of salsas with varying intensities of spice on the side. Border Grill also serves up a nice burrito ranchero stuffed with shredded beef or chicken, topped with ranchero sauce, cheese, and sour cream, and served with rice and beans. Finish with a nice cup of *horchata* drink with cinnamon and rice, or *aguas frescas,* fresh, natural-flavored waters.

Cafe Tu Tu Tango, 8625 International Dr., Orlando, FL 32819; (407) 248-2222; cafetututango.com; Parking Lot; Tapas; $$. Cafe Tu Tu Tango is an inspired and artistic restaurant featuring creative tapas dishes. Local artists paint and belly dancers perform and entertain throughout the evening while guests share and dine on the small appetizer portions of such dishes as calamari with crispy pepperoncini, marinara, and chipotle aioli and the signature Tango alligator bites served with horseradish remoulade and chipotle aioli. The Cajun chicken egg rolls stuffed with roasted corn, cheddar, and goat cheese and the 5-cheese pizza (featuring cheddar, mozzarella,

Manchego, goat, and Parmesan cheeses) are also popular items here.

Cala Bella, 9939 Universal Blvd., Orlando, FL 32819; (407) 996-3663; calabellarestaurant.com; Parking Lot and Valet; $$$$. Cala Bella, Rosen Shingle Creek's upscale Italian restaurant, features inspired Italian classics with a Mediterranean and American twist, accompanied by an extensive wine list. The inspiration of the name Cala Bella, or "Beautiful Creek" in English, comes from owner Harris Rosen's celebration of Florida's history and the unique history of Shingle Creek itself. Visitors can sit in the main dining room and enjoy the sunset over the golf course outside or view the open kitchen and watch the chefs prepare dishes over open flames at this AAA Three Diamond–rated restaurant. Many of the restaurants at Rosen Shingle Creek hearken back to the resort's Floridian roots. Start with the Cala Bella sampler platter, a hearty platter filled with house meatballs, calamari *fritti,* bruschetta Cala Bella, and antipasto. For seafood lovers, the Cala Bella seafood *pescatore* is a must-try: The slightly spicy, very flavorful, and earthy saffron tomato broth serves as the base for this dish, in which Australian lobster tail, littleneck clams, mussels, shrimp, and scallops are braised. For meat lovers, try the marinated, herb-roasted Cala Bella lamb chops with pickled garlic, shallots, and rosemary-minted Marsala, accompanied by the daily risotto.

David's Club Bar & Grill, 6001 Destination Pkwy., Orlando, FL 32819; (407) 313-4300; thehiltonorlando.com; Valet Parking; $$$. This stylish bar and grill at the Hilton hotel has all the markings of an upscale sports pub: servers in sports jerseys, large flat-screen TVs, and plenty of drinks at the bar. The menu, however, consists of more than your average pub fare. The Drums & Flaps are grilled chicken wings, Korean style, with a sweet and spicy barbecue sauce. David's Wagyu Pub Burger is a huge burger topped with Kerrygold Irish cheddar, pickled tomato relish, bacon, caramelized onions, baby red oak lettuce, and blue corn chips. Other popular items include the BLTE steak-house sandwich, composed of smoked bacon, fried green tomato, egg, roasted garlic herb aioli, and Irish cheddar, and a side of sweet potato fries, and chicken and waffles made with a lemon thyme waffle and bourbon maple syrup.

Emeril's Orlando, 6000 Universal Blvd., Orlando, FL 32819; (407) 224-2424; emerilsrestaurants.com/emerils-orlando; Parking Garage; $$$$. Located at Universal Resort's CityWalk, Emeril's features an open kitchen and a food bar where guests can view the chefs putting out their creative dishes inspired by the celebrity chef. Start off with some cornmeal-fried oysters with sweet potato slaw or fried cilantro-garlic marinated quail. For those hankering for some of Emeril's Cajun classics, try the chef's chicken and andouille gumbo, Creole marinated calamari, or smoked wild and exotic mushrooms with *tasso* cream and angel-hair pasta. Kurobuta pork chop, slow-roasted lamb shank, andouille-crusted redfish, and seared snapper are some entree favorites.

Emeril's Tchoup Chop, Universal Orlando Resort's Loews Royal Pacific Resort, 6300 Hollywood Way, Orlando, FL 32819; (407) 503-2467; emerilsrestaurants.com/emerils-tchoup-chop; $$$$. Emeril's Tchoup Chop (pronounced chop-chop) is the second eatery by Emeril Lagasse at Universal Orlando Resort, serving up dishes with Asian and Pacific influences. The restaurant's name is a nod to New Orleans's famous Tchoupitoulas Street, where Emeril's flagship restaurant is located. Start off with some spicy Vietnamese-style escargot, Mongolian glazed slow-roasted pork belly in Chinese-style steamed buns with spicy Napa kimchee slaw, or kiawe-smoked baby back ribs. For entrees, popular dishes include the banana leaf–wrapped roasted pork shoulder with taro root, sweet potato, and baby bok choy, as well as pan-roasted Maple Leaf Farms duck breast, Chinese 5-spice braised lamb shank, and tender sake-braised beef short ribs. End the meal with some decadent chocolate Kahlua cake with peanut butter mousse filling and bananas Foster sauce, or Emeril's signature banana cream pie for dessert.

Japan Food Aki Restaurant, 7460 Universal Blvd., Orlando, FL 32819; (407) 354-0025; aki-japanfood.com; Parking Lot; Sushi/Japanese; $. Since opening in 1995, this restaurant provides traditionally cooked Japanese food by Chef Aki Yoshida, with a family-type atmosphere in a small strip mall setting. The decor is definitely no frills, and a little cafeteria-like, but the menu is authentic homemade Japanese comfort food. Try the *nabeyaki udon* noodle soup, house-made ramen, curry katsu pork, or the deep-fried chicken *namban* with sweet vinegar sauce. Sushi and sashimi lovers will enjoy the half-price rolls and dollar *nigiri* happy hour Monday through Friday from 5:30 to 6:30 p.m.

Magic Wok, 6700 Conroy Windermere Rd., Orlando, FL 32835; (407) 522-8688; magicwokorlando.com; Parking Lot; Chinese; $$. Don't let the name mislead you. This is not your typical to-go Chinese take-out joint, but rather a nice little family-owned restaurant with authentic Chinese food made to order. The restaurant specializes in both traditional Shanghainese and Americanized Chinese food with a variety of vegetarian and healthy choices and no MSG. Shanghainese cuisine is often thought of as the youngest of Chinese regional cuisines, with elements of Cantonese-, Szechuan-, and Peking-style foods. The small Shanghainese dim sum menu here features steamed pork buns (similar to soup dumplings, but without broth), honey ham and bean curd skin in a steamed bun, and steamed fish dumplings, among other items not found at most other dim sum places. The chef's specialties feature crunchy, delectable Shanghai-style sweet and sour ribs and Peking duck. There is an extensive list of home-style soups, such as ham with winter melon, sea cucumber with fish maw, and stuffed fried dough and bean curd. Braised meatballs, braised pork belly with bean curd knots, and spicy stir-fried snapper are some other must-tries here.

Ming Court Wok & Grille, 9188 International Dr., Orlando, FL 32819; (407) 351-9988; ming-court.com; Parking Lot; Chinese; $$$. Ming Court is an International Drive landmark, with its palatial green roof and Chinese stone lions guarding the entrances. Modeled after Ming dynasty–style architecture, this Chinese restaurant serves up a wide selection of dim sum, stir-fry dishes, and sushi rolls in a comfortable, spacious setting. Perfect for dining parties, Ming Court features such Chinese classics as steamed sole with ginger and scallion, baby clams with black bean sauce, and 5-spice beef and white noodles in soup. At times the flavors are toned down for the tourist crowd, but you may find some hidden treasures, particularly on the dim sum menu here.

Nile Ethiopian Restaurant, 7048 International Dr., Orlando, FL 32819; (407) 354-0026; nile07.com; Parking Lot; Ethiopian; $. Ethiopia has one of the oldest civilizations in the world (according to some historians, dating back to around 10,000 BC) and yet many do not know much about this ancient land or its cultures. Luckily for us here in Orlando, you don't have to travel internationally to have a taste of Ethiopian culture; all you have to do is travel to a small strip mall off of International Drive to find Nile Ethiopian Restaurant. Here, servers don traditional Ethiopian wear and serve up beers and wines imported straight from Mother Africa and also have authentic dishes. *Sambusa,* reminiscent of the Indian Samosa, is a pastry crust filled with lentils, green pepper, and onions. Ethiopian cuisine has plenty of both vegetarian and meaty dishes to order here at Nile. This authentic restaurant features various popular styles: *wots* (stewed) and *tibs* (sautéed) all served with *injera*. *Injera,* a staple carb in the Ethiopian diet, is a sour, slightly spongy, crepe-like bread used as a complement for all the other dishes. You tear off a piece of the *injera* and use your hands (traditionally there are no utensils here, unless you ask) to take in the meats, sauces, and veggies like a dip. Go in a group and order the Nile meat combination, which has a combination of *doro alicha* (tender chicken stewed with house spices and turmeric powder and served with a hard-boiled egg), beef *key wat* (finely chopped lean beef with spiced butter and special red pepper called *mitmita,* and served with cheese), beef *alicha* (fresh and tender beef braised in turmeric powder and assorted spices), and *zilbo* (beef cubes with collard greens). There is also a Nile vegetarian combination with split peas, red lentil, collard greens, and cabbage. Many of the dishes are seasoned with *berbere,* a strong spice mixture containing chile peppers, garlic, ginger, basil, fenugreek, and other spices and herbs, and *niter kibbe,* a clarified butter infused with ginger, garlic, and several spices. While you are here at Nile, make sure you request the coffee ceremony, a traditional Ethiopian ritual where incense is lit and coffee beans are roasted in a small pan, filling the air with their aroma. The beans are then ground by hand and served with a blessing.

Pao Gostoso Bakery, 5472 International Dr., Orlando, FL 32819; (407) 447-8946; paogostoso.net; Parking Lot; Brazilian/Bakery; $. Pao Gostoso is a bakery in the heart of the Little Brazil area of International Drive, specializing in Brazilian baked goods, sweet and savory pastries, and much more. Since 2004 the baked goods have been made daily on the premises, from Brazilian cheese breads to coconut cakes. Some of the specialty items include the condensed flan, caramel "napkin" pastries, and the dulce de leche cake with nuts. For more savory fare, try the empanadas and the *coxinha,* literally "little chicken thigh," a popular Brazilian snack made from shredded chicken and spices, and enclosed in flour, battered, and fried. For lunch, try the *moda da casa,* a popular gargantuan hamburger topped with chicken breast, sausage, bacon, ham, a fried egg, potato sticks, corn, lettuce, and tomato.

Passage to India, 6129 Westwood Blvd., Orlando, FL 32821; (407) 351-3456; passagetoindiarestaurant-orlando.com; Parking Lot; Indian; $$. For those looking for Indian fare done well, pay a visit to this restaurant, serving up naan, curries, and all the favorite Indian dishes. Start off with the vegetable Samosas, 2 flaky pastries stuffed with spiced peas and potatoes. The chicken tikka is made of tender pieces of boneless chicken marinated in mild spices and yogurt and roasted in a clay oven, the tandoor. Shrimp vindaloo, juicy chunks of shrimp marinated in vinegar and spices and cooked in a hot sauce with potatoes, is a popular seafood dish. For lovers of *biryani,* try the lamb *biryani,* a dish made of basmati rice and lamb flavored with herbs and spices. Wash it all down with a cool glass of mango *lassi.*

Pio Pio Restaurant, 5752 International Dr., Orlando, FL 32819; (407) 248-6424; piopiointernational.com; Parking Lot; Latin; $$. Despite its strip-mall locale, inside you will be pleasantly surprised by the dark browns, soft lighting, and overall elegant decor of Pio Pio, a restaurant specializing in Peruvian/Colombian cuisine. Salads here are topped with a gratuitous amount of buttery avocado, just like they do in Peru. The specialty, though, is Peruvian-style rotisserie chicken, succulent and juicy, served with a side of yellow rice, beans, and sweet plantains. Try also the fantastic *sancocho,* a rich, hearty, homemade chicken soup with cassava, green plantains, and potatoes, with corn on the cob and cilantro. Additional location: Pio Pio Latin Cuisine, 2500 S. Semoran Blvd., Orlando, FL 32822; (407) 207-2262.

Q'Kenan Venezuelan Restaurante, 8117 Vineland Ave., Orlando, FL 32821; (407) 238-0014; qkenanrestaurante.com; Parking Lot; $. This little hole-in-the-wall of a restaurant near Walt Disney World serves up some authentic Venezuelan fare, with many dishes containing their homemade Venezuelan style *queso blanco* cheese. Try their *patacon,* a sandwich with green, unripened plantain sliced and fried, encasing shredded beef, roasted pork, chicken, cheese, lettuce, tomato, and tartar sauce. The *maduritos* are the sweet plantain version of this popular dish. *Tequeños,* shaped like bread sticks, are stuffed with homemade Venezuelan white cheese and fried, whereas the *cachapas* are corn cakes stuffed with the popular mild-tasting, slightly sweet and salty cheese. Both are popular street foods in Venezuela. *Arepas,* flat corn cakes found throughout

Latin America and particularly Venezuela and Colombia, are aplenty here. Try the Arepa Q'Kenan Santa Barbara, a hearty *arepa* sandwich stuffed with beef, cheese, pico de gallo, lettuce, and tartar sauce.

Spencer's for Steaks and Chops, 6001 Destination Pkwy., Orlando, FL 32819; (407) 313-8625; thehiltonorlando.com/dining/spencers/index.cfm; Valet Parking; $$$$. Spencer's for Steaks and Chops at the Hilton Orlando features hand-cut USDA prime beef, dry aged, as well as fresh local seafood and local organic produce. Unlike at most traditional, clubby steak houses, the decor is rather modern and sleek. The chefs and culinary team, with a rather innovative and creative touch, compose such dishes as the diver scallops, served with smoked cheddar cauliflower puree, verde sauce, and crispy leeks. For something traditional, try the cowboy-cut rib chop, 18 ounces of USDA prime bone-in rib eye aged 21 days and cooked at 1,600 degrees to seal in the natural beef juices under the charred crust. End with a decadent dessert like the New York–style cheesecake topped with strawberry rhubarb compote or the bittersweet chocolate soufflé with bourbon *anglaise.*

Stonewood Grill & Tavern; 5078 Dr. Phillips Blvd., Orlando, FL 32819; (407) 297-8682; stonewoodgrill.com; Parking Lot; Steak House; $$$. Stonewood Grill is one of those places you'd take your significant other for a nice night out on the town. The decor is decidedly American, with a lot of woods and dark tones, yet is also very homey. It is one of three Stonewood Grills in the area, with the original Stonewood Grill founded in Ormond Beach near Daytona Beach. For starters, I recommend an order of the blue cheese chips, homemade potato chips drizzled with blue cheese aioli, lightly baked and served with blue cheese crumbles and topped with a balsamic reduction. Try also the buffalo shrimp, drizzled with buffalo sauce and blue cheese crumbles, delightful and fresh to taste. For an entree, try the 12-ounce oak-grilled rib eye steak, a tender, flavorful, juicy cut of aged steak grilled using oak-wood chips—skillfully done, cooked to perfection. The herb-encrusted grouper, part of the seafood selection here, is thick and meaty with a texture reminiscent of crab meat, very tasty and luscious. Sides are not their strong point, however. For dessert, try the signature chocolate bread pudding, made in house and topped with Häagen-Dazs ice cream. More like a hybrid of chocolate cake and bread pudding, it is sweet, comforting, and moist.

Taverna Opa, 9101 International Dr., Orlando, FL 32819; (407) 351-8660; tavernaopaorlando.com; Parking Garage; Greek; $$$. This lively restaurant in Pointe Orlando serves up loud Greek music and belly dancing to accompany the Greek dining experience. Piles of paper napkins fill the air as patrons shout out, "Opa!" throughout the night and the belly dancers make their way around the spacious dining room. The menu runs the gamut of Greek cuisine from hot and cold meze appetizer dishes to seafood and lamb. Try the delicious octopus, grilled over an oak-wood fire, for an appetizer. The *kleftiko,* slow-roasted lamb in parchment paper with carrots, potatoes, rosemary, whole garlic, and Greek cheese, is a specialty, as are the slow-roasted lamb and the braised lamb shank. If you are in the mood for sharing, try the *thallasino* or the seafood *pikilia,* a 7-ounce lobster tail, shrimp, scallops, mussels, calamari, king crab legs, and fish of the day in a tomato garlic sauce with white wine.

Teak Neighborhood Grill, 6400 Time Square Ave., Orlando, FL 32835; (407) 313-5111; teakorlando.com; Parking Lot; $$. This neighborhood restaurant located in the MetroWest area near Universal Studios is known for its creative and filling burgers. Start off with some of Danny's award-winning beanless chili, made with slow-stewed Angus beef, fresh diced onions, roasted red peppers, and fresh herbs and spices topped with diced tomato, red onion, and cheddar Jack cheese. The burgers here at Teak, each with its own cultural theme and ingredients, are made with half-pound certified Angus beef, grilled to order, and served with your choice of side: garlic bistro fries, sweet-potato tots, risotto, or house-made potato chips, among others. Try the sweet and savory PB&J burger, topped with a smooth almond and peanut butter spread, orange marmalade, crispy potato strings, and provolone cheese on a toasted pretzel bun. The Colombian burger here is topped with grilled pineapple, provolone cheese, lettuce, beefsteak tomato, and herb-crusted potato chips, and drizzled with a garlic cilantro sauce served on a toasted brioche bun. For those looking to try a taste of Brazil, the Brazilian burger will do the trick, topped with sliced Black Forest ham over a medium egg, crispy potato strings, and provolone cheese piled high with lettuce, beefsteak tomato, and ranch dressing served on toasted brioche bun. For those competitive eaters and fans of *Man v. Food,* try the Teak's Burger Challenge, where you face off against 2 burgers with 2 full pounds of Angus beef, 9 slices of American cheese, 9 slices swiss cheese, 9 slices provolone cheese, 24 slices smoked bacon, 2 fried fresh-mozzarella rounds, beefsteak tomatoes, lettuce, beer-battered onion rings, Danny's award-winning beanless chili, and sliced jalapeños, all covered in cheddar cheese sauce.

Trey Yuen Chinese Restaurant, 6800 Visitors Circle, Orlando, FL 32819; (407) 352-6822; Parking Lot; Chinese/Dim Sum; $$. Hidden away from busy International Drive in the midst of the tourist district, Trey Yuen serves up some of the most authentic and tasty Cantonese dishes in town in addition to American Chinese favorites. The interior is also one of the most ornate, with scenes from Chinese mythology and ornate dragons spread throughout the ceilings and walls, giving the illusion of dining in an old Chinese teahouse. And much like what happens in teahouses today, when patrons go to *yum cha,* or drink tea, it often calls for some dim sum. Here at Trey Yuen, the dim sum is ordered by marking a long paper list on the menu with the desired number of each item. The shrimp dumplings, chicken feet, *chiu chow fun gor,* and all the rest—all very good—are then prepared and presented to the table still fresh and hot from the steamers. Enjoy it all with some nice hot jasmine tea (ask for rock sugar) to help it go down smoothly. For dinner-size options, try some of the beef *chow fun,* homemade wide, flat rice noodles with chunky slices of beef and stir-fried with onions and bean sprouts, a hearty noodle delight. Add hot chile oil for some extra kick. Other highlights of their main menu include the hearty Trey Yuen Delight, a delicious combination of sliced chicken, lobster chunks, shrimp, scallops, and roasted pork sautéed with an assortment of vegetables, and the Peking duck, Long Island duckling slowly roasted and served boneless, with the skin and shredded tender meat served with Chinese pancakes and a side of special hoisin dipping sauce and spring onions.

Vito's Chop House, 8633 International Dr., Orlando, FL 32819; (407) 354-2467; vitoschophouse.com; Parking Lot; Steak House; $$$. A classic, intimate steak house with an Italian flair, Vito's Chop House provides some of the best aged steaks in Orlando. The specialty martini list, 1,000 wine selections, and over 50 varieties of cigars in house make Vito's quite the classy affair. The menu features USDA prime and choice corn-fed beef, aged 4 to 6 weeks on the premises, and the steaks and chops are hand cut daily. After you choose your cut of steak from the display plate, they are flame broiled over oak and orange wood. Try the tomahawk long-bone rib eye, a 30-ounce Greg Norman Ranch Wagyu steak, or the Vito's master cut, a 52-ounce Harris Ranch porterhouse, for those extra hungry for some meaty fare. For those looking for seafood options, try the cedar plank–roasted salmon or the yellowtail snapper *aqua pazza*.

Zorba's Greek Taverna, 4898 S. Kirkman Rd., Orlando, FL 32811; (407) 219-4326; zorbasgreektaverna.com; Parking Lot; Greek; $$. This restaurant features all the classic Greek dishes with belly dancers entertaining guests on weekend evenings. The place is known for their gyro sandwiches and platters, but try some of their wonderful appetizer sampler, the Zorba Platter, composed of tzatzki spread, hummus, baba ghanouj, *dolmades*, and *tirosalata* feta cheese with pita.

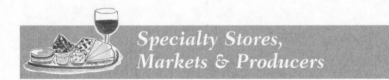

Specialty Stores, Markets & Producers

Whole Foods Market, 8003 Turkey Lake Rd.; Orlando, FL 32819; (407) 355-7100; Parking Lot. See listing description under the Winter Park entry, p. 75.

Restaurant Row/ Sand Lake Road

The stretch known as Restaurant Row along Sand Lake Road just west of I-4 is home to a high concentration of restaurants, ranging from fine dining and high-end chains to sushi lounges and Indian hot spots. It's a popular place not only among conventiongoers, but also among the more affluent residents in the Dr. Phillips and Windermere areas, many of whom are involved in the thriving hospitality industry nearby.

Best of the Neighborhood

Big Fin Seafood Kitchen, 8046 Via Dellagio Way, Orlando, FL 32819; (407) 615-8888; bigfinseafood.com; Parking Lot; Seafood; $$$$. Big Fin Seafood Kitchen ships in fresh seafood twice daily from around the globe. Start off with some of Chef James Slattery's Thai-inspired crab, corn, and coconut soup or a few grilled or raw oysters and Manhattan-style seafood chowder, made with fresh bacon and potatoes. They also have a bevy of fresh snow crab clusters, king crab claws, and king crab legs. From the sushi menu, try the Hawaiian sunset roll with avocado, cream cheese, and albacore tuna topped with torched Hawaiian orange *nairagi,* mango, *tobiko* caviar, and ginger-soy gastrique, or the Krakatoa roll, a California roll made with king crab and topped with lobster, *surimi, masago,* jalapeño oil, and spicy mayo, and then baked. Main entrees include a plethora of grilled, broiled, fried, pan-seared, or blackened-style fish, such as black grouper, salmon, ahi tuna, mahimahi, and swordfish fillets. Try the delicious pan-seared Bahamian yellowtail snapper cioppino style in tomato broth, made with Alaskan king crab meat, bay scallops, shrimp, clams, mussels, new potatoes, and sweet corn.

Chatham's Place, 7575 Dr. Phillips Blvd., Orlando, FL 32819; (407) 345-2992; chathamsplace.com; Parking Lot; Continental/European; $$$$. When Chatham's Place was founded in 1988, Orlando's Restaurant Row along Sand Lake Road was far from the restaurant mecca it is today. Despite the restaurant's being located in a rather drab office complex, the locally inspired Continental cuisine shines through, offering up what has been rated as some of the best dishes in the country. The setting is intimate and impressive, like you're inside an affluent friend's personal library along with its own private dining room in the chef's wine cellar. The kitchen is led by Co-Owner/Chef Tony Lopez and the exemplary, suited waitstaff is led by Co-Owner and maître d' Maurice Colindres. The appetizers and entrees, interspersed with little amuse-bouche plates from the kitchen, are divine. Start with some of the cream of portobello mushroom soup or the oven-baked brie a la *carozza,* with arugula, hearts of palm, and silverback anchovies drizzled with balsamic vinegar. Signature dishes include the pecan-buttered Florida black grouper with scallions and the savory rack of lamb in rosemary au jus.

The Table, 8060 Via Dellagio Way, Suite 106 (across from Regions Bank), Orlando, FL 32819; (407) 900-DINE; thetableorlando.com; Reservations Required; Parking Lot and Garage; Modern American; $$$$. The Table is unique in Orlando, as it features only 22 seats together around one beautiful, magnificent table for Friday and Saturday nights only. Created by Chef-Owner/husband-and-wife team Tyler Brassil and Loren Falsone, the menu here is prix-fixe, local, sustainable, and seasonal New American cuisine, consisting of hors d'oeuvre and five courses with wine pairings. Designed by Brassil himself, the dining room resembles a modern home decked out with a large painting of a foggy bridge on one wall, a large mirror and candles on another, and a beautiful hanging chandelier in the center over the large, black dining table. The ingredients all come fresh from local farms and local fishermen who bring whatever they caught that day, and the kitchen then uses these items for the meal. You can really feel their passion for food flowing into The Table, calling to you to sit, relax, and enjoy the epicurean journey with them. Also available for private parties and special events.

Foodie Faves

Anatolia Orlando, 7600 Dr. Phillips Blvd. #108, Orlando, FL 32819; (407) 352-6766; anatoliaorlando.com; Parking Lot; Turkish; $$$. This restaurant in the Marketplace at Dr. Phillips shopping plaza is perfect for those looking to try out an authentic, exotic meal from Turkey. The menu is extensive and the dishes are so generous, you could even share some with a friend. The atmosphere is cozy yet classy, with a soundtrack of the latest popular Turkish music playing in the background while you eat. For starters, I would recommend the *lavas,* or "balloon bread," a thin Turkish bread made from flour, water, and salt that's puffed up with air like a balloon and topped with sesame seeds. The *lavas* is fun to eat, especially dipped in *cacik,* a yogurt made with finely chopped cucumbers, herbs, and a hint of garlic. For the entree, you can choose from one of the many kebab dishes on the menu, all served with rice, mixed vegetables, or red potatoes. The *karisik* kebab is a mixed grill platter, more than enough for 2 people, with *tavuk adana* (chicken) kebab, lamb shish kebab, chicken kebab, *doner* kebab, and lamb chops with a serving of *kofta* kebab, all quite delicious and very satisfying. Finally, if you aren't full to the brim yet, for dessert you can choose from the traditional baklava, a layered phyllo pastry filled with pistachio and drizzled with homemade syrup, or the *kunefe,* a large shredded dough layered with a mild cheese and syrup, and big enough to feed a family of 4. Simply one of the best authentic ethnic restaurants in town.

Bee Won Korean Cuisine, 5100 Dr. Phillips Blvd., Orlando, FL 32819; (407) 601-7788; Parking Lot; Korean; $$$. Inside Bee Won, Korean for "secret garden," photos of Korean pro golfers and patrons, wooden tables and chairs, and traditional Korean decor fill the space. It is definitely larger and more airy than the popular Shin Jung (see p. 100), leaving you plenty of space to breathe in case you decide to cook up some *bulgogi* or *kalbi* beef ribs at your table. Try the spicy seafood noodle soup, pleasant with a spicy and thick seafood broth full of shrimp, clams, mussels, and Korean noodles. The *kalbi* beef short ribs are excellent, marinated in a sweet soy sauce and chargrilled. Other staples at this Korean joint include the *kimchijigae,* a spicy kimchee-based soup, and *bulgogi,* a very popular Korean marinated barbecue beef dish.

Cedar's Restaurant of Orlando, 7732 W. Sand Lake Rd., Orlando, FL 32819; (407) 351-6000; orlandocedars.com; Parking Lot; Mediterranean; $$$. Cedar's, a local, family-owned restaurant, features Middle Eastern fare, with strong roots in authentic Lebanese cuisine. Start off with old classics, such as stuffed grape leaves, tabbouleh, fried falafel, and hummus topped with roasted beef. Here the kibbe *bi laban,* kibbe balls made with ground meat, cracked wheat, onions, and pine nuts, are cooked in a yogurt sauce with garlic and cilantro. Skewered kebabs of ground meat, lamb, and chicken are available, or order the mixed grilled for a combination of each. Cedar's *farrouj musahab,* a deboned and grilled Cornish game hen, is worth a try as well. Finish off the meal with a slice of sweet, flaky, crunchy baklava.

Christini's Ristorante Italiano, 7600 Dr. Phillips Blvd., Orlando, FL 32819; (407) 345-8770; christinis.com; Parking Lot; Italian; $$$$. Christini's, an old-fashioned, classic restaurant accented by dark woods and attentive servers, serves up Italian dishes with a fine-dining flair. Owner Chris Christini welcomes guests and provides that extra touch to bring some of the best service in town. Start with the carpaccio *di manzo,* thin slices of rare filet mignon served with flakes of Parmigiana Reggiano cheese, lemon juice, and extra-virgin olive oil, or the *prosciutto e melone,* melons with thin slices of prosciutto served with sun-dried figs. For pasta lovers, try the fettuccine alla Christini, or the *fra diavolo aragosta,* made with lobster served over linguine in a spicy pescatore sauce. For meatier fare, try the signature *costata di vitello,* a thick-cut chop of juicy veal. End the meal with a slice of sweet, traditional tiramisu cake.

Dragonfly, 7972 Via Dellagio Way, Orlando, FL 32819; (407) 370-3359; dragonflyorlando.com; Parking Garage; Sushi, Japanese; $$$. Originally from Gainesville, Florida, this classy offshoot is the place to be for sushi in the area. Large, sweeping white curtains surround the restaurant and inside, dark reds and dim lighting set an urban, modern ambience like a swanky Miami nightclub. Try the signature Dragonfly roll, made with tuna and albacore, wrapped with grouper, and baked with spicy sauce, then topped with scallions and finished with eel sauce. The unique thing at Dragonfly is the *robata* grill, which uses fine binchotan charcoal heated up to 1,000 degrees and used to grill produce and proteins quickly, thus capturing the flavors of the food. The grilled appetizers are served up tapas style: Try the bacon-wrapped enoki mushrooms or the Wagyu rib eye. They also serve a decent ramen noodle bowl with pork belly and braised short ribs, topped with soft-poached egg, bok choy, scallions, bean sprouts, *togarashi,* and *nori.*

Fleming's Steakhouse & Wine Bar, 8030 Via Dellagio Way, Orlando, FL 32819; (407) 352-5706; flemingssteakhouse.com; Parking Garage; Steak House; $$$$. Fleming's in Dellagio Plaza is probably best known for its aged prime beef and an extensive wine list featuring 100 wines by the glass and a world-class Reserve List. Their porcini-rubbed filet mignon and peppercorn New York strip steak are fine staples that show off their prime steaks, cooked to perfection. The setting is very modern, and rather formal. Try their happy hour, available at the bar till 7 p.m., featuring a list of splendid appetizers and their signature prime burger with cheese and bacon at a more affordable price for those not using the company account.

Le Cafe de Paris, 5170 Dr. Phillips Blvd., Orlando, FL 32819; (407) 293-2326; Parking Lot; French; $. This little French cafe is a bit hidden away in a small shopping plaza. You may be transported to the streets of Paris with the smell of their fresh baguettes, croissants, quiches, and pastries. The special breakfast sandwich, made with bacon, egg, and cheese, is served here on a flaky, buttery croissant, and the slightly crunchy, grilled *croque madame* sandwich, made with ham and béchamel cheese, and topped with a sunny-side-up egg, are all classic favorite morning breakfast items. Try their *pan bagnat* chicken sandwich, made with chicken, lettuce, tomatoes, egg, black olives, and mayonnaise, or the simple Le Parisien, made with French baguette, butter, brie cheese, and tomato. The Pro's sandwich is a hearty sandwich consisting of baguette, prosciutto, pesto, mozarella, basil, and tomato. Try one of the many homemade gelato flavors for something sweet to finish off your visit.

MoonFish, 7525 W. Sand Lake Rd., Orlando, FL 32819; (407) 363-7262; fishfusion.com; Parking Lot; Seafood; $$$. MoonFish features a classy atmosphere with some of the freshest fish and aged steaks in town. The restaurant serves up a fusion-style blend of pan-Asian, Cajun, Pacific, and Floridian fare with flair, ranging from sashimi and sushi to citrus and oak wood–fired grilled and blackened fish. Guests can sit at the raw bar and enjoy fresh shucked oysters and clams or have a more elegant sit-down meal in the main dining room. Known for the fresh fish, MoonFish also serves up such popular dishes as sesame duck carpaccio and crispy almond-fried lobster tail.

Nagoya Sushi, 7600 Dr. Phillips Blvd., Orlando, FL 32819; (407) 248-8558; nagoyasushi.com; Parking Lot; Japanese/Sushi; $$. Tucked away and hidden in a hallway, Nagoya Sushi isn't the easiest place to find. But for those who seek fresh, delicious sushi, know that this gem is worth the search. The sushi chefs here prepare their rolls, or *maki*, with great care and attention to detail. The *nigiri* sushi pieces here range from sea urchin (*uni*) and octopus to tuna and salmon, each flavorful and fresh. Some of the more innovative rolls here include the Popeye roll, made with cold salmon, baby spinach, cream cheese, and rice wrapped in a spicy sauce, as well as the mango tango roll, made with shrimp tempura, imitation crab meat, slices of mango, and rice with a sweet mango glaze drizzled on top. The particularly delicious Fire Mountain roll is made with spicy raw tuna, white tuna, and salmon on top of a California roll with 5 types of caviar.

The Oceanaire Seafood Room, 9101 International Dr., Orlando, FL 32819; (407) 363-4801; Parking Garage and Valet; theoceanaire.com; Parking Garage and Valet; Seafood; $$$$. The Oceanaire Seafood Room features some of the freshest seafood in town, with a classic, sleek, and sophisticated atmosphere. Fish dishes are a specialty here, from the stuffed flounder Florentine, with spinach, shrimp, and crab meat stuffing with tomato-chive butter sauce, to the seafood mixed grill with grilled fish, shrimp, and scallops, and baked stuffed shrimp. The Oceanaire's got it all for that sea lover in you. Try their signature pan-seared Florida triggerfish Louie, topped with jumbo lump crab meat and served in a lemon caper butter sauce.

Press 101 Sandwich & Wine Bar, 7600 Dr. Phillips Blvd., Orlando, FL 32819; (407) 351-2101; press101.com; Parking Lot; Sandwiches; $$. This popular restaurant on Restaurant Row features a multitude of sandwich options along with a nice wine and craft beer list. During lunch the restaurant operates with counter service, where patrons walk up to the register to order, and later on a server brings out the order inside the restaurant or out on the covered patio. At night the service changes to sit-down, and some nights feature live jazz and a slightly different sit-down menu. The sandwiches here are wonderful and creative. For example, the *banh mi* steak sandwich, inspired by the Vietnamese sandwich, is served on a baguette, with flatiron steak, a sweet chile mayonnaise sauce, sliced cucumber, fresh cilantro, fresh baby arugula, pickled carrots, daikon and onions, soy sauce, and sport peppers. Choose from an extensive list including delicious prosciutto *di parma,* french dip, meatball sub, or grilled cheese with swiss, fontina, and shrimp cheddar cheese, applewood-smoked bacon, and tomatoes on wheat bread. Also try the roasted duck confit sandwich, served on *lavosh* bread with balsamic deglazed onions, sun-dried mission figs, brie cheese, and fontina finished with balsamic glaze, or the crab niçoise, made with marinated lump crab meat, French-cut baby green beans, roasted fingerling potatoes, hard-boiled egg, mixed olives, caper berries, sun-dried tomatoes, seasonal greens, micro mix blend, alfalfa sprouts, and feta cheese.

Roy's, 7760 W. Sand Lake Rd., Orlando, FL 32819; (407) 352-4844; roysrestaurant.com; Parking Lot; Asian; $$$$. This Hawaiian chain founded by James Beard Award winner Roy Yamaguchi was one of the first to establish itself on Restaurant Row, and continues to bring the spirit of the Hawaiian fusion cuisine and aloha spirit to central Florida today. Dishes here take influences from Japan, China, Vietnam, Thailand, and more to come together through macadamia nut–crusted mahimahi and Hawaiian-style braised short ribs with honey mustard, broccolini, and Yukon mash. The Hawaiian-style *misoyaki* butterfish, made with flaky black cod, is buttery and divine.

Saffron Indian Cuisine, 7724 W. Sand Lake Rd., Orlando, FL 32819; (407) 674-8899; saffronorlando.com; Indian; $$. Saffron is a relatively new Indian restaurant that opened in the Restaurant Row district along Sand Lake Road. The decor and interior, with its decidedly modern feel, is warm and sophisticated with dark wood and bright walls. The lunch prices are very reasonable, from $7.95 and up. Servers are very accommodating, checking in often during the meal and making sure your red glasses are filled with water. Try the lamb *xacutti,* a signature dish that comes from the Indian coastal state of Goa, known for its beautiful beaches and coconut trees. The *xacutti* is a savory, rich curry-like dish with grated coconut, tender chunks of lamb, and notes of blended spices in a creamy sauce. The sauce is light and delicious and goes well with the charred tandoor clay oven–baked naan and basmati rice.

Seasons 52 Fresh Grill, 7700 W. Sand Lake Rd., Orlando, FL 32819; (407) 354-5212; seasons52.com; Parking Lot; Modern American; $$$. Seasons 52 is an upscale American chain developed by Darden Restaurants, whose headquarters and test kitchens are located here in Orlando. The concept focuses on a casual yet sophisticated atmosphere with seasonally changing menus that emphasize fresh, healthy ingredients and lower calories (most dishes contain fewer than 475 calories). Favorite entrees here include the flavorful cedar plank–grilled Atlantic salmon, caramelized sea scallops, and grilled rack of New Zealand lamb. The desserts highlighted the most here are the mini-indulgences, featuring mini-desserts in a shot-size glass, and filled with such classics as key lime pie, chocolate peanut butter mousse, and pecan pie, and seasonal desserts, such as pumpkin pie, in the fall.

Vines Grille & Wine Bar, 7533 W. Sand Lake Rd., Orlando, FL 32819; (407) 351-1227; vinesgrille.com; Parking Lot; Modern American; $$$$. This local hot spot serves up classic yet creative fare set in a smooth, sophisticated environment accentuated by lively jazz and a selection of over 500 different wines. Small plates are popular here, ranging from seared *foie gras* with pan-roasted pear, to porcini-crusted prime steak carpaccio, to oysters Rockefeller with pork belly, to grilled octopus. Start off with some french onion soup, or one of the salads made with organic and locally grown greens. For dinner try one of the many hearty dishes, such as the pan-seared Chilean sea bass with lobster risotto, a cut of their USDA prime steaks, such as filet mignon, the Wagyu burger with truffle aioli, or the slow-braised bone-in beef short ribs with cheddar grits. Sit up by the bar and enjoy the live jazz throughout the night, amid the busy company of nearby conventioneers.

Specialty Stores, Markets & Producers

Funky Monkey Wine Company, 9101 International Dr., Orlando, FL 32819; (407) 418-9463; funkymonkeywine.com. **See** listing description under the Central Orlando entry, p. 80.

Disney/ Lake Buena Vista

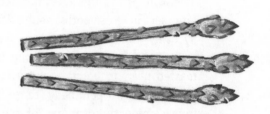

Since opening in 1971, the Walt Disney World Resort (also known informally as Disney World) has irrevocably changed the face of central Florida and was a major impetus for growth in Orlando. The sprawling complex includes four theme parks (Magic Kingdom, Epcot, Disney's Hollywood Studios, and Disney's Animal Kingdom), two water parks (Blizzard Beach and Typhoon Lagoon), 23 on-site themed resort hotels, five golf courses, and a downtown-themed shopping district. Nearby there are countless other hotels, shops, and restaurants that have sprung up to meet the ever-growing demands of the tourism industry.

Best of the Neighborhood

Bull & Bear Steakhouse at Waldorf Astoria, 14200 Bonnet Creek Resort Lane, Orlando, FL 32821; (407) 597-5500;

bullandbearorlando.com; Valet Parking; Steak House; $$$$. **Bull & Bear**, set with chandeliers and fancy decor, offers a menu of classic fare, with an emphasis on serving USDA-certified Angus prime beef, the highest-quality grade available in the US, much like the original Bull & Bear in New York City. The 36-ounce, 28-day dry-aged Tomahawk rib eye steak, served with a candle made of the steak's own fat drippings, is sure to delight any meat lover. Other popular dishes here include the yellowfin tuna carpaccio, pan-roasted Dover sole, and oak plank–grilled wild salmon.

Jiko—The Cooking Place at Disney's Animal Kingdom Lodge, 2901 Osceola Pkwy., Lake Buena Vista, FL 32830; (407) 939-3463; disneyworld.disney.go.com/dining/jiko-the-cooking-place; Valet Parking; $$$$. Jiko, which means "cooking place" in Swahili, serves up masterful dishes that pay homage to Africa, ranging from grilled wild boar tenderloin with mealy *pap* (porridge) to *peri-peri* roasted chicken, to bunny chow, to falafel, to Durban curry vegetables with naan bread, to Kenyan coffee–rubbed Atlantic black grouper. Popular items also include wood-fired flatbreads, such as African-spiced fire-roasted chicken and roasted mushrooms with masala curry and crispy fennel. Jiko has one of the largest offerings of South African wines anywhere in the US, with more than 65 of South Africa's boutique wineries available in the wine room. The restaurant has also been awarded AAA Four Diamond status and the *Wine Spectator*'s Award of Excellence. End the meal with some coconut bread pudding or Tanzanian chocolate and Kenya coffee mousse with cinnamon mascarpone nutty chocolates and hot chocolate.

La Luce by Donna Scala at the Hilton Bonnet Creek, 14100 Bonnet Creek Resort Lane, Orlando, FL 32821; (407) 597-3600; laluceorlando.com; Valet Parking; Italian; $$$. Beautifully haunting scenes created with chalk hang inside the restaurant at La Luce inside the Hilton Orlando at Bonnet Creek: a fountain, a street scene—all images that will be swept away in a few months. La Luce's Chef Donna Scala (of Napa Valley's Bistro Don Giovanni) has earned a reputation throughout the culinary community as a food purist, with dishes prepared with the freshest local ingredients. The menu at La Luce melds together Italian traditions and Napa Valley's unique approach to fresh cuisine. The dishes here, from the thin pizzas, lasagnas, and other fresh Italian cuisine, are prepared "the way it was meant to be: hearty, yet not overwhelming."

The Venetian Room, 8101 World Center Dr., Orlando, FL 32821; (407) 238-8060; thevenetianroom.com; Valet and Parking Lot; Continental/European; $$$$. The Venetian Room, an AAA Four Diamond–rated restaurant located inside the Caribe Royale convention resort hotel, off of World Center Drive near Disney World, is probably best reserved for special occasions or events like a romantic evening or an anniversary night out, or if you just feel like a boss. Waiters at your table, dressed in black ties and coats, stand ready to offer great, classic service that is welcoming yet also unobtrusive. In a setting that is intimate and luxurious, with deep reds along the walls and in the chairs, and a grand chandelier hanging in the middle of the copper dome, the decor reflects the old-world charm of the Venetian Renaissance period. Some of the

Continental-inspired dishes that will surprise you range from luscious diver scallops and gnocchi stroganoff, to filet mignon and Chilean sea bass, to the heavenly Grand Marnier soufflé, an experience served table side with a sweet crème *anglaise,* all standouts at The Venetian Room.

Victoria & Albert's at Disney's Grand Floridian Resort & Spa, 4401 Grand Floridian Way, Lake Buena Vista, FL 32830; (407) 939-3862; victoria-alberts.com/index.html; Valet Parking; Modern American; $$$$. The definition of fine dining in central Florida and one of the finest restaurants in the Southeast, Victoria & Albert's features a changing daily menu of contemporary American cuisine with fresh, seasonal ingredients sourced from around the world. Led by James Beard Award–nominated Chef Scott Hunnel, Victoria & Albert's is central Florida's only recipient of AAA's highest achievement, the Five Diamond Award, and is characterized by a knowledgeable maître d'hôtel and chefs in traditional Victorian attire and classic white toques. Diners can enjoy seven courses of haute cuisine in the dining room, or 10 to 12 at the chef's table or in Queen Victoria's Room. In a room inside the kitchen, guests at the chef's table get a front-row seat where Chef Hunnel starts the evening with a Champagne toast and discusses ideas to craft a personal menu. At Queen Victoria's Room, guests experience an elegant, intimate setting behind closed doors with tableside French *gueridon* service. With a selection of over 500 wines, Victoria & Albert's is also continually ranked with Best of Award of Excellence from *Wine Spectator*. The dinner may include premium ingredients such as tender Monterey abalone, Niman Ranch lamb, Wagyu strip loin, prosciutto-wrapped Gulf shrimp with Florida melons and *jamón ibérico,* paired with wine and spirits, and often provides 3 to 4 hours of foodie delights.

Foodie Faves

Boma—Flavors of Africa at Disney's Animal Kingdom Lodge, 2901 Osceola Pkwy., Lake Buena Vista, FL 32830; (407) 938-4722; disneyworld.disney.go.com/dining/boma-flavors-of-africa; Valet Parking; African; $$$$. Designed to resemble an African marketplace, Boma serves dishes, buffet style, inspired by flavors of the many countries of Africa. Guests can watch as Boma's chefs prepare seafood and meat dishes in an open kitchen with a wood-fire rotisserie grill. *Boma* in Africa is "an open, natural space that provides safety and shelter in the bush." Curries, chutneys, and other Indian and Asian influences can be found in the Durban-spiced roasted chicken, fresh fish, and other offerings. Beef and lamb *bobotie,* baked salmon, cinnamon raisin rice, couscous Marrakesh, and the sweet, signature zebra dome pastries are not to be missed.

California Grill, 4600 N. World Dr., Lake Buena Vista, FL 32830; (407) 824-1576; disneyworld.disney.go.com/dining/california-grill; Valet Parking; Sushi/Modern American; $$$$. California Grill, set high atop Disney's Contemporary Resort, serves up breathtaking views of the Magic Kingdom theme park alongside its inspired contemporary American fare with an emphasis on California fusion cooking. The menu changes regularly to showcase the freshest produce, but guests can look forward to flavorful renditions of brick oven–baked flatbreads, sushi rolls, handmade Sonoma goat cheese ravioli, oak-fired beef fillets and pork tenderloins, and a wine list featuring selections from California's finest estates. Note: The California Grill will be closed for refurbishment from January 6, 2013, through late summer 2013.

Citricos at Disney's Grand Floridian Resort & Spa, 4401 Grand Floridian Way, Lake Buena Vista, FL 32830; (407) 939-3463; disneyworld.disney.go.com/dining/citricos; Valet Parking; Continental/European; $$$$. Citricos restaurant serves up the inspired cuisine of southern Europe stemming from the cuisine of Provence, Tuscany, and the Spanish Riviera. These dishes, with a contemporary, seasonal, American twist, include oak-grilled steaks, creative risottos, pastas, and seafood. Guests can also choose to dine at the Chef's Domain at Citricos, ordering from the traditional menu or choosing to have the chef create a menu for them in a private dining room that seats up to 12. The first includes items such as *arancini,* crispy risotto with cremini mushrooms, Asiago, and charred tomato coulis and yellow tomato gazpacho served with smoked rock shrimp, tomato and cucumber salsa *cruda, piquillo* coulis, and a 25-year sherry vinegar–lime ice. For an entree, choose from Madeira-braised short ribs, grilled Colombia River wild king salmon, Berkshire pork tenderloin, and roasted pork belly. Warm chocolate banana torte, lemon-scented cheesecake, gelato tastings, and tiramisu round out the dessert favorites.

Earl of Sandwich, 1750 E. Buena Vista Dr., Lake Buena Vista, FL 32830; (407) 938-1762; earlofsandwichusa.com; Parking Lot; Sandwiches; $. Legend has it that the first sandwich was named after John Montagu, the fourth Earl of Sandwich. Often found gambling, he did not have time to have a meal during play, so he would ask his servants to bring him slices of meat between two slices of bread during his long hours at the card table. This habit became well known among his gambling friends and thus the sandwich was born. The Earl of Sandwich at Downtown Disney was actually founded by a real-life descendant of the original Earl of Sandwich, along with one of the founders of Planet Hollywood. The hot sandwiches are the draw here at the Earl's, and at $5.99, they are a great bargain for the family. Inside, there is a lineup system—the same familiar one perfected by Disney at its parks—where customers move through to the cashier to give their order. Try the Italian hot sandwich, filled with salami, capocollo, roasted ham, mortadella, mozzarella cheese, and roma tomatoes, and topped with a nice Italian dressing. The sandwich is definitely meaty, but my favorite part is the sandwich's crunchy, flaky bread.

Flying Fish Cafe, 2101 Epcot Resorts Blvd., Lake Buena Vista, FL 32830; (407) 939-3463; disneyworld.disney.go.com/dining/ flying-fish-cafe; Valet Parking; Seafood; $$$$. Flying Fish Cafe serves up fresh seafood at the nostalgic Atlantic seaboard pier–themed Disney's BoardWalk. At this restaurant named for a Coney Island roller coaster called the Flying Turns, with cars emblazoned with "flying fish," guests can dine at the chef's counter by the show kitchen to watch the culinary team prepare dishes such as oak-grilled Maine diver scallops and steak, rain forest pepperberry–grilled Kurobuta pork tenderloin, char-crusted New York strip steak, or potato-wrapped red snapper. Start off with the signature Flying Fish Cafe Crispy Maine Coast Jonah Crab Cake, with savory vegetable slaw, roasted red pepper coulis, and ancho chile remoulade. For an entree, the potato-wrapped red snapper is a signature dish here, served with a leek fondue with a veal glacé, red wine, and cassis butter reduction. For dessert, the caramelized banana napoleon is not to be missed: served with crisp phyllo, banana mousse, crème caramel, exotic fruit coulis, and bitter chocolate.

Les Chefs de France at Disney's Epcot, 1830 N. Avenue of the Stars, Lake Buena Vista, FL 32830; (407) 939-3463; disneyworld

.disney.go.com/dining/les-chefs-de-france; Parking Lot; French; $$$$. Les Chefs de France is located at Disney's Epcot's France Pavilion, set to the look of an authentic brasserie that could be found along the Rue de Seine. The chef-owners here are renowned across the world: Paul Bocuse, Gaston Lenôtre (who died in 2009), and Roger Verge. Bocuse's son, Jerome, oversees the culinary operations, and Executive Chef Bruno Vrignon trained under Bocuse in his Lyon restaurant. Start off with some *soupe a l'oignon* gratinée, the classic onion soup topped with gruyère cheese, or fresh flatbreads baked with crème fraîche, onion and bacon. Entree favorites include braised lamb shank and *canard aux cerises,* duck breast, and leg confit. End the meal with some famous French vanilla crème brûlée or chocolate profiteroles pastries.

Ohana, 1600 Seven Seas Dr., Lake Buena Vista, FL 32830; (407) 939-3463; disneyworld.disney.go.com/dining/ohanas; Valet Parking; Asian; $$$$. Ohana restaurant in Disney's Polynesian Resort offers family-style dining, with a character breakfast in the morning and a Polynesian-themed dinner in the evening. The entree items are served *rodizio* style, with servers arriving at tables with giant skewers of sirloin steak, turkey, shrimp, and pork that have been roasted over an expansive 18-foot oak-fire pit, and side dishes including stir-fried vegetables, coriander chicken wings, pork fried dumplings, lo mein noodles, and a salad starter.

Raglan Road Irish Pub and Restaurant, 1640 E. Buena Vista Dr., Lake Buena Vista, FL 32830; (407) 938-0300; raglanroadirishpub

.com; Parking Lot; Irish; $$$. Located at Downtown Disney, Irish celebrity Chef Kevin Dundon's Raglan Road features traditional Irish favorites like shepherd's pie and bangers and mash with a contemporary twist. In the evening guests can experience an entertaining dance show featuring Irish dancers who jig away on tabletops at the center of the restaurant. Start off with some mighty mussels in a coconut-infused curry broth or some salmon swoon, choice Irish smoked salmon served with capers, shallots, and crème fraîiche. Try some of the *lambo,* a lamb shank braised in rosemary *jus* with mash, leeks, shiitake mushrooms, and baby carrots, or the mighty mixed grill, a plate of lamb chop, Guinness banger, sirloin steak, black pudding, chicken drumstick, and bacon.

Shula's Steak House, 1500 Epcot Resorts Blvd., Lake Buena Vista, FL 32830; (407) 934-1362; donshula.com/shulas-steak-house-orlando; Valet Parking; Steak House; $$$$. Shula's Steak House, with its low lighting and classic clubby steak-house setting, features a decor punctuated by photos and memorabilia of Coach Don Shula's Miami Dolphins. The steaks are where the action is here at Shula's with choice cuts of the custom Shula cut as well as New York sirloin, porterhouse fillet, and filet mignon, along with fresh seafood including 3- to 5-pound Maine lobsters. Servers here bring the menu on a custom-designed football and a display tray of various cuts of steak for choosing. Start off with some barbecued shrimp stuffed with basil or jumbo lump crab cake. Choose from one of the many steaks available, including the Kansas City strip, cowboy rib eye, and porterhouse cuts, with options of adding red-wine herb reduction, béarnaise, Mary Anne, or horseradish cream sauces. The sauces are hardly needed, however, as the succulent steaks can stand on their own.

Todd English's bluezoo, 1500 Epcot Resorts Blvd., Lake Buena Vista, FL 32830; (407) 934-1111; thebluezoo.com; Valet Parking; Seafood; $$$$. Celebrity Chef Todd English brings together the freshest seafood with coastal cuisines from around the world at Todd English's bluezoo, located at Walt Disney World Dolphin Hotel, set in an exotic underwater-themed decor designed by renowned architect Jeffery Beers. Dishes include savory shellfish, swordfish, tuna, salmon, and Chilean sea bass. Creative veal and pork dishes with braised bacon brussels sprouts are available for those who want an alternative to fish. Try the teppan-seared jumbo sea scallops with braised beef short rib and silky cauliflower puree, or the miso-glazed *mero*, Hawaiian sea bass, shiitake-ginger rice, black garlic, and sticky soy. For lobster lovers, try the 2-pound Maine Cantonese lobster fried and tossed in a sticky soy glaze.

Wolfgang Puck Cafe, 1482 E. Buena Vista Dr., Lake Buena Vista, FL 32830; (407) 938-9653; disneyworld.disney.go.com/dining/wolfgang-puck-cafe; Parking Lot; Asian/Modern American; $$$$. Wolfgang Puck Cafe, located in Downtown Disney, serves up the famous chef's unique fusion of Asian and California cuisine. Signature offerings at Wolfgang Puck Cafe include sushi, vegetarian dishes, wood-fired gourmet pizzas, hand-tossed salads, piquant pastas, savory sandwiches, and decadent desserts. Try some of the Wolfgang classics, such as oven-roasted salmon with tomato, fennel, roasted potatoes, and horseradish cream, or the pan-seared sea bass, pumpkin ravioli, and steak frites.

North Orlando

A little bit farther north of Orlando are the suburban cities of Sanford, Altamonte Springs, Casselberry, Maitland, Apopka, and Longwood. Headquarters for such corporations as AAA and Ruth's Hospitality Group, this area is generally a suburban paradise with a good school system and where a few Orlando Magic players call home. Crane's Roost Park at the Altamonte mall is popular for Fourth of July festivities, with the Red, Hot & Boom concert event with thousands of attendees each year. Nearby Wekiva Springs and Rock Springs have provided relaxing, cool spring waters for central Florida residents for generations. The Senator tree, located in Longwood, at more than 3,000 years old, was easily central Florida's oldest tourist attraction until it burned down in early 2012.

Best of the Neighborhood

Cress Restaurant, 103 W. Indiana Ave., DeLand, FL 32720; (386) 734-3740; cressrestaurant.com; Street Parking and Parking Lot;

Modern American/Indian; $$$. Helmed by James Beard Award–nominated Chef Hari Pulapaka (who is also a doctor of mathematics and adjunct professor for nearby Stetson University) and his wife, Dr. Jenneffer Pulapaka, Cress restaurant in Deland is one of the best restaurants in central Florida, with inspired, creative flair and dishes that are rich in flavors. Drawing from his Indian roots and Southern sensibilities, Le Cordon Bleu–trained Chef Hari brings together a constantly changing menu inspired by the seasons. When they are available, you can start off with some fresh Florida fish seviche, cured to order with cilantro, fresh citrus, shaved Florida onion, ginger, coconut milk, and signature Cress chips. The shrimp and grits, a Southern mainstay, are delicious, rustic, and soulful here (the recipe for this tasty dish is available, as are other menu items, on their website as well). Popular dishes include the tikka masala curry, served with your choice of New England sea scallops, braised local goat, Ashley Farms free-range chicken, wild shrimp, or roasted vegetables and tofu. For dessert, don't miss the Scotch whiskey–infused, sweet banana-pecan croissant pudding. Book ahead to try the very special chef's table menu for a "gastronomic adventure." See Cress Restaurant's recipe for **Slow-Roasted Jerk-Spiced Local Pork** on p. 246.

Fresh on the Fly, 1210 S. International Pkwy., Lake Mary, FL 32746, (407) 878-5808; fresh-on-the-fly.com; Parking Lot; $$. Fresh on the Fly serves up fresh, wild-caught fish, hormone-free chicken, and grass-fed beef, stressing their dedication to serving chemical-free entrees and making healthy environmental choices in their operations. Start off with some oyster shooters, served here with a spicy cocktail sauce in a shot glass with key lime cocktail sauce, or share an order of blackened mahi Cali fish tacos, served with a chipotle sauce, Monterey Jack cheese, cilantro, and diced red onions. Some menu highlights include their mahimahi cheesesteak, made with blackened mahimahi with sautéed peppers and onions, melted American and provolone cheeses, topped with a chipotle aioli sauce, and served in a wrap. Bronzed diver scallops served with roasted red pepper risotto and wilted spinach in a Sauvignon blanc butter sauce are also a popular entree. Though seafood is their specialty, the prime burgers here are also made with extra care, sourcing their beef from local Deep Creek Ranch in DeLeon Springs. Finish the meal with a sweet ending: a slice of the homemade key lime pie.

Hollerbach's Willow Tree Cafe, 205 E. 1st St., Sanford, FL 32771; (407) 321-2204; willowtreecafe.com; Parking Lot; German; $$. In historic downtown Sanford north of Orlando, near the banks of Lake Monroe, Hollerbach's Willow Tree Cafe is an ode to the great German beer halls, a place where it is always Oktoberfest on weekend evenings. Through the Willow Tree Cafe, Owners Theo, Linda, and daughter Christina Hollerbach do their best to bring the experience of authentic German *Gemütlichkeit,* a sense of well-being and happiness that comes from enjoying the company of friends and family while savoring good food and drink. When it first opened in 2011, the cafe took up about 1,000 square feet, and now it is up to 14,000 square feet with over 75 employees and an impressive outdoor dining area. You can often see the jovial, bearded Chef Theo Hollerbach walking from table to table, welcoming guests, and sharing the festive air and drinking with restaurant patrons as he makes his rounds. The Willow Tree serves over 50 different German beers and wines and live entertainment in the form of the popular oompah band, complete with tuba and accordions. The beer is always flowing freely here, where every few minutes you can hear cheers of the German drinking toast "Zicke, Zacke, Zicke, Zacke, Hoi, Hoi, Hoi!" Bring a group of friends and family and enjoy some beer in a "boot," which comes in 1-, 2-, and 3-liter sizes. The Hollerbach family comes from the small town of Kyllburg in Germany where Theo's grandfather was a master butcher and the family was famous for their sausages. Their recipes include many of the old-world traditionals plus family specialties, and they serve up dishes such as bratwurst sausages, *numbergers,* and veal, pork, and chicken schnitzels. Start off with some nice freshly baked *Wiesn Brezn* (giant pretzel) with a sweet mustard sauce. My favorites include the potato cakes and the *Eisbein,* the very flavorful, tender, and lightly smoked pork shank, served with sauerkraut and Heaven and Earth mashed potatoes. End the meal with some German *apfel* strudel, made in house with fresh apples, rum-soaked white raisins, cinnamon, and sugar. The Willow Tree Cafe is festive and fun and definitely a place to enjoy yourself with family and friends. *Prosit!*

That Deli!, 3801 W. Lake Mary Blvd., Lake Mary, FL 32746; (321) 363-1394; thatdelifl.com; Sandwiches; $. The owners here at That Deli! take pride in their sandwiches, made large just the way they like them. The sandwiches are served on rye, white, or wheat bread or with a spinach wrap, pita wrap, or gluten-free rice wrap. Start off with some of their house-made "clam chowda" or the gluten-free farmhouse stew and fresh mac and cheese. Some of their more popular specialty sandwiches here include the I-4 Deluxe, consisting of a com- bination of chunks of real cold turkey, hot bacon, sliced avocado, provolone, tomato, and a tarragon mayo sauce. Try also the Hen House sandwich, made with chicken sausage, red onion, cheddar cheese, and tarragon mayo in a toasted steak roll, or the Beef Me Up Scotty, a hot roast beef sandwich with cheddar, porto- bello mushroom, and garlic mayo sauce. Veggie lovers can find their inner child with the Looney Shrooms, a playful sandwich made with hot portobello mushrooms, sautéed peppers and onions, romaine, tomato, cheddar, and garlic mayo.

Foodie Faves

Aladdin's Cafe, 1015 E. Semoran Blvd., Casselberry, FL 32707; (407) 331-0488; aladdinscafeorlando.com; Parking Lot; Mediterranean; $.

Aladdin's Cafe serves up authentic Middle Eastern cuisine, with an emphasis on Lebanese favorites. Located in a strip mall, this hole-in-the-wall serves up fresh hummus, grilled kebabs, seasoned *kofta*, tender leg of lamb, and more. Try the falafel, made with a mix of ground fava beans, chickpeas, spices, and herbs, deep fried, and served with tahini sauce, or start with some of the grilled quail with garlic and cilantro. End the meal with a slice of sweet, baked baklava or rice pudding made in house.

Angel's Soulfood and BBQ, 114 S. Sanford Ave., Sanford, FL 32771; (407) 302-6167; Street Parking; Soul Food/Southern; $. This little restaurant in downtown Sanford serves up hearty, home-cooked, Southern soul food and barbecue. Try some of their tasty renditions of such classics as fried chicken, mac and cheese, and fried catfish. Open Thurs through Sat.

Beard Papa's Fresh'n Natural Cream Puffs, 4922 W. SR 46, Sanford, FL 32771; (407) 322-3456; beardpapas.com; Parking Lot; Desserts/Bakery; $. Known as the bakery of the "World's Best Cream Puffs," Beard Papa's is an offshoot of the first Beard Papa's, located in Osaka, Japan. They offer a variety of puff pastries including chocolate éclair, strawberry, vanilla, and cookie crunch flavors. Start by choosing a pastry shell for the cream puff—original, cookie, éclair, Paris-Brest—and then choose a custard cream filling. Beard Papa's also serves up some nice shaved ice desserts, like the mango ice shower and sweet *mochi* ice cream.

Bagel King, 1455 E. Semoran Blvd., Casselberry, FL 32707; (407) 657-6266; bagelking.net; Bagels/Jewish; $. Founded in 1977, Bagel King reigns supreme among bagel shops in central Florida. This bakery makes its dough fresh every day, hand rolled, kettle dipped, and baked, resulting in a classic New York–style bagel. They also serve up *bialys,* those traditional rolls from the Polish city of Bialystok and staples of Polish Ashkenazi cuisine that were almost lost as a result of the devastation of World War II. The bagels at Bagel King range from cinnamon raisin to poppy, everything, pumpernickel, and more. They also serve up knishes, Reuben sandwiches, and over a dozen varieties of homemade cream cheese (including almond amaretto and sun-dried tomato). A popular breakfast and brunch spot (they also provide baked goods for Disney's Main Street), Bagel King offers up many great combos including the King's Breakfast special: 2 eggs topped with American cheese, home fries, toasted butter bagel, and coffee. I like the Fresh Fish Fantasies, a bagel served with romaine lettuce, tomato, sweet Bermuda onion, capers, and fresh sliced belly lox and nova with cream cheese schmear. Satisfy your sweet tooth with their pastries, such as chocolate and strawberry rugalach, black and white cookies, Danishes, and almond cookies.

Cafe Rouge, 129 W. 1st St., Sanford, FL 32771; (407) 324-7887; sanfordcaferouge.com; Street Parking; Continental/European; $$$. This little cafe in historic downtown Sanford (also a food truck known as Cafe Rouge Express) serves up traditional dishes stemming from cities in Europe all with a connection to the owners and the menu, namely London, Manchester, Paris, Toulouse, and Dublin. The English shepherd's pie and the traditional English-style beer-battered haddock and chips, consisting of a huge portion of fried haddock and long-cut potato fries, will bring you back to the docks on London's Thames. Cafe Rouge also serves up a great pan-seared jumbo sea scallop dish with leek and chile-butter sauce, as well as a delicious New Zealand rack of lamb served with garlic herb and sweet mint shallot butter.

Cuban Sandwiches on the Run, 2956 S. US 17-92, Casselberry, FL 32707; (407) 339-2272; Parking Lot; Cuban/Latin; $. This tiny hole-in-the-wall features some of the best authentic Cuban sandwiches in Orlando, done well. Try the *medianoche,* a cousin of the Cuban sandwich, consisting of roasted pork, ham, mustard, swiss cheese, and dill pickles, made with soft bread rather than the traditional Cuban bread.

Cypriana Restaurant, 505 E. Semoran Blvd., Casselberry, FL 32707; (407) 834-8088; cyprianausa.com; Parking Lot; Greek; $$. This popular Greek restaurant serves up classic Mediterranean staples that transport you to the Greek isle of Cyprus. Start off with an order of hummus and the *dolmathakia,* stuffed, marinated grape leaves with rice and beef, or rice, dill, and olive oil for vegetarians. The *kotopita,* a Greek version of the chicken potpie, is made with chunks of

boneless rotisserie chicken blended with fresh mushrooms, peppers and Greek herbs, wrapped in a flaky phyllo pastry and baked. Try some of their fresh spanokopita as well, a baked spinach pie made with feta cheese, and Greek herbs wrapped in a crispy pastry. For entrees, try the grouper Athenian, a filet stuffed and filled with spinach, feta cheese, and fresh mushrooms and broiled in a garlic wine sauce.

Enzo's Restaurant on the Lake, 1130 S. US 17-92, Longwood, FL 32750; (407) 834-9872; enzos.com; Italian; $$$$. In 1979 Enzo Perlini founded Enzo's on the Lake at the quaint lakefront house where the restaurant stands today, specializing in classic Italian dishes found in Enzo's Roman culinary heritage. With its antipasto bar, full-service bar, main dining room, and private dining areas for parties, it's no wonder that this lakeside home complete with sculpture gardens is popular for weddings and other special gatherings. Try this longtime Orlando institution's fettuccine *al aragosta e gamberi,* a favorite pasta dish served with lobster and shrimp in a light saffron and green onion sauce, or the fresh Dover sole sautéed in olive oil and lemon. Also popular are the veal scaloppine sautéed with artichokes in white wine sauce, and the *bucatini alla* Enzo with a sauce of prosciutto, peas, bacon, mushrooms, and Parmesan. For meat lovers, try the *agnello scottadito,* grilled Australian lamb chops marinated in extra-virgin olive oil, garlic, fresh oregano, and lemon and served with creamy polenta. Desserts are made fresh daily.

Imperial Dynasty Chinese Restaurant and Lounge, 2045 SR 434 West, Longwood, FL 32779; (407) 786-2266; imperialdynasty .com; Parking Lot; Chinese; $$. This Chinese-American restaurant serves up old favorites like General Tso's chicken in a sweet-spicy glaze sauce, and sesame chicken. Tony Chen and his wife, Kathy, have been offering these fresh dishes, with no MSG or preservatives, for years and continue to provide central Florida with some of the best American-style Chinese food in town. Try also the jalapeño beef, beef chow fun, lemon chicken, or hot and spicy noodle soup. See Imperial Dynasty's recipe for **Honey Walnut Shrimp** on p. 264.

Kobé Japanese Steakhouse & Sushi Bar, Multiple Locations, 468 W. SR 436, Altamonte Springs, FL 32714; (407) 862-6099; kobesteakhouse.com; Parking Lot; Japanese; $$$. Kobé Steakhouse is the most prominent teppanyaki grill–style restaurant chain in central Florida, with locations from International Drive to Altamonte Springs. Upon reaching Kobé, you are immediately awestruck by the majesty of the towering blue temple-like building that houses the restaurant. Inside, the place is teeming with people and the loud clangs of spatulas and knives flipping in the air from the hibachi chefs. Over 20 teppanyaki grill tables inhabit Kobé Steakhouse, an amazing number of grill tables. Part show, part food party, playing with your food is something these guys do with charm and wit. Watch for when they construct a volcano of onion, dousing it in vegetable oil and exploding it in volcanic fire spewing out puffs of white smoke. Overall, it's a nice place to go with a party for a special event.

Kohinoor Indian Cuisine, 249 W. SR 436, Altamonte Springs, FL 32714; (407) 788-6004; kohinoorindianrestaurant.com; Parking Lot; Indian; $$. Kohinoor, located just off I-4 on SR 436 in Altamonte Springs, offers an authentic menu of traditional Indian cuisine. Start off the meal with the Kohinoor special appetizer platter, consisting of vegetable Samosas, vegetable *pakoras, aloo pakoras,* chicken *pakoras,* chicken tikka, and *seekh* kebab. The chicken tandoori is marinated in yogurt and fresh Indian spices, then skewered and grilled in the tandoor, an Indian-style clay oven. You can also order *seekh* kebab, made with mildly spiced minced lamb on a skewer; *paneer* tandoori, made with cubes of marinated cheese curds, or *paneer;* and tandoori shrimp, among others that are cooked in the tandoor. *Aloo gobi,* a dish made with potatoes and cauliflower cooked with herbs and spices, and *paneer* masala, homemade cottage cheese cooked with bell peppers, onions, and spices in a tomato-based sauce, are popular vegetarian dishes and Indian cuisine staples. For chicken lovers, there are 9 ways the restaurant serves the dishes here, from chicken curry to chicken vindaloo to the popular chicken tikka masala in a tomato-based sauce, all served with a side of rice. Similar treatment of curries and sauces can be found with the lamb, fish, shrimp, and lobster courses. Order some fresh tandoori naan bread to dip in the sauces. For dessert, try some of their *rasmalai,* a sweet cottage cheese cake soaked in cardamom and rose-flavored milk, or the rice pudding, made with basmati rice, almonds, cashew nuts, raisins, and milk, and garnished with pistachio powder.

Korea House Restaurant, 1155 SR 434 West, Longwood, FL 32750; (407) 767-5918; koreahouseorlando.com; Parking Lot; Korean; $$. Open since 1982 and one of the first Korean restaurants in the state, Korea House has continued to provide excellent traditional and authentic Korean cuisine to all of central Florida. The kitchen is led by Head Chef Kisoo Choi with 40 years of experience in both Korean and Korean-Chinese cuisine. Korean cuisine is marked by the use of *gojuchang* (fermented Korean spicy chile pepper pastes) and sesame oil, and the dominance of kimchee, the national spicy pickled cabbage. The cuisine is often spicy, flavorful, and fresh. For appetizers, start off with the *gun-mandu,* Korean pan-fried dumplings made with pork, and the *haemul-pajun,* a Korean-style seafood pancake with green onions and hot pepper, and made from a batter of eggs, wheat flour, and rice flour. The version at Korea House is absolutely the best I've had in Orlando—slightly crunchy, crispy, and stuffed with green onion and bits of calamari and imitation crab. Add a dab of spicy chile soy sauce to the slice of *haemul-pajun* and enjoy. *Dolsot*-bibimbap, a mixed-rice dish served sizzling in a hot stone pot, is full of vegetables and sliced beef, and topped with a fried egg. To eat, just add some of the sweet pepper paste provided, and mix it all with your metal spoon while relishing the crunchy, slightly burnt rice on the bottom of the pot. The *jjambbong*, a huge bowl of spicy seafood noodle soup, and the *jajang-myun,* black soybean paste noodles with beef and vegetables, are said to be particular favorites of the locals at Korea House. Other popular dishes here include the hot Korean stews, such as the *sundubu-tzigae,* a spicy, soft tofu stew with shrimp and seafood, and the *gom-tang* oxtail soup, prepared by simmering for 10 hours and served with clear noodles and beef. There is also an extensive list of fish prepared Korean style with a little bit of salt, grilled or fried, such as cod, monkfish, and mackerel, to be eaten with white rice. When you order large portions of the Korean barbecue menu, the dining party can opt to use the grills built into the tables or have the kitchen prepare the dishes and bring them out on hot sizzling plates. The *gal-bi,* thick chunks of beef short ribs marinated in Korean barbecue sauce, are excellent here, as are the *bulgogi,* available in pork, chicken, and beef varieties. Korea House is known for quality Korean cuisine, and its reputation as one of the best Korean restaurants in Orlando is well deserved.

LaSpada's Original Philly Cheese Steaks & Hoagies, 1010 Lee Rd.; Orlando, FL 32810; (407) 539-0067; laspadas.com; Parking Lot; Sandwiches; $. Located just off Lee Road off the I-4 exit in a strip mall/plaza, La Spada's is a small hole-in-the-wall place known for the best Philly cheesesteaks in town. Stemming from an Italian family with roots in Chester, Pennsylvania, LaSpada's was founded in the Orlando area by John LaSpada Jr., who moved his operation to Orlando in the 1980s. Inside, this old '80s-era shop is decorated with Philly memorabilia and *Rocky* posters, and also sells Tastykakes, Herr's chips, and Hank's sodas. Yup, a slice of Philly in Orlando. You'll see the shop is in need of some tender, loving care, but I think that might be part of the appeal. Order the Philly cheesesteak on the fresh, delicious Amoroso roll and you won't regret it. It comes out piping hot; try it with provolone instead of Cheez Whiz to make it a little bit healthier if that's your thing. They also serve up some great Italian hoagies and deli sandwiches.

Polonia Polish Restaurant, 750 S. US 17-92, Longwood, FL 32750; (407) 331-1933; polonia-restaurant.com; Parking Lot; Polish; $. Polonia provides some of the most authentic Polish cuisine in Orlando, with many of their dishes made from scratch using real butter, farmer cheese, and real mashed potatoes. Start off with an order of potato pancakes and handmade pierogis stuffed with farmer cheese and topped with caramelized onions. The *golabki,* or stuffed cabbage, is made with pork, cabbage, beef, and rice, and the *bigos* here are made with a mixture of kielbasa, pork, cabbage, and kraut. The meat is fresh and the cutlets are made to order, pounded and breaded for each customer.

RanGetsu Restaurant & Orchid Lounge, 901 S. Orlando Ave., Maitland, FL 32751; (407) 345-0044; rangetsu.com; Parking Lot; Japanese/Sushi; $$$. Longtime visitors to and residents of Orlando may remember RanGetsu on International Drive, where it stood for decades in a grandiose Japanese imperial castle-style building. RanGetsu at Maitland's Lake Lily is a rebirth of the restaurant, bringing together traditional Japanese cuisine with a modern twist in a sleek, hip lounge atmosphere. They've added a *robata* grill to the list of tempura and sushi items, allowing guests to order tapas-style grilled small plates on the super-hot *robata* grill. Try the bacon-wrapped enoki mushroom, seared chicken thigh, or some of the seafood items cooked on the *robata*. In addition to serving modern sushi *maki* rolls, such as the *naruto,* a cucumber-wrapped roll with tuna, salmon, imitation crab, yellowtail, and avocado, RanGetsu is one of the few places that serves *sukiyaki* and Shabu-shabu, cooked tableside. One of their most popular entrees remains the broiled Chilean sea bass, glazed and marinated with a sweet miso sauce. Finish the meal with a refreshing green tea–infused crème brûlée for dessert.

Ravalia's Pasta Bar & Italian Rotisserie, 3950 US 17-92, Casselberry, FL 32707; (407) 571-9912; ravalias.com; Parking Lot; Italian; $. Ravalia's is a bit of a hole-in-the-wall, mom-and-pop Italian place where they make the pasta fresh in house. The pasta is freshly made before your eyes from high-quality semolina flour without any preservatives and comes as whole-wheat pasta, or pasta made with red sweet peppers, spinach, beets, and other fresh seasonal vegetables creating different vibrant colors and earthy flavors. Try any of the pasta varieties, including traditional favorites like spaghetti, fettuccine, penne, rigatoni, cavatelli, shells, ravioli, or tortellini, each with your choice of sauce: tomato, vodka, Alfredo, cherry tomato and ground sausage, meat, and more.

Try also one of their grinder sandwiches, Tuscan rotisserie chicken, or one of many pizzas. Finish the deal with some dessert: house-made gelato made from *fior di latte,* cream naturally extracted from the milk.

Rolando's Cuban Restaurant, 870 E. Semoran Blvd., Casselberry, FL 32707; (407) 767-9677; rolandoscubanrestaurant.com; Parking Lot; Cuban/Latin; $$. This traditional Cuban restaurant has been a central Florida staple for decades. The old-school Rolando's still continues to serve up such Cuban classics as chicken croquettes, made with seasoned ground chicken rolled with cornmeal, breaded, and fried, and *masitas de cerdo,* fried marinated pork chunks topped with grilled onions and a garlicky mojo sauce. For entrees, try the *ropa vieja,* or shredded flank steak, made with pulled beef slowly stewed in a tomato-based sauce with green peppers, onions, olives, and potatoes, or the *arroz con pollo,* yellow rice served over a very tender quarter piece of chicken meat.

Stefano's Trattoria, 1425 Tuskawilla Rd., Winter Springs, FL 32708; (407) 659-0101; stefanos-trattoria.com; Parking Lot; Italian; $$$. Headed by Chef-Owner Stefano LaCommare, who was raised in Sicily before immigrating to New York and finally Florida with dreams of opening a restaurant, Stefano's Trattoria has become a dream fulfilled. With loyal customers and attentive staff, the restaurant churns out traditional Italian favorites such as pastas, with your choice of penne, spaghetti, or linguini, and served with marinara, Bolognese, Alfredo, or one of a multitude of other sauces and combinations. Start off with antipasto, such as the calamari *fritti* or the bruschetta Siciliana. For an entree, choose from the extensive list of pizza, chicken, veal, and seafood entrees, such as the *pollo alla* scaloppini, *vitello alla* Bolognese, or *zuppa di mare di* Stefano.

Terramia Brick Oven Pizza, 7025 CR 46A, Lake Mary, FL 32746; (407) 333-1233; terramiaorlando.com; Parking Lot; Pizza; $. Terramia Brick Oven Pizza uses a specially designed brick oven to make the pizzas with a thin, delicious crust using some of the freshest ingredients in the area. Try some of their delicious pizza *salamino* with ham, or the pizza *quattro formaggi,* made with 4 cheeses. For lunch, also try one of the popular panini sandwiches while being taken care of by the warm and attentive waitstaff.

Terramia Wine Bar and Restaurant, 1185 Spring Centre S. Blvd., Suite 1040, Altamonte Springs, FL 32714; (407) 774-8466; terramiaorlando.com; Parking Lot; Italian; $$$. Terramia serves up fine Italian cuisine with roots in Naples, Italy. Traditional pasta dishes as well as the antipasto Terramia are house specialties. The antipasto Terramia comes with olives, Caprese, salami, bruschetta, and cheeses for sharing, or start with some mussels and clams for an appetizer. Try the tender, savory, and slow-cooked osso bucco, seafood lobster pasta, or the veal chops, all while enjoying a nice glass of wine from their extensive collection.

Bake Me a Cake, 1161 E. Altamonte Dr., Altamonte Springs, FL 32701; (407) 830-9006; bakemeacake.net; Parking Lot. **Bake Me a Cake** is a family-owned cake design studio and pastry shop that not only designs cakes for special events and weddings, but also features a shop that showcases their creative flavors in cupcake form. In addition to custom fondant cakes, Bake Me a Cake also serves up a variety of cupcake flavors including almond, amaretto, mocha, guava, hazelnut, chocolate malt, chocolate chip, banana, lemon, and Grand Marnier.

Hollerbach's Magnolia Square Market, 117 Magnolia Ave., Sanford, FL 32771; (407) 878-4942; magnoliasquaremarket.com; Parking Lot. Around the corner from **Hollerbach's Willow Tree Cafe** (see p. 170) in historic downtown Sanford is this hidden gem of a German market. They feature authentic German deli meats, cheeses, beers, sausages, bratwursts, chocolates, and even gluten-free baked goods. On one side is an entire section with home-brewing materials and grains so that you can bring home the joys of the Willow Tree Cafe and make the beer yourself. They even have classes so you can learn more about home brewing. You can even buy a "boot" and other beer mugs as seen at the Willow Tree. One of my favorite items from this shop is the chocolate rum balls—decadent, rich chocolate cake balls that are just amazing.

The staff members here are all very kind and gracious, and happy to offer suggestions.

Hoover's Market & Sunflower Cafe, 1035 Academy Dr., Altamonte Springs, FL 32714; (407) 869-0000; hoovers market.com; Parking Lot. This organic market features, in addition to organic products and produce, a splendid little juice bar and cafe with fresh salads, daily soups, sand-wiches, and organic cheeses. Choose from a variety of organic fresh juices with fresh-produce apples, kelp, broccoli, carrots, pineapples, and more. The Green Supreme is a popular juice choice, made with kelp, broccoli, kale, bell peppers, parsley, and apple, as is the organic wheatgrass juice. Try some of their daily soups, such as the plantain coconut or butternut squash and sweet potato, when available.

Petty's Meat Market, 2141 W. SR 434, Longwood, FL 32779; (407) 862-0400; pettysmeats.com; Parking Lot. Petty's Meat Market has been a central Florida mainstay for fresh seafood, meats, and cheeses for over 30 years. They have custom sandwiches as well as a salad bar, homemade spreads, artichoke-heart cakes, and prepared foods to go for those wanting to forgo cooking at home. Choices for prepared foods range from homemade lasagna, to meat loaf, spaghetti pie, chicken fiesta, chicken potpie, stuffed pork chops, barbecue pork, and several varieties of stuffed chicken. Try some of their free beer while you shop for fresh seafood catches, such as American red snapper, Scottish salmon, and oysters. For those looking for meats, Petty's has a great selection of USDA choice and prime beef and veal, as well as chicken and pork, all cut to order.

West Orlando

This area covers the neighborhoods of Pine Hills, Ocoee, Winter Garden, and Clermont. Winter Garden's downtown area is a quaint little district with many unique, outstanding restaurants. This area has experienced a renaissance recently, and the Saturday morning crowds at the local farmers' market at the city pavilion downtown are a testament to this. The rolling hills in the area are where you will find probably the highest elevations in central Florida, popular with cyclists who savor the challenge of riding on steep terrain in a typically flat and sea-level Florida. Pine Hills is an area known for its large Caribbean immigrant and African American communities with a host of markets and restaurants featuring authentic West Indies and Jamaican cuisine. This is the place to go if you want some authentic island food. There is also a substantial new development known as the Chinatown shopping center, which is home to the largest Asian supermarket in central Florida, 1st Oriental Supermarket, as well as some local Taiwanese bakeries and restaurants. As with any neighborhood, always be aware of your surroundings.

Chef's Table at the Edgewater Hotel, 99 W. Plant St., Winter Garden, FL 34787; (407) 230-4837; chefstableattheedgewater .com; Street Parking; Modern American; $$$. Located in historic downtown Winter Garden, the Chef's Table at the Edgewater Hotel provides creative, fresh cuisine and intimate service in a cozy little dining room. Chef-Owners Kevin and Laurie Tarter bring to life their extensive experience from Disney's acclaimed Victoria and Albert's (see p. 159) and New Orlean's Arnaud's in a full-view kitchen, visiting your table during the evening to ensure the dining experience is up to par, accompanied by wines from their extensive wine list. The dinner is prix fixe featuring 3 courses, with addition of wine pairing and cheese plate optional. Appetizers include dishes like delectable *foie gras* with Vidalia onion and Granny Smith apple crème brûlée, and a mushroom and chive crepe torte with roasted shallot cream and truffle salt. The menu also includes fresh fish, delicious beef short ribs Wellington, house-cured and -smoked pork chop, and succulent pork belly.

Donut King, 208 US 27, Minneola, FL 34715; (352) 243-4046; thedonutking.com; Parking Lot; Bakery; $. Open 24 hours a day 7 days a week, Donut King is a treat for those who love handmade, fresh daily doughnuts. Located out in Minneola, north of SR 50 and way out west of Orlando, this unassuming little bakeshop packs a big punch in terms of sweet flavors. Strangely enough, there are several menus featured here at Donut King: the doughnut menu, a breakfast menu, a slider-style burger menu, and a New Orleans–style Cajun menu (including an impressive list of po' boy sandwiches). Doughnuts reign supreme here at Donut King, soft, fluffy, and delicious. The glazed doughnut is heavenly, sweet, soft, and fluffy, like something you'd find on cloud nine with a touch of vanilla flavor. The red velvet chocolate cake doughnut and the sourdough cake doughnut are also great, though they tasted more like cakes in doughnut form than a traditional doughnut. Custard-filled doughnut holes, chocolate Oreo-crusted doughnuts, strawberry glazed doughnuts, and even a University of Florida Gator–themed sprinkled, chocolate glazed doughnut are some of the many flavors available. The Cajun menu here is surprisingly good. The catfish has a spicy, flavorful batter and is fried to a golden crisp. A whopping platter of gumbo with okra, sausage, Cajun spices, and sauce over rice and french bread has a home-cooked though mild taste. One of my favorite things on the menu here is the chicken wings, fresh, crispy little wings dipped in a mild hot sauce. Just the sheer amount of variety here will have you liking something on the menu.

The Tasting Room at the Chef's Table at the Edgewater, 99 W. Plant St., Winter Garden, FL 34787; (407) 230-4837; chefs tableattheedgewater.com; Street Parking; Modern American; $$$. The Tasting Room is a new concept from the **Chef's Table** (see p.

189), featuring small plates tapas style, wines by the glass, craft beers, and exotic cocktails from the full bar in an intimate area with just 20 tables. The plates here are playful and tantalizing, from the goat cheese ravioli, to the lobster mac and cheese with house-made bacon and cheddar-truffle sauce, to the jambalaya *arancini* with braised venison. Try The Tasting Room's eggroll made with *tasso* ham, collards, local Zellwood corn, and local shrimp, and served with a spicy peach mustard. Their "parts" platter features wild boar ribs, house-made pâté, and fried chicken livers. Don't miss Chef Kevin's famous boudin balls, house-made pork sausage rolled in panko, fried, topped with Lake Meadows egg sunny-side-up, and served with a Cajun mayo sauce

Yellow Dog Eats Cafe, 1236 Hempel Ave., Gotha, FL 34734; (407) 296-0609; yellowdogeats.com; Parking Lot; Sandwiches; $$. This quaint cafe, nestled in a neighborhood, features a variety of delicious sandwiches, salads, barbecue, and daily specials created by Chef-Owner Fish Morgan, a graduate of the Culinary Institute of America. The sandwiches here are made with lean, flavorful deli meats, locally grown baby greens, and multigrain "Pioneer" bread. Also, the bacon, pork, and other meats are smoked on the premises over apple and other natural woods. Some of the high-lights of the menu (with fanciful dog-themed names) include the Fire Pig, a savory pulled-pork wrap with applewood-smoked bacon, Gouda cheese, Yellow Dog–style coleslaw, and Sriracha topped with citrus barbecue sauce and fried onions in a chipotle wrap, and the Rufus, made with pulled pork topped with brie cheese and cherry ring peppers, and drizzled with famous raspberry Melba sauce with shoestring potatoes, fried onions, and smoked applewood bacon add-ons. Try also the Forest Hambone, a sandwich made with sweet Black Forest smoked ham and smoked Gouda cheese, layered with wood-smoked pineapple, lettuce, tomato, sweet smoky pommery grain mustard and a hint of Yellow Dog's orange-cointreau mayo, served on multigrain bread.

Foodie Faves

The Big Easy, 15502 Stoneybrook West Pkwy., Winter Garden, FL 34787; (407) 654-3279; Parking Lot; Cajun; $$. *Laissez les bons temps rouler!* The Big Easy is a new authentic New Orleans–style Cajun "home-cookin'" restaurant located in Winter Garden, serving up some mighty fine dishes from the heart of Louisiana country. Inside The Big Easy, memorabilia such as gold and purple beads, newspaper clippings, dolls, and umbrellas hang along the walls, all symbolizing the good times found in New Orleans. Vibrant purple and yellow walls frame the interior. Brass-band and jazz music compose the soundtrack to The Big Easy, and I even caught myself tapping my foot to the beat once or twice. For an entree, try Estrelle's Crawfish Etouffée, a dish found in Cajun cuisine typically served with shellfish over rice with a dark roux base.

Caribbean Sunshine Bakery, 2528 W. Colonial Dr., Orlando, FL 32804; (407) 839-5060; caribbeansunshinebakery.net; Parking Lot; Caribbean Market; $. This Caribbean restaurant serves up all the traditional home-style Jamaican dishes, such as freshly baked Jamaican beef patties, succulent oxtail, *roti,* and other dishes complete with spices and herbs from the West Indies. Try some of their jerk wings, curry chicken and rice, or a spicy beef patty. House specialties include the snapper *escovitch,* fried and topped with sliced and chopped onions, carrots, sweet peppers, and hot peppers, served with rice and beans, steamed or tossed vegetables, and sweet plantains. They also serve up a nice bakery selection of buns, breads, spice buns, coconut breads, and cakes.

Flyer's Wings & Grill, 5621 W. Colonial Dr., Orlando, FL 32808; (407) 297-9464; Parking Lot; Wings; $. Flyer's Wings and Grill has some of the best wings in Orlando if you are willing to brave the trip out to West Orlando. It looks a bit run-down on the outside, and on the inside things look a bit like your charming aunt's living room that hasn't seen a renovation since the '80s, but hey, it's all about the wings, right? This place has been serving these tasty fried bits of chicken wings for over 20 years on the northwest corner of Kirkman Road and Colonial Drive in its yellow and red building. Their wings, though they appear small, are actually quite meaty and fresh, crispy yet also tender. The favorite sauce here is definitely the lemon pepper, a delicious buttery flavor that is one of the best chicken wing sauces I have had. The most popular sauce flavors here are the lemon pepper, hot, and garlic mix. The sweet tea at Flyer's has a perfect mix of tea and sugar, not overly sweet and not too bitter from the tea. The all-you-can-eat wings night on Monday is really popular as well.

Harry & Larry's Bar-B-Que, 54 W. Plant St., Winter Garden, FL 34787; (407) 614-5950; harryandlarrys.com; Street Parking; Barbecue; $. Harry and Larry's Bar-B-Que, a family-run restaurant started by sisters Ashlee and Katie Grimes and lovingly named after their two grandfathers, applies that same love and care to their beef brisket and smoked barbecue ribs. Located in historic downtown Winter Garden, Harry and Larry's serves up mouthwatering smoked ribs, turkey, sausage, brisket, and barbecue sandwiches on garlic-butter Texas toast.

Lee & Rick's Oyster Bar, 5621 Old Winter Garden Rd., Orlando, FL 32811; (407) 293-3587; facebook.com/pages/lee-and-ricks-oyster-bar/205952767800; Parking Lot; Seafood; $$. Founded in 1950, the legendary Lee and Rick's Oyster Bar is an Orlando institution. The place started when the owners began selling oysters in their front yard, eventually turning the business into the restaurant you see today. It's a dive for sure, but a beloved dive. Sit at the bar, where they will shuck buckets and buckets of oysters right there in front of you, and after you're done, you can shuck the oyster shells right back into the trough behind the bar. Get there early because the place gets packed very quickly in the evening.

Perrotti's NY Deli, 4056 Winter Garden Vineland Rd., Winter Garden, FL 34787; (407) 347-5913; perrottisnydeli.com; Parking Lot; Sandwiches; $. Perrotti's NY Deli is a family-run local deli that serves up some of the best sandwiches in town. Their deli stocks Thumann's deli meats and cheeses as well as Just Bagels, true water bagels from the Bronx. The small deli shop is decked in Pittsburgh Steelers memorabilia, due to the owner's love for the football team, but the family has roots in New York. Try the signature Perrotti-Petro sandwich, made with corned beef, pastrami, provolone, coleslaw, potato chips, and tomatoes, and topped with spicy mustard on rye bread. The New Yorker sandwich, corned beef, pastrami, and swiss cheese on rye with Dusseldorf mustard, and the Pastramageddon, hot pastrami, Pepper Jack cheese, jalapeños, Thousand Island dressing, and creamy horseradish on rye bread, are also popular choices here. In addition to their mouthwatering sandwiches, Perrotti's also dishes out fresh hot dogs and sweet cannolis.

Singh's Roti Shop and Bar, 5244 Old Winter Garden Rd., Orlando, FL 32811; (407) 253-2900; singhsrotishop.com; Parking Lot; Caribbean; $$. For those adventurous foodies, Singh's Roti Shop offers its West Indies cuisine (particularly deriving from the tropical island nation of Trinidad) in West Orlando, an area where most of the Caribbean community in Orange County resides. The food of Trinidad featured at Singh's has strong influences from Indian cuisine, with blends of Native American, European, African, Creole, Chinese, and Lebanese traditions. The woman working at the register has the look of the angry cafeteria lunch lady with a heart of gold, if only you give her a chance and a smile. The atmosphere is very relaxed, but there is a Caribbean no-nonsense attitude that you get from the staff here, like you should just know what you want, order, eat, and enjoy. Their menu boasts the best doubles in town, which is made of 2 fried flatbreads stuffed with spicy curried chickpeas. You eat it with your hands like a small delicious sandwich. The doubles sandwich is exquisite and hearty, served fresh and hot out of the back counters. Rotis are a specialty here and include options like *aloo* (potato), *channa* (chickpeas), chicken, goat, beef, shrimp, conch, duck, curry/stew snapper, and curry gilbacker fish. Curry duck, a brownish stewed dish, is a savory, heaping hot mess over fluffy basmati rice full of spices like cumin, turmeric, and curry of course. Overall, it's a nice place to start your adventure into the food of the West Indies.

Sun Pearl Bakery, 5082 W. Colonial Dr., Orlando, FL 32808; (407) 299-3256; Parking Lot; Asian Bakery; $. This Taiwanese bakery located in the Chinatown development features unique bakery items and home-cooked dishes. The Taiwanese-style baked goods are lighter and fluffier than Chinese-style pastries, ranging from scallion egg rolls, to taro buns, to egg tarts and more. They have a Szechuan-style spicy beef noodle soup for about $5 . . . very good.

Teriyaki House, 5600 W. Colonial Dr., Orlando, FL 32808; (321) 281-8088; Parking Lot; Chinese; $$. Teriyaki House is a paradox. Though it appears to be a typical hole-in-the-wall Chinese takeout joint, Teriyaki House keeps its essence within its traditional Taiwanese dishes. A true mom-and-pop shop (run entirely by an elderly Taiwanese couple), Teriyaki House seats just 4 tables with a mostly Asian clientele. If you come here, make sure you are not in a hurry, as dishes can take awhile to get out of the kitchen, especially with the limited staff. But it's worth the wait. Their crispy yet succulent salt-and-pepper fried chicken is addictive. My heart stops for the braised pork belly, served with a hearty, savory cabbage broth in a clay pot. It melts in your mouth like butter. Other popular dishes include the fried tofu stuffed with garlic and their home-style sweet Taiwanese sausage. Eating at Teriyaki is like being invited over for a home-made meal by your Taiwanese grandma.

Thai Blossom, 99 W. Plant St., Winter Garden, FL 34787; (407) 905-9917; mythaiblossom.com; Street Parking; Thai; $$. Thai Blossom serves up tasty Thai fare in sleepy downtown Winter Garden at the historic Edgewater Hotel. Start off with some soft-shell crab, deep fried and served with sweet and sour sauce, or some New Zealand steamed green mussels sautéed with bell peppers in a sweet chile garlic sauce. For noodle soup lovers, try out Thai Blossom's signature silver noodle soup, a clear noodle soup, slow cooked in a special broth of Thai herbs, fried garlic, chicken, shrimp, and vegetables. House specials include the *param* steamed chicken, sliced chicken and mixed vegetables steamed and then tossed in a peanut sauce, and roasted duck curry, boneless roasted duck with tomatoes, bell peppers, pineapple, and carrots simmered in coconut-milk red curry.

Specialty Stores, Markets & Producers

Caribbean Supercenter Grocery, 5111 W. Colonial Dr., Orlando, FL 32808; (407) 523-1308; caribbeansupercenter.com; Parking Lot. This huge Caribbean supermarket provides not only Caribbean food products and goods, but also fresh fruits from all over the Caribbean, such as carambola, also known as starfruit, papaya, sweet sop, and breadfruit, among others. The meat department has hard-to-find parts popular in Caribbean cuisine, such as cow heel, pig's feet, and neck bones, as well as over 50 varieties of fish in the seafood department. The braided plait bread, soft rolls, and hand-crafted sweet breads are baked fresh in house as well as a selection of sweet pone, sugar cakes, and other Caribbean pastries.

1st Oriental Supermarket. 5132 W. Colonial Dr., Orlando, FL 32808; (407) 292-3668; 1storiental.com; Parking Lot. 1st Oriental Supermarket is the largest Asian market in central Florida, carrying over 13,000 items from China, the Philippines, Hong Kong, Korea,

Taiwan, Japan, and all over Asia. From an extensive produce section with plenty of bok choy, *gai lan,* winter melon, and more to the bakery with Chinese pastries and baked goods, 1st Oriental Supermarket has pretty much all you need for an Asian meal from start to finish. Drop by their barbecue area, where Hong Kong–style roasted duck glistens in the display case next to roasted pork, *char siu* barbecue pork, roasted chicken, and baby-back ribs. The supermarket also carries a wide variety of seafood, including live lobster, tilapia, striped bass, Dungeness crab, white eel, and black grouper, all in huge fish tanks in the seafood department.

East Orlando

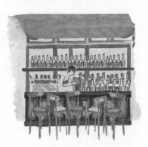

East Orlando consists of the suburban neighborhoods of Waterford Lakes/Avalon Park, University of Central Florida, and Oviedo. The main thoroughfares include Colonial Drive and Alafaya Trail. Waterford Lakes is known primarily for its sprawling outdoor shopping center, where you can pick up all the basics that you need from big-box retailers, such as Target and Best Buy, but there are also quite a few notable eateries out that way. As you travel north toward the University of Central Florida, the third-largest university in the US, you will notice more and more apartments as well as the customary college bars and bookstores. There are quite a few good, cheap eats along the University Boulevard stretch that services not only the budget-constrained college students but also the local lunch crowd coming from the corporations located in the Central Florida Research Park. Farther north along Alafaya Trail is the Oviedo area, known as one of the last frontiers of the greater Orlando area, where much of the land is still rural and agriculture based, but also increasingly affluent as families move to the area for their grade-A schools. Oviedo is probably the only place where you'll find not only chickens that roam free in the historic downtown area (near the local Popeye's Chicken, no less), but also some of the most exciting modern sushi cuisine in central Florida at Sushi Pop.

Best of the Neighborhood

Brianto's Original Hoagies, 12001 Avalon Lake Dr., Orlando, FL 32828; (407) 382-2667; briantos.com; Parking Lot and Street Parking; Sandwiches; $. Inside, the walls are adorned with photos of the Philadelphia Phillies baseball team and sports memorabilia from decades gone by, thank-you plaques from local little leagues that have been beneficiaries of Brianto's charitable giving, and a huge sign regarding the Philly way of "How to Order a Cheese Steak" by I. M. Hungry: "wit or wit-out" onions, of course. Go original with the Cheez Whiz sauce or take it easy with provolone cheese. You could also order the pizza steak, which comes with steak, marinara, mozzarella, and Parmesan cheese. The cheesesteaks and hoagies are served on authentically Philly-made Amoroso bread. The crispy, rich, golden-brown Amoroso bread is specially shipped in by air to ensure Brianto's has the authentic taste of true Philly cheesesteaks and hoagies. Truly Philadelphia: Brianto's also has a stockpile of direct-from-Philly Tastykakes cupcakes and pies as well as Herr's potato chips.

Guavate Puerto Rican Eatery & Bistro, 422 S. Alafaya Trail, Orlando, FL 32828; (407) 281-4700; guavateinorlando.com; Parking Lot; Latin; $$. Orlando has one of the largest populations of Puerto Rican immigrants and with that come all the restaurants, food trucks, and markets that cater to the ethnic needs of this thriving community. One of the most popular restaurants that features the cuisine of Puerto Rico is Guavate in east Orlando. The decor inside is elegant with various paintings and scenes, and flat-screen TVs with a DVD playing aerial views from across Puerto Rico. Order the small empanadas called *pastelitos* stuffed with ground beef and served with salsa, or the *bacalaitos con guineitos,* mini salted codfish fritters with green bananas. The *pastelillitos de carne* are quite delicious—tiny bite-size finger food–style pastries, instead of the larger pocket-size empanadas. For lunch they serve up many traditional Latin dishes, such as the flavorful *pernil,* marinated roasted pork shoulder, with pigeon peas and rice, and the *carne guisada,* a rather enjoyable beef stew. *Mofongo* is a specialty dish of Puerto Rico, made with crushed green plaintains and pork cracklings. Guavate has some of the best *mofongo* in town and this is actually their specialty. Get the *mofongo* with churrasco skirt steak in chimichurri sauce.

Mi Viejo San Juan, 7229 E. Colonial Dr., Orlando, FL 32807; (407) 380-2061; miviejosanjuanrestaurant.com; Parking Lot; Latin; $$. This slightly hidden mom-and-pop restaurant is named after the famous bolero song "En mi Viejo San Juan," considered a second national anthem by many Puerto Ricans, especially those who live far away from Puerto Rico. The restaurant is run with the heart and soul of a loving grandma, Doña Irma, and her family who moved here to central Florida from Puerto Rico over a decade ago. Their appetizers include authentic local dishes like *sorullos* (sweet, plump corn fritters), *papa rellena* (mashed potato balls stuffed with ground beef), and beef empanadas. The portions are plentiful and the *mofongo,* a dish made with plaintains mashed with garlic, olive oil, and pork cracklings, is made fresh daily here. Try their *pernil* roasted pork dish accompanied with a side of yellow rice with pigeon peas and some sweet plaintains, or feast on the *arroz con mariscos,* a seafood rice dish similar to paella, made with yellow rice, shrimp, mussels, and peas and carrots. Wash it all down with a piña colada and end it on a sweet note with some *tres leches* cake or *tembleque,* a coconut jelly custard.

Sushi Pop Seafood and Chops, 310 W. Mitchell Hammock Rd., Oviedo, FL 32765; (407) 542-5975; sushipoprestaurant.com; Parking Lot; Sushi; $$$. Sushi Pop Seafood and Chops is set up out in far-flung Oviedo, but the location belies its truly masterful creations and creative takes on Japanese cuisine. Helmed by Chef-Owner Chau Trinh, Sushi Pop upholds an impeccable dedication to freshness and quality of food, all in a wonderful, modern setting. Glowing pink squid-like lamps light the room, accented by neon pinks and plush white leather-seated booths as anime films play on the large flat-screen TVs along the walls. A large open kitchen area overlooks the room where diners can watch as Chef Chau and his team prepare the dishes. The waitresses here take their cues from the streets of Harajuku, popular for the counterculture and costume plays. For an appetizer, start off with an order of the *hamachi* pop, shichimi pepper–seared *hamachi* fish grilled and topped with guacamole, purple and green *shiso*, toasted garlic, fried rice, kimchee vinaigrette, and spicy honey mayo, all bursting with *umami* flavors. For those wishing to sample something besides the sushi, the kitchen, led by Chef de Cuisine Isaac Romero, provides an adventurous menu featuring dishes like savory Kurobuta tacos, made with braised Berkshire pork belly, hoisin sauce, scallions, micro cilantro, and avocado. The sushi rolls here are also not to be missed, like the Hot Mess roll, made with smoked salmon, avocado, and tempura flakes with honey *kabayaki* and topped with baked tuna, salmon, yellowtail, flounder, spicy mayo, smelt roe, chives, and rendered bacon. The luscious seviche roll is constructed with *hamachi* with avocado, tempura shallots, and chipotle lime sauce topped with seasonal whitefish, Sriracha hot sauce, micro cilantro greens, Hawaiian pink salt, and a wedge of lime. If you are not sure what to get, put your trust in the chef and preorder the Chef's Omakase, a multicourse tasting menu created personally by Chef Chau, sure to delight the taste buds. For dessert, order some of their popular PMS, made with powdered peanut butter, molten chocolate, and salted caramel ice cream. See Sushi Pop's recipes for **Tuna Tataki** on p. 256 and **Sautéed Garlic Edamame** on p. 257.

Thai Basil, 5800 Red Bug Lake Rd., Winter Springs, FL 32708; (407) 699-8889; thaibasil.org; Parking Lot; Thai; $$. Thai cuisine, much like the food of all peoples around the world, is a reflection of Thai culture: a belief in an intricate balance of the senses and tastes, sweet, salty, spicy, and sour, that all interplay in the Thai palate. One of the best places in town for Thai food has consistently been at Thai Basil. The restaurant has an elegant, magical feeling: Huge framed mirrors line the walls, creating infinite reflections of the dining area; long, sweeping purple curtains adorn the front end, and artifacts and paintings of scenes from Thailand are scattered throughout the restaurant. The service here is always attentive and friendly. The menu features traditional dishes done very well, such as pad thai, a 5-spice duck noodle soup, green curry fried rice, and more. For an appetizer choice, try the homemade steamed dumplings, topped with roasted garlic and soy vinaigrette.

Foodie Faves

Anmol Indian Cuisine, 12239 University Blvd., Orlando, FL 32817; (407) 384-8850; anmolindiancuisine.com; Parking Lot; Indian; $$. The decor inside Anmol features framed engravings of ancient gods in pose, paintings of decorated Indian elephants, and a television set interchanging between CNN International and some old Bollywood musical. The menu is diverse, ranging from vegetarian dishes to chicken and lamb curry. Visit during lunchtime, when the special includes lentil soup, an entree dish, a plate of yellow and white basmati rice, and naan bread. Naan, a light flatbread made from a dough of superfine flour and baked in a tandoor, or clay oven, is slightly glazed with ghee butter and is luscious when dipped into curry sauces. The chicken tandoori is made of little pieces of chicken marinated in yogurt and mild spices, roasted in the tandoor. The lamb curry comes with tender lamb chunks, potatoes, and a curry sauce. The chicken *pasanda,* my personal favorite, comes in a small dish with savory morsels of chicken in a rich, almond-flavored creamy sauce. The mountain of airy basmati rice accompanies the entrees well. Wash it down with a mango *lassi,* a sweet yogurt-based, smoothie-like Indian drink that balances the spicier tastes of India. Service is not their strongest point, so prepare for long waits between check-ins.

Bayridge Sushi and Steakhouse, 3680 Avalon Park East Blvd., Orlando, FL 32828; (407) 282-8488; brsushi.com; Parking Lot; Japanese; $$. Bayridge Sushi and Steakhouse in Avalon Park has a sleek, modern, upscale ambience with smooth black tabletops and colorful neon lights. The restaurant hosts a lively bar area with a large drink selection and tables for diners waiting for a spot in the hibachi area or the main sushi dining area. The restaurant tends to get noisy with the chatter around the room. The service here is attentive; waiters visit often and are courteous, although it may take awhile for some dishes to be prepared especially during busy periods. Sometimes the staff may appear disorganized. Give it some time to improve. The Spicy Tuna-tini appetizer is an interesting,

unique appetizer made from
chunks of spicy tuna in a ses-
ame-oil base on top of seaweed
salad, all inside a martini glass (p.s.
it's a nonalcoholic appetizer). For
sushi rolls, try one of their many spe-

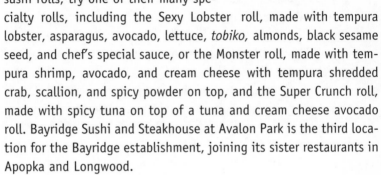

cialty rolls, including the Sexy Lobster roll, made with tempura
lobster, asparagus, avocado, lettuce, *tobiko,* almonds, black sesame
seed, and chef's special sauce, or the Monster roll, made with tempura shrimp, avocado, and cream cheese with tempura shredded
crab, scallion, and spicy powder on top, and the Super Crunch roll,
made with spicy tuna on top of a tuna and cream cheese avocado
roll. Bayridge Sushi and Steakhouse at Avalon Park is the third location for the Bayridge establishment, joining its sister restaurants in
Apopka and Longwood.

Goodfella's Pizzeria, 11865 E. Colonial Dr., Orlando, FL 32826;
(407) 658-6615; goodfellasorlando.com; Parking Lot; Pizza; $. The
menu is simple Italian fare and the building is dated, but their
authentic New York–style pizza is where Goodfella's shines. The
crust is thin and crispy, the cheese is fresh and flavorful, and the
tomato sauce is seasoned well. The pizza is as close to New York as
you can get here in Orlando. Try also their garlic knots, made with
tons of freshly shaved garlic and butter.

Gino's Pizza Italian Restaurant, 43 Alafaya Woods Blvd.,
Oviedo, FL 32765; (407) 366-1000; ginositalianrestaurant.net;

Italian; $. Gino's is a cozy little neighborhood spot that has been serving home-style Italian food in the Oviedo area since 1986. The Gino's Special pizza pie is a delight, topped with tons of pepperoni, sausage, ham, fresh green peppers, fresh mushrooms, onions, and black olives. The extensive traditional Italian menu includes calzones, strombolis, panini, oven-baked pastas, lasagna, and chicken, veal, and seafood dishes.

Lazy Moon Pizza, 12269 University Blvd., Orlando, FL 32817; (407) 658-2396; eatdrinkandbelazy.com; Parking Lot; Pizza; $. Located right across from the University of Central Florida, Lazy Moon, with its laid-back, hang-out type atmosphere, is the perfect place to go on a late weekend night to grab a slice of pizza (they're open until 3 a.m. on Friday and Saturday). The unique feature about these pizzas, in addition to being pretty tasty yet mild, is the ginormous size of their slices with toppings that include artichokes, anchovies, basil, wood-smoked bacon, and more. Wash it all down with something from their impressive list of imported and craft beers. Or if you want to go simple, shoot for the Boxcar Willy, a slice of cheese pizza with a pint of PBR.

Jeremiah's Italian Ice, 12271 University Blvd., Orlando, FL 32817; (407) 277-7769; jeremiahsice.com; Parking Lot; Desserts; $.

This popular walk-up dessert stand is known for serving up a simple and sweet concept: soft-serve ice cream, Italian ice, or a combination of both in the form of gelato. It's a simple enough idea but as we know, it's the simple things that are hard to do well. Jeremiah's definitely does it well. Their Italian ice is made by using fresh fruit, fruit puree, water, and sugar, and throwing it into an ice cream machine. My particular favorite style is the gelati, where you can get layers of soft-serve vanilla or chocolate ice cream on top of layers of your choice of Italian ice. There are over 40 flavors to choose from, such as the Scoop Froggy Frog, Jeremiah's signature mint chocolate chip flavor, as well as black raspberry, P-Nutty peanut butter flavor, piña colada, mango, strawberry banana, and much more. Prices here are very reasonable for a generous small cup.

Olympia Restaurant, 8505 E. Colonial Dr., Orlando, FL 32817; (407) 273-7836; olympiaorlando.com; Parking Lot; Greek; $$$. An Orlando staple, this restaurant owned and operated by the Vasiliadis family has been serving up authentic Greek food since 1979. Located inside a rather older looking building, Olympia serves up gyro sandwiches with homemade tzatziki sauce and traditional dishes like the moussaka, made with layered potatoes, eggplant, and lean ground beef topped with creamy béchamel sauce, or the Greek lasagna, *pastitsio,* made with layered Greek pasta, lean ground beef, and feta cheese. There are a few dishes named after Greek gods and goddesses—Olympia is the home of the gods, after all—such as the Aphrodite chicken, made with marinated oven-baked chicken breast stuffed with spinach and feta cheese, topped with a zesty lemon sauce. Try a bit of everything, if you are up to the task, with the Hercules platter, a combination of roasted lamb, gyro meat, dolma grape leaves, spanakopita spinach pie, and moussaka served with tzatziki, pita, rice, and vegetables. Belly dancers show up to entertain on some Friday and Saturday evenings. Prepare to wait, as service can be a bit slow.

Royal Thai, 1202 N. Semoran Blvd., Orlando, FL 32807; (407) 275-0776; royalthai-orlando.com; Thai; $. Royal Thai is one of those restaurants tucked inside a cozy house off of busy Semoran Boulevard that is a go-to place for something you know will be consistently good. In this case, some of the best Thai food in Orlando can be found here, with all the wonderful basics like *tom yum* soup, pad thai noodles, *param* chicken, and various Thai curries. Unique dishes at Royal Thai include the *toong thong,* a delicious little appetizer made with minced chicken, potato, and onion, with a dash of Thai spices wrapped in a pouch. For something hotter, try the prawns in chile sauce, or the chile jam, a dish with your choice of meat stir-fried in chile jam, onion, celery, and carrot. Or you could order any of the entree dishes "Thai hot," the way it should be. A few desserts are available seasonally, including sliced mango with sweet, sticky rice, and the black sticky rice with shredded coconut.

Sweet! by Good Golly Miss Holly, 711 N. Alafaya Trail, Orlando, FL 32828; (407) 277-7746; sweetbyholly.com; Parking Lot; Bakery/

Desserts; $. Celebrity Chef—and two-time Food Network *Cupcake Wars* winner—Hollis Wilder is no stranger to the sweet and savory life. This little cupcake shop in Waterford Lakes Town Center whips out 30 rotating flavors of gourmet cupcakes baked from scratch daily, along with 12 flavors of self-serve frozen yogurt and 48 toppings. Moist, delicate, and definitely sweet, the cupcake flavors—both inspirational and playful—range from German chocolate cake and banana pudding, to red velvet and orange Creamsicle. Sizes range from regular to more manageable mini sizes, allowing you to sample more flavors in one outing. On Monday the minis are at a special $1 each. See Chef Hollis Wilder's recipe for **Crystallized Ginger Olive Oil Cupcakes with Lime Buttercream, Opal Basil, Mint, and Lime Zest** on p. 270.

The Town House Restaurant, 9 E. Broadway St., Oviedo, FL 32765; (407) 365-5151; oviedotownhouse.com; Lot and Street Parking; Breakfast/American; $. This family-owned Oviedo institution is a popular place with locals for down-home Southern-style cooking and breakfast. Inside the yellow brick building with blue accents, the Town House restaurant, filled with various kitschy memorabilia that you'd probably find in your eclectic aunt's house, there is an ambience of a small-town diner, with probably not much changing since it was founded in the 1950s. The staff here is kind and welcoming with that good Southern hospitality. Nearby you can see the famous Oviedo chickens roaming the grassy areas in the historic downtown area. Try one of their many omelets, the biscuits and gravy, or the country-fried steak, all coming with a side of home fries (very tasty) or grits. They also have lunch and dinner items, such as the 3-D grilled cheese sandwich, a triple decker made with swiss, provolone, and American cheeses, bacon, and tomato. There are also a few Greek dishes here in case you are hankering for a gyro.

Specialty Stores, Markets & Producers

Cavallari Gourmet, 1954 W. SR 426, Oviedo, FL 32765; (407) 365-8000; cavallarigourmet.com; Parking Lot. This local gourmet Italian market features a meat department with a nice selection of premium USDA prime and top choice beef, marinated meats, fresh chicken cut and trimmed to order, premade burgers, and sausages. Their imported Italian specialty meats include genuine prosciutto di Parma, dried salami, *soppressata,* and *mortadella.* There is also a nice selection of side salads to go with your dinner preparations, as well as Boar's Head meats and cheeses in the deli. Premade meals are available here, too, such as meat lasagna, chicken Parmesan, chicken Marsala, and other Italian favorites.

Eastside Asian Market, 12950 E. Colonial Dr., Ste 106, Orlando, FL 32828; (407) 615-8881; eastsideasianmarket.com. This sparkling new market is stocked with the essentials of Asian cooking: soy sauces, noodles, rice, dried mushrooms, produce, and more. They even have a large selection of ramen for those of you who are on a tight budget or are going to college at the nearby University of Central Florida. The local family owners are devout Buddhists and vegetarians, so you will notice that they have a large variety of vegetarian items at this Asian market. In addition to veggies and fruits, they have tofu products and faux meat items that spice up the typical vegetarian diet. They also have quartered off a section of the market into a cafe with a developing menu specializing in Taiwanese dishes and, of course, all vegetarian. At their cafe, they currently serve *boba* milk tea, taro slush, flavored black tea (passion fruit, mango, strawberry, lychee), shaved ice, fruit slush, fruit smoothies, special buns, egg rolls, dumplings, and egg pancakes, and are adding items as time goes on. Their vegetarian "special buns" are a must-try: scrumptious, spicy flavored slices of tofu and mushroom in sweet *mantou* wheat buns.

South Orlando

South Orlando includes the areas surrounding the Orlando International Airport (MCO), the developing Lake Nona area, Kissimmee, Semoran Boulevard (SR 436). We are lucky in central Florida to live in an area relatively rich in Latin American culinary offerings. Puerto Rican *lechoneras,* Colombian and Peruvian chicken joints, Cuban establishments, and more abound in the Orlando landscape, especially here in the southern part of town. They are mostly mom-and-pop-type operations with small storefronts and the customary hole-in-the-wall atmosphere. Near the Lake Nona area, a new medical city is sprouting up, with hospitals and universities ready to address the needs of our aging community.

Best of the Neighborhood

Norman's, 4012 Central Florida Pkwy., Orlando, FL 32837; (407) 393-4333; normans.com; Valet and Parking Lot; Caribbean/Latin; $$$$.

Norman's is the product of legendary Chef Norman Van Aken, who is also known as the "founding father of New World Cuisine," a fusion of Latin, Caribbean, Asian, African, and American flavors, and a winner of the prestigious James Beard Award for "Best Chef in the Southeast" in 1997. Norman's at the Ritz-Carlton hotel in Orlando is the sister restaurant to the Norman's in Coral Gables, Florida. Start off with some small-plate tapas, like the fried green tomatoes with *escabeche*-spiced mayo and queso fresco, or Key West shrimp seviche with a touch of Patron tequila, salsa, and avocado. For an entree, try some of Norman's famous pan-cooked fillet of yellowtail snapper with asparagus spears, citrus butter sauce, and garlicky mashed potatoes, or the pork Havana with smoky plantain *crema*, mole, black bean corn salsa, and golden grits.

Padrino's Cuban Bistro, 13586 S. John Young Pkwy., Orlando, FL 32837; (407) 251-5107; padrinosbistro.com; Parking Lot; Cuban/Latin; $$. Padrino's Cuban Bistro, founded on family recipes and based out of south Florida, offers delightful, beautifully crafted traditionally Cuban dishes with a modern twist. The decor is slightly upscale with dark brown walls decorated with paintings of various scenes from Cuba. On one side is a stage area for live musicians and performances, and a small bar. Meals begin with a complimentary plate of fried banana slivers with garlic and oil dipping sauce. The beefy empanadas come beautifully arranged with a unique, sweet guava-based salsa and taste as great as they look. For entrees, try the *vaca frita,* marinated shredded flank steak pan-fried to a crisp and topped with sautéed onions. Also good is the lush *ropa vieja,* made with shredded flank steak slow-cooked with green peppers and onions in a tomato-based sauce and served with white rice, black beans, and sweet plantains. On the second Saturday of each month, they host an all-you-can-eat pig roast featuring a whole roasted pig.

Primo by Melissa Kelly, 4040 Central Florida Pkwy., Orlando, FL 32837; (407) 393-4444; grandelakes.com/Primo-78.html; Valet and Parking Lot; Italian/Modern American; $$$$. Chef Melissa Kelly prescribes to the eat-local movement here at the upscale yet casual Primo at the JW Marriott Orlando, Grande Lakes. The restaurant sources its food from responsible growers and producers who practice sustainable methods of farming, and buys local and organic whenever possible. These ingredients, with some of the fresh produce coming directly from the hotel's own organic gardens, brings out the wonderfully prepared, contemporary Italian cuisine here with Chef de Cuisine Gilberto Ramirez at the helm when Chef Kelly is away. Start off with some of the Primo antipasti Misti, consisting of house-cured meats, house-made pickles, *peperonata,* prosciutto-stuffed *arancini,* marinated olives, and Italian sausage–stuffed artichokes, or the *foie gras* duo, made of *foie gras au torchon* with cherry *mostarda* and a *foie gras* with cappuccino truffle foam. Pasta lovers can try any of the specialty pastas, such as smoked paprika tagliatelle *arrabbiata,*

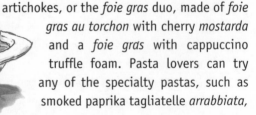

made with littleneck clams, mussels, Florida rock shrimp, Calabrian chile, garden basil, and kale. Try also the pan-roasted local Florida snapper with fennel *gnocchetti,* Florida rock shrimp, marinated mussels, clams, and an orange fennel *nage,* or the grilled Lake Meadow Naturals farm duck breast, served with local orange blossom honey–roasted apricots, ricotta cheese, dried apricot gnocchi, and roasted Hakurei turnips. For dessert, have a slice of warm chocolate *budino* cake served with coffee gelato and warm caramel, or the *affogato* espresso float with vanilla, chocolate, and caramel gelato with a crisp cinnamon *zeppole.*

Foodie Faves

Beto's Mexican, 7135 S. Orange Blossom Trail, Orlando, FL 32809; (407) 859-7030; Parking Lot; Mexican; $. This popular Mexican hole-in-the-wall, housed in a former McDonald's, is open 24 hours and serves up authentic Mexican fare, such as tasty burritos and tacos. The *machata* burrito, stuffed with onions, green peppers, cheese, eggs, and steak, is a popular breakfast item. The chimichangas, stuffed with chicken or beef, and the *carne asade* fries are also popular here at Beto's, especially on late nights.

Bombay Cafe, 1137 Doss Ave., Orlando, FL 32809; (407) 240-5151; bombaycafeorlando.com; Parking Lot; Indian/Vegetarian $. Located inside a plaza, past an Indian grocery store, the hidden

Bombay Cafe is a vegetarian Indian restaurant specializing in Indian street food, particularly from the Mumbai and Udipi regions. Appetizers include *thali,* side dishes served with onions, tomatoes, chutneys, and curries. Try one of the many *dosa,* or stuffed fermented rice pancakes, or the Chinese *bhel chaat,* made with crispy noodles and chopped vegetables in a Chinese-inspired sweet and spicy chutney sauce. A few other Indo-Chinese favorites here include the Paneer 65, made with cubes of cheese curds cooked with ginger, onion, and bell peppers in a dry hot-and-sour sauce, and the gobi Manchurian, composed of crispy cauliflower fritters in a Manchurian sauce made with ginger, garlic, onions, soy, and chile.

Eastern Pearl, 5749 T. G. Lee Blvd., Orlando, FL 32822; (407) 373-6888; Parking Lot; easternpearlrestaurant.com; Chinese; $$. With 2 locations, one in Altamonte Springs and the other near the Orlando International Airport tucked off of a side street of Semoran Boulevard, Eastern Pearl is one of the better Chinese restaurants around town. It is actually a sit-down restaurant with a full menu of dishes ranging from Szechuan specialties to traditional fried rice and seafood tofu hot pot as well as your standard General Tso's chicken. Try the sizzling pepper steak, a huge plate of sliced beef served literally sizzling on a hot plate. Also try the seafood tofu hot pot, a tricky dish to master, as it comes out a bit bland in most Chinese restaurants.

Fortuna Bakery & Cafe, 12701 S. John Young Pkwy., Orlando, FL 32837; (407) 855-7070; Parking Lot; Latin/Bakery; $. This Colombian and Venezuelan bakery and cafe showcases an impressive and intoxicatingly sweet array of traditional Latino pastries as well as coffee. *Pandebono,* a type of Colombian bread made of corn flour, cassava starch, cheese, and eggs, is popular here and is traditionally consumed warm with hot chocolate right out of the oven. Other popular pastries include *dulce de leche* napoleons, *choclo con queso, almojabanas, pastel de* guava, and cookies. For more savory fare, try the beef empanadas or the cheese and chorizo *arepa* corn cakes. Don't forget to enjoy a cup of cappuccino or espresso coffee here with your pastries, too.

Golden Lotus Chinese, 8365 S. John Young Pkwy., Orlando, FL 32819; (407) 352-3832; Parking Lot; Chinese/Dim Sum; $. Golden Lotus specializes in Cantonese and Szechuan dishes, serving dim sum until 4 p.m. daily. Their dim sum is among the best in central Florida, with fresh ingredients and skillful preparation, and the largely ethnic Chinese clientele is a testament to its authenticity. The egg tarts here are flaky and bite-size sweet delights, a perfect dessert to go with hot tea, a drink cultivated for thousands of years by the Chinese for its healthy qualities. The shrimp dumpling (*ha gow*) and pork dumpling (*siu mai*) are both plump and savory, freshly steamed to order in the kitchen. They also serve up some great authentic noodle dishes like the beef chow fun noodles, hand made right on the premises from scratch, as well as heartwarming, aromatic bowls of braised beef noodle soups. Another specialty at

Golden Lotus includes the tea-smoked duck, which takes hours to make. The duck is first salted and spiced inside, then hung over night. The duck is then dry smoked with Chinese tea leaves using wood chips to absorb the flavors into the duck.

Middle East Market, 8100 S. Orange Blossom Trail, Orlando, FL 32809; (407) 855-6555; Parking Lot; Mediterranean; $. This little Lebanese deli prides itself on serving authentic Middle Eastern cuisine, such as baba ghanoush, stuffed grape leaves, hummus, baklava, and Lebanese rice. You order at the counter and pick your desired sides from the glass case. Try any of their pitas, such as the chicken, gyro, or beef shawarma garnished with lettuce, pickles, tomatoes, turnips, parsley, hummus, and tahini sauce and hot-pressed like panini. Enjoy one with a cup of Turkish coffee and a slice of baklava pastry. There is also a small grocery section in the back with assorted Middle Eastern goods and supplies for hookah.

Mikado Japanese Cuisine, 13586 Village Park Dr., Orlando, FL 32837; (407) 851-9933; mikadosushiorlando.com; Parking Lot; Sushi, Japanese; $$. This Japanese sushi restaurant is known for its fresh, flavorful, and inspired rolls. Start off with some *tai* seviche, consisting of seasonal snapper sliced sashimi-style, with a yuzu citrus sauce, seasoned with Hawaiian pink salt and Sriracha hot sauce, then topped with black *tobiko* and micro cilantro. The conch salad here is also very fresh and delicious, consisting of thick slices of Bahamian conch on a bed of asparagus and cucumber, served with a spicy kimchee sauce. Some signature sushi rolls here include the Hot Mama roll, consisting of smoked salmon rolled with avocado and crunchy flakes, topped with a mix of baked spicy crab, bay scallops, scallions, and *masago* and drizzled with a sweet cinnamon honey sauce, as well as the Drama Queen roll, made with spicy tuna, avocado, and crunch roll, laced with seared yellowtail, escolar fish, *tobiko,* and jalapeño slices dressed with special spicy sauce and scallions.

NaraDeva Thai Restaurant, 4696 Millenia Plaza Way, Orlando, FL 32839; (407) 903-0300; naradevathai.com; Parking Lot; Thai; $$. When you first walk into this restaurant, you are immediately transported into a world resembling a wooden village in the jungles of Thailand. The decor is lush and earthy, with all the pieces hand picked by the charming owners Tammy, a native of Thailand, and Ali. Over the fireplace by the eastern wall, a solemn statue of Buddha sits watching over the restaurant. The most popular item on the menu is their Thai red barbecue fried rice, a uniquely delectable dish made with Asian-style sweet barbecued pork, eggs, and chopped scallions. Many of the items, such as the whole fried snapper and curry duck, are all part of their large menu of authentic Thai dishes. For desserts, try the Thai doughnuts with pandan coconut custard, a sweet dip with lovely aromas of the pandan, a fragrant leaf found in Southeast Asia.

Nona Tap Room, 9145 Narcoossee Rd., Orlando, FL 32827; (407) 440-4594; nonataproom.com; Parking Lot; Pub Food; $. The up-and-coming Lake Nona area will soon be home to some of the nation's best hospitals and a medical research center. In the meantime, the culinary scene is still growing here, and one of the few bright spots around town is the Nona Tap Room, a neighborhood sports bar featuring 50 draft beers, a nice selection of wine, cocktails, and over 50 bottled beers from around the world. Try some of their famous burgers, such as the half-pound Guinness-marinated Tap Room burger with crispy bacon, sautéed mushrooms and onions, lettuce, tomato, and your choice of cheese, or the fried egg burger topped with cheddar cheese and crispy bacon.

Sushi Tomi, 8463 S. John Young Pkwy., Orlando, FL 32819; (407) 352-8635; Parking Lot; Sushi/Japanese; $$$. Headed by sushi Chef and Owner Ochiai Hidehiko, Sushi Tomi serves up some of the best in traditional Japanese cuisine in Orlando, with particular emphasis on fresh sushi and sashimi. Start off with some traditional grilled chicken *yaki-tori,* crisp and moist, or some *gyoza* pork dumplings. The sushi here is extra fresh, from the common tuna, salmon, and eel to the more exotic live jumbo orange clam, mackerel *battera,* and sea urchin. For those who are extra hungry, try the dinner special, consisting of beef teriyaki, shrimp and vegetable tempura, salad, miso soup, half a Florida roll, and pieces of fresh tuna and mackerel sashimi.

Technique Restaurant, 8511 Commodity Circle, Orlando, FL 32819; (407) 888-4000; techniquerestaurant.com; Parking Lot; American; $. Despite being located in a drab office/commercial complex, the campus is very lively within the walls, full of the clattering of pots and pans from Le Cordon Bleu students perfecting their techniques in beautiful kitchen classrooms. As part of 6 weeks at Technique, the students are taught appreciation for not only the kitchen in the back of the house, but the front of the house, where they spend 3 weeks working as servers and hosts before flipping to the kitchen side. The dining room at Technique is rather simple, much like any dining room you would find in a hotel, with white tablecloths and blue accents, and a nice view of the open kitchen from the dining room. The servers are of course students at the school and can at times be nervous or unsure, but all are genuine and attentive, trying their hardest to please. If you are to dine at Technique, know that walk-ins are okay, but be sure to call ahead to make sure they are open, as dates vary according to the class schedule. The dinner has a 3-course meal option for $12 and 4-course meal for $15, which are great deals, often featuring wonderful Caprese salads, filet mignon, and house-made desserts.

Vitale Spa Cafe, 4012 Central Florida Pkwy., Orlando, FL 32837; (407) 206-2400; ritzcarlton.com/en/properties/orlando/dining/vitalespa-cafe/menu.htm; Parking Lot and Valet; Modern American; $$$.

Inside the award-winning Ritz-Carlton hotel, just downstairs from the spa, is the Vitale Spa Cafe, where you can enjoy some delicious offerings while sipping tea with a beautiful view of the pool side. The Vitale Spa Cafe offers some very healthy dishes, ranging from salads to wraps and sandwiches, and also, surprisingly, bento boxes. If you choose the bento box, you can have your pick of mains such as citrus-marinated grilled chicken, grilled shrimp, teriyaki-glazed salmon, grilled snapper, grilled marinated tofu, or filet mignon brochette with accompaniments such as soba noodles, heirloom tomatoes, fresh fruits, and more. What I enjoyed most about Vitale Spa Cafe was its emphasis on fresh, simple ingredients while also making the full flavors of the ingredients jump out in their dishes, all while enjoying the Florida sun poolside.

Specialty Stores, Markets & Producers

All Italian Market & Deli, 13526 Village Park Dr., Suite 214, Orlando, FL 32837; (407) 704-1856; allitalianmarket.blogspot.com; Parking Lot. This little Italian market features all sorts of delicious food products from the Italian pantry: fresh buffalo milk mozzarella cheese, fresh panini, homemade pastas, pestos, ciabatta bread, and hundreds of different wines and olive oils from Italy. Deli meats, a gelato counter, and an espresso bar also help bring the flavors of Italy to life here. Some of the popular lunch items include the *friuli* panini, bruschetta al prosciutto, *calabria* panini, and the sweet and savory pear and gorgonzola *sacchetti* pasta.

International Food Club Specialty Food Market & Cafe, 4300 L. B. McLeod Rd., Orlando, FL 32811; (321) 281-4300; international foodclub.com; Parking Lot. With groceries from over 25 countries all over the world, International Food Club, located in a rather industrial part of town, features specialty foods from Europe, Africa, the Mediterranean, the Middle East, South Asia, and more, with a substantial selection of international beers. Walk around the aisles and pick up some feta cheese from Greece, Cortas fava beans from Lebanon, Ülker cookies from Turkey, basmati rice and curry spices from India, tea and biscuits from London, and much more.

Food Trucks

The food truck movement hit Orlando hard. Hundreds of chefs and entrepreneurs have banded together in the past few years to bring together their own takes on cuisine to the masses via food trucks. From the Korean BBQ Taco Box food truck to the Yum Yum Cupcake Truck, the variety runs the gamut of the culinary spectrum. Several events throughout the month, including the Daily City's Food Truck Bazaars, Tasty Tuesdays in the Milk District, and the Winter Park Food Truck Stop, allow foodies to try multiple food trucks in one spot and create a sense of community.

The Food Truck Bazaar, produced by local proponent Mark Baratelli of TheDailyCity.com, is the premier food truck event in central Florida, a movable feast traveling each weekend to different cities and towns and drawing crowds of thousands. This community event, usually occurring Friday through Sunday, brings together friends and family to enjoy an evening meal from some of the finest food trucks in town in a festive setting. Patrons are recommended to bring their own tables and chairs (much like at a tailgate event) and to expect long lines. Find out more information at thefoodtruckbazaar.com.

Arepas El Cacao, 5350 International Dr., Orlando, FL 32819; (321) 202-4983; twitter.com/ArepasElcacao; Latin; $. This bright, little blue food truck features Venezuelan street fare favorites like *arepas* and *cachapas*. Salty and sweet, *arepas* are corn cakes stuffed with homemade Venezuelan cheeses, veggies, and your choice of black beans, beef, pork, ham, shrimp, or chicken. Try also their *cachapas*, sweet corn cakes filled with handmade Venezuelan cheeses.

The Batter Bowl Truck, thebatterbowltruck.com; twitter.com/batterbowltruck; facebook.com/BatterBowlTruck; Desserts; $. The Batter Bowl truck features delicious desserts that range from classic comforts like key lime pie to more creative sweets like red velvet cake and chocolate–peanut butter push pops. The goat cheese brownie, oatmeal cream pie, crème brûlée, and chocoholic are all crowd favorites. Recently The Batter Bowl began partnering with other food trucks in the area, such as C & S Brisket Bus, serving their salted caramel bacon brownies topped with bacon sprinkles.

Big Wheel Food Truck, (407) 494-4297; bigwheeltruckmenu .com; facebook.com/BigWheelTruck; twitter.com/bigwheeltruck; Modern American; $. Helmed by Chef Tony Adams and a part of the Big Wheel Provisions company that provides boutique catering and handmade charcuterie in Orlando, Big Wheel Food Truck uses creative techniques to bring locally sourced, handmade food to the central Florida community. The food truck has won wide acclaim since its opening, winning "Best Food Truck" awards left and right, noted for the chefs' love of locally sourced creations. The menu changes weekly and can be found by viewing their website, ranging from local fried brussels sprouts with local honey, Sriracha, soy, and lime dressing to local soft-shell crab, tomato, avocado, and mayo sandwiches. Pork belly, Titusville octopus, handmade sausage, bacon fries, *foie gras,* and other local ingredients can be found on the menu here as well. See Chef Tony Adams's recipe for **Lump Crab–Stuffed Florida Avocado** on p. 283.

C & S Brisket Bus, (407) 913-2333; twitter.com/csbrisketbus; brisketbus.com; facebook.com/CSBrisketBus; Deli/Sandwiches; $. C & S (which stands for Chris and Stew's) Brisket Bus is a "mobile gourmet delicatessen" that cures, smokes, and braises their own meats served with fresh-baked bread and house-made condiments. Their delicious deli truck features sandwiches like the Texas, made with juicy smoked brisket, topped with barbecue sauce and served on Texas toast, and the Black and Blue, with smoked brisket, lettuce, and roasted garlic blue cheese mayo, served on a blackened brioche bun. C & S Brisket Bus also serves up their own root-cured bacon BLT sandwich with herb mayo on Texas toast, and a classic Reuben with pastrami, sauerkraut, Thousand Island dressing, and swiss cheese on rye bread, among many other tasty sandwiches.

Cafe Rouge Express, sanfordcaferouge.com; twitter.com/cafe rougebistro; facebook.com/caferougeexpress; French/British; $. This food truck offshoot of the original **Cafe Rouge** in Sanford (see p. 174) serves up English and French cuisines with a modern flair. They are most popular for their authentic fish and chips, bangers and mash, Parisian burgers, and savory shepherd's pie.

The Crooked Spoon, (407) 927-1587; facebook.com/thecrooked spoon; twitter.com/thecrookedspn; Burgers/American; $. This food truck serves up some of the best burgers and dishes in town. Their Crooked Spoon Burger is a meaty Angus beef burger with soft buns made locally from the Olde Hearth Bakery topped with a chipotle aioli sauce, sweet caramelized onions, swiss cheese, lettuce, and tomato. My favorite, however, was the mac and cheese, made with a 6-cheese blend, roasted red and yellow peppers, bacon, and toasted bread crumbs. The decadent serving was enough to fill up 2 people, so be sure to bring along a friend to share this heavenly, cheesy, mac-y creation. They are also known for their 420 Burger, a sweet and savory burger made with Angus beef, pineapple relish, spicy candied bacon, swiss cheese, a honey whole-grain mustard aioli, and fried onion rings all between 2 buns.

5 Gastronomy, 5gastronomy.com; twitter.com/5gastronomy; facebook.com/5gastronomy; Modern American; $. Chef Bruno Fonseca serves up seasonally-inspired dishes including hand-crafted Perfect Burgers, 48-hour braised pork tacos, and gourmet mac and cheese to central Floridians throughout the week. The

Perfect Burger is topped with confit tomatoes, lettuce, hickory bacon jam, mushroom duxelles, and melted gruyère on a soft bun, while the braised pork tacos are served with smoked corn puree, pickled onions, jicama cilantro salad, cream, and avocado drizzle. Try also their 24-hour braised pork belly confit sandwich with arbol pepper–pineapple marmalade, arugula, pickled onions, and *queso fresco* on a bun, one of many gourmet concoctions at 5 Gastronomy.

Fork in the Road, forkintherd.com; twitter.com/forkintherdlive; facebook.com/EatForkInTheRoad; Modern American; $. Fork in the Road, helmed by Orlando native and French Culinary Institute–trained Chef Bryce Balluff, serves up gourmet yet familiar comfort fare as well as extraordinary dessert treats. Start off with some paella saffron rice balls, blue and black truffle mac and cheese pops, or the Kurobuta pork egg rolls. Their signature pork belly and beef short rib sandwiches, served on Tribeca Oven baguettes, are braised for 72 hours to achieve their desired tenderness and flavor. For dessert, try some of their fabulous Peanut Butter Cup on Steroids, made with peanut butter and swiss chocolate mousse with a chocolate ganache center. See Chef Bryce Balluff's recipe for **"A Short Rib by Any Other Name . . . Still Tastes Delicious"** on p. 267.

Gokudo, twitter.com/gokudoorlando; facebook.com/gokudo orlando; Asian/Japanese; $. Gokudo specializes in modern Japanese fusion and Malaysian cuisine. From curry rotis, to homemade ramen noodles and *yakisoba* noodles, Gokudo serves up spicy, curried renditions of classic Japanese favorites. The signature OG (Original Gokudo) uses a Malaysian *roti* bread filled with your choice of chicken or beef topped with purple cabbage, caramelized onions, fresh pico de gallo, and cilantro aioli, and topped off with a signature Gokudo white sauce.

Korean BBQ Taco Box, kbbqbox.com; facebook.com/KBBQBox; twitter.com/koreanbbq_2011; Korean; $. The first of the new wave of food trucks in Orlando, Korean BBQ Taco Box is known for bringing together Korean and American fusion cuisine much like another famous truck based out in Los Angeles known as the Kogi Truck. The tacos here, often greasy, use flour tortillas and are stuffed with traditional Korean marinated meats like *kalbi* short ribs, spicy pork, and marinated chicken teriyaki. Most of the meals here are served with salads and side dishes, which depending on the day can be a combination of spicy chicken wings, fried cheese rolls, fried tofu, or egg omelet rolls.

La Empanada Food Truck, laempanadatruck.com; Latin; $. La Empanada is a lovely food truck brought to you in partnership with the good people of **Black Bean Deli** (see p. 55), the famous Cuban sandwich shop on US 17/92 in Winter Park. Some of the best empanadas in Orlando can be found at La Empanada; not too greasy or overly fried, these delicious pockets of joy are a delight. The empanadas sit inside a glass case by the main window of the truck, where usually there are 6 choices daily (changing seasonally) of savory and sweet for empanadas ($3) and also a side like soup or salad. Try their *picadillo* empanada, a Cuban classic, stuffed with tasty ground beef and bits of carrots, potatoes, green olives, and golden raisins. See Chef Gabrielle's recipe for **Spinach Empanada** on p. 285.

Tasty Tuesdays at the Milk District, 2424 E. Robinson St., Orlando, FL; facebook.com/TastyTuesdaysOrlando; twitter.com/ TastyTuesdaysFL; $. A rotating roster of the best food trucks in Orlando gather in the back parking lots of The Milk Bar/Etoile Boutique and Spacebar/Sandwich Bar every Tuesday night, hosted by the Milk District on Robinson Street, east of Bumby, right next to the T. G. Lee milk factory. The convenient thing about this event setup is that all the bars (The Milk Bar, Sandwich Bar, Spacebar, etc.) open up to allow you to bring in the food. There you can order an alcoholic or nonalcoholic beverage of your choice, and enjoy the food without having to stand around awkwardly or lean on the hood of your car.

Treehouse Truck, treehousetruck.com; facebook.com/pages/ Treehouse-Truck/185883788108647; twitter.com/treehousetruck; American; $. The Treehouse Truck features an eclectic mix of burgers and sandwiches, with a twist on traditional favorites. Besides a list of blackened burgers, Cheez Whiz-ed Philly cheesesteaks, and a western bacon-infused cheddar burger, this truck's calorie-busting signature dish is the Luther sandwich, an all-American cheeseburger with lettuce, tomato, and pickles served between two Krispy Kreme doughnut "buns." Or try also the Mamma's PBJ, a deep-fried peanut butter, jelly, Nutella, and banana sandwich, topped with powdered sugar. For dessert, try some of the fried Oreos or handmade fried glazed doughnut bread pudding.

Winter Park Food Truck Stop, 1127 N. Orlando Ave., Winter Park, FL; facebook.com/WPFoodTruckStop; $. This food truck stop, located at the pothole-ridden parking lot of Tom and Jerry's Lounge, hosts several trucks throughout the week, with the most prominent time being Thursday night, when the community comes out to live music and a full house of trucks. Find out what trucks are open at the Winter Park Food Truck Stop by following them on Twitter.

The Yum Yum Cupcake Truck, theyumyumcupcaketruck.com; facebook.com/theyumyumtruck; twitter.com/yumyumtruck_fl; Desserts; $. This retro-decked truck is known for quirky cupcakes and a loyal fan following. In addition to favorites like chocolate and red velvet cupcakes, the Yum Yum Cupcake Truck serves up seasonal and changing items like the Duchess of Tiramisu, a fluffy coffee cake filled with a chocolate-mascarpone mousse, topped with a rich mascarpone buttercream and chocolate dusting—and more chocolate-mascarpone mousse. When available, try the salted caramel, a chocolate caramel cake topped with a rich caramel buttercream, drizzled with caramel and sea salt, and finally topped with Peterbrooke Chocolatier of Winter Park's famous chocolate-covered caramel popcorn. See The Yum Yum Cupcake Truck's recipe for **Orange Cream Dream Cupcake** on p. 272.

Recipes

Le Coq au Vin's Coquille St. Jacques, 238

Veal Sweetbreads, 240

Julie Petrakis's Crème Caramel, 242

Honey Earl Grey Tuile Cookies, 244

The Original Gin & Jam, 245

Slow-Roasted Jerk-Spiced Local Pork, 246

Glazed Duck, 248

Farro Salad with Corn, Tomato, Basil, and Goat Cheese Bruschetta, 250

The Rio Cocktail, 251

The Cetriolo Cocktail, 252

Lake Meadow Green Goddess–Stuffed Eggs, 253

Waterkist Meets Lake Meadow Bloody Mary, 255

Tuna Tataki, 256

Sautéed Garlic Edamame, 257

Quinoa Salad, 258

Smoked Salmon Tartine, 259

4Rivers Bacon-Wrapped Jalapeños, 260

Cowboy Steak by Cowboy Kitchen, 261

Coca-Cola & Potato Chip Cupcake, 262

Honey Walnut Shrimp, 264

Grilled Blue Cheese–Crusted Filet, 265

"A Short Rib by Any Other Name . . . Still Tastes Delicious", 267

Crystallized Ginger Olive Oil Cupcakes with Lime Buttercream, Opal Basil, Mint, and Lime Zest, 270

Orange Cream Dream Cupcake, 272

Fresh Fruit 'n' Nut Salad with Citrus Goat Cheese Dressing, 274

Blood Orange Tofu Cheesecake, 276

Citrusy Champagne Sangria, 278

Florida Seafood Pasta in a White Wine Sauce, 279

Strawberry Sangria, 281

Grandma's Potato Salad, 282

Lump Crab–Stuffed Florida Avocado, 283

Spinach Empanada, 285

Grilled Swordfish with Heirloom Tomatoes, 287

Le Coq au Vin's Coquille St. Jacques

Le Coq au Vin Restaurant was among the first, open in 1976, and is still among Zagat America's top restaurants (2009). Le Coq au Vin is now owned and operated by Chef Reimund Pitz and his wife, Sandy, in partnership with Chefs Louis and Magdalena Perrotte. The cuisine reflects traditional classical cooking techniques as well as different cultural influences. For 20 years, Chef Pitz served as area chef, sous chef, chef de cuisine, and executive chef at Walt Disney World/ MGM Studios theme park. Trained as a chef in his native Germany, Pitz has earned many culinary awards, citations, and honors. In 1992 he was named southeast region and national ACF Chef of the Year. At the 1988 international Culinary Olympics in Frankfurt, Germany, he earned five gold medals, one perfect score, and the grand gold medal. He also helped lead the 1992 Culinary Team USA to victory at the international Culinary Olympics and served as adviser for the 1996 Culinary Team USA.

Makes 8 servings

Oil for sautéeing

2 teaspoons chopped garlic

½ teaspoon each: thyme and tarragon

12 ounces white button mushrooms, washed and sliced

Salt and pepper to taste

⅓ cup dry white wine

48 medium fresh sea scallops

2 cups heavy cream

1 stick butter

Infusion of fresh herbs and oil

Seasoned bread crumbs

Thinly shaved Parmesan

Put oil in a sauté pan and add chopped garlic. Add thyme and tarragon. Add mushrooms next and salt and pepper to taste.

Deglaze pan with white wine. Add scallops and cook until opaque.

With a colander positioned over a metal bowl, drain scallop mixture.

Divide scallop mixture evenly among 8 shell-shaped, ovenproof serving dishes. Set aside.

Pour the drain pan juices back into the sauté pan. Add cream and butter and cook, stirring, until mixture thickens.

Pour mixture over scallops in serving dishes. Drizzle with herb-infused oil. Sprinkle each serving with bread crumbs and shaved Parmesan. Broil until tops are golden and serve.

Courtesy of Chef Reimund Pitz of Le Coq au Vin (p. 80).

Veal Sweetbreads

Chef-Owners James and Julie Petrakis of Orlando, who trained at the prestigious Culinary Institute of America in Hyde Park, New York, and worked in some of the finest kitchens in the eastern US, returned to their hometown of Winter Park to realize their dream of opening their own restaurant—The Ravenous Pig, an American Gastropub. The Petrakis family has achieved great success with their passion for food and been nominated multiple times for the James Beard Award for Best Chef of the South. The couple has also recently opened the Southern pubhouse–themed Cask and Larder restaurant in Winter Park.

Chef's notes: Vindaloo curry powder is a hot-tangy blend sold at Penzey's Spices, Williams-Sonoma, and other shops. A microplane is a grater. European cukes are sometimes marked "English."

Makes 6 servings

Pickled heirloom carrots

- 2 cups cider vinegar
- 1 cup each: water and sugar
- ¼ cup coarse salt
- 1 tablespoon each: coriander and fennel seeds, black peppercorns
- 2 teaspoons chile flakes
- 3 to 4 cups ¼-inch sliced heirloom carrots

Cumin-spiced yogurt

- 2 cups Greek yogurt
- 1 European cucumber, microplaned
- 1 lime, juiced and zest removed
- 2 teaspoons cumin
- 1 teaspoon vindaloo curry powder
- Coarse salt to taste

Sweetbreads

2 pounds veal sweetbreads	Vegetable oil
2 quarts whole milk	Coarse salt and black pepper

1 large yellow onion, diced	1 head garlic, top cut off
2 large carrots, peeled and cut into ½-inch pieces	8 sprigs thyme
	4 fresh bay leaves
2 celery stalks, cut into ½-inch pieces	½ bottle dry white wine
	2 quarts chicken stock

Mix vinegar, water, sugar, salt, coriander, fennel, peppercorns, and chile in pan on medium; boil. Cool to room temperature. Pour over carrots. Marinate 12 hours.

Mix yogurt ingredients. Refrigerate.

Submerge sweetbreads in milk; soak overnight in fridge. Bring pot of salted water to simmer. Drain sweetbreads. Poach 2 minutes. Transfer to pan lined with towels; trim fat and as much connective tissue as possible. Cover with towels, a second sheet pan, and a heavy pot to slightly compress sweetbreads, not flatten. Refrigerate for several hours or overnight. Heat oil in flat-bottomed pan on medium-high. Season sweetbreads with salt and pepper. Lightly sear, 2 minutes per side. Transfer to plate. To pan, add onion, carrot, celery, garlic, thyme, and bay leaves. Reduce heat to moderately low. Stir vegetables 5 minutes. Add wine, loosening bits on bottom. Add stock and sweetbreads; bring to boil. Reduce heat to low. Simmer with pan partially covered with lid, until sweetbreads are firm but springy, 15–20 minutes. Cool sweetbreads in liquid. Portion into 6 servings. Heat oil in pan. Sear sweetbreads until golden.

Serve with yogurt and carrots.

Courtesy of Chefs James and Julie Petrakis of The Ravenous Pig (p. 47).

Julie Petrakis's Crème Caramel

Makes 8 (4-ounce) servings

For the caramel

1 cup sugar

¼ cup water

Squeeze of fresh lemon juice

For the vanilla cream

5 egg yolks and 1 whole egg

½ cup sugar, divided

1 teaspoon vanilla extract

2 cups cream

1 cup milk

Pinch salt

For the citrus compote (*makes about 4 cups*)

2 cups honey

1 cup water

1 tablespoon vanilla

1 teaspoon salt

Juice of 2 lemons

1 grapefruit, seeded and cut into segments

2 oranges, seeded and cut into segments

1 blood orange, seeded and cut into segments

1 lemon, seeded and cut into segments

To make the caramel:

Mix together sugar, water, and lemon juice in a heavy-bottomed saucepan over low heat, stirring to dissolve sugar. Brush sides of pot with a little water to prevent the sugar from crystallizing on sides.

Cover and cook over low heat until the syrup turns golden brown. Remove from heat, and divide hot caramel among 8 ramekins. Let cool for at least 2 minutes.

To make the vanilla cream:

Preheat oven to 325°F.

Stir together egg yolks and egg with half of sugar in a large mixing bowl; set aside.

Stir together vanilla, cream, milk, salt, and remaining sugar in a medium saucepan over medium heat; bring to just below a boil and remove from heat.

Gently whisk 2 tablespoons of hot milk mixture into egg mixture. Slowly whisk in remaining hot milk mixture ⅓ at a time.

Place 8 ramekins in a baking dish, and pour 4 ounces into each ramekin. Carefully pour boiling water into the baking dish until ⅔ of the way up sides of ramekins. Cover with aluminum foil pierced in a few places to vent.

Bake 35 minutes, or until custard is set. Remove from oven, and use tongs to remove ramekins from hot water. Let stand at room temperature for 20 minutes, then refrigerate until ready to serve.

To serve, dip ramekin in very hot water for 15 to 20 seconds, and run a sharp knife around sides. Invert custard onto serving plate; serve with fruit compote and tuile cookies.

To make the citrus compote:

Bring honey, water, vanilla, salt, and lemon juice to a boil in a medium saucepan over medium heat. Remove from heat, and cool slightly.

Place fruit in bowl, and pour syrup over fruit; stir to combine. Refrigerate until ready to serve.

Courtesy of Chef Julie Petrakis of The Ravenous Pig (p. 47).

Honey Earl Grey Tuile Cookies

Makes approximately 6 dozen (4-inch) cookies

1 cup all-purpose flour
1 tablespoon Earl Grey
tea, finely ground
(approximately 3 tea bags)
Pinch salt

4 ounces unsalted butter
(1 stick)
1 cup powdered sugar
¼ cup honey
¼ teaspoon vanilla extract
3 egg whites

Place oven rack in middle position, and preheat oven to 325°F. Line a large baking sheet with nonstick liner.

Whisk together flour, tea, and salt; set aside.

Cream together butter, sugar, honey, and vanilla in a large bowl with an electric mixer at medium speed until well combined and fluffy.

Add egg whites, one at a time, beating well after each addition.

Reduce mixing speed to low, and slowly add flour mixture. Mix on medium-low until just combined. Do not overmix.

Transfer batter to a piping bag fitted with a plain, round piping tip. Pipe thin 2½-inch circles onto an ungreased baking sheet, with 4 inches of space between. Smooth circles with an offset spatula.

Place pan in oven. Bake 8 to 10 minutes or until lightly brown around the edges, rotating pan halfway through baking. Remove pan from oven; let stand 5 minutes before transferring cookies to a cooling rack. Repeat until all batter is used.

Courtesy of Chef Julie Petrakis of The Ravenous Pig (p. 47).

The Original Gin & Jam

Yields 1 serving

2 ounces gin (we like Nicholas Gin from Tampa)

1 ounce sour mix (see notes)

1 teaspoon tangelo marmalade (see notes)

Combine gin and sour mix in shaker with ice. Shake and strain into a rocks glass with ice.

Serve with spoonful of marmalade (to be stirred in by guest).

Notes: *To make sour mix: Combine 3 parts lime juice, 1 part lemon juice, and 1 part simple syrup. Make sour mix the day you make the drink; it is essential that it is fresh.*

To make marmalade:

10 pounds tangelos, thinly sliced cross-wise, pithed and peeled

4 cups sugar

1 tablespoon salt

1 vanilla bean

1 cinnamon stick

Combine all ingredients in a pot over low heat until a thick consistency is reached (around 45 minutes), stirring occasionally. Store in fridge.

Courtesy of Larry Foor of The Ravenous Pig (p. 47).

Slow-Roasted Jerk-Spiced Local Pork

Hari Pulapaka, executive chef and co-owner of Cress Restaurant, was born and raised in the bustling metropolis of Mumbai (formerly Bombay). After getting his doctorate in mathematics at the University of Florida, Hari went on to graduate from Orlando's Le Cordon Bleu. Today Hari is a classically trained, James Beard–nominated chef as well as an active tenured associate professor of mathematics at Stetson University. Hari teaches full-time at Stetson University during the day and returns to the kitchen at Cress at night.

Chef's note: Instead of cooking the pork in a conventional oven, one could use a wood-burning smoker for added authenticity and deeper flavor.

Yields 8-10 servings

> 5 pounds high-quality free-range pork shoulder (Boston butt is best) from a local source

Jerk paste

- 1 bunch scallions (cleaned, greens and whites)
- 5 cloves fresh garlic
- 1 tablespoon grated fresh ginger
- 4 Scotch bonnet peppers (substitute with habañero, if necessary)
- 4 tablespoons fresh thyme
- 4 fresh sage leaves with stems
- 1 fresh orange (juice plus zest)
- ½ bunch fresh cilantro (with stems)

Spices

- 3 tablespoons whole all spice berries
- 1 tablespoon whole black peppercorns
- 1 tablespoon whole cumin seeds
- 1 teaspoon whole coriander seeds
- 1 large cinnamon stick

Other Ingredients

1 tablespoon kosher salt

2 tablespoons red wine vinegar

1 teaspoon light brown sugar

¼ cup canola oil

Toast the spices in a dry sauté pan for a few minutes on medium-low heat. Grind in a spice/coffee grinder to a medium coarse consistency. Add all the jerk paste ingredients, other ingredients, and ground spices to a food processor and blend until well incorporated.

"Butterfly" the pork shoulder to a 1½-inch-thick slab. Pat the pork shoulder dry with paper towels and pierce several uniformly spaced slits with a paring knife. Stuff each slit with a whole garlic clove. Rub the jerk paste liberally and vigorously on all sides. Cover and marinate for at least 24 hours. Preheat oven to 450°F. Reseason the pork well with more of the jerk paste, kosher salt, and pepper. Roast the pork for about 25 minutes. Note: The oven might smoke a bit with the pungent spices. Turn the oven down to 275°F. Cover the pork with foil and roast for an additional 5 hours, until the meat is tender. Let it rest before cutting off pieces or tearing apart. Serve with stewed cabbage and rice and peas.

Courtesy of Chef Hari Pulapaka of Cress Restaurant (p. 168).

Glazed Duck

A graduate of the California Culinary Academy, Executive Chef Brandon McGlamery of Luma on Park and Prato has gained an array of international culinary experience during his tenure at some of the most prestigious restaurants across the nation. McGlamery has held positions at California's Stars Restaurant, French Laundry and Chez Panisse, The Dining Room at the Ritz-Carlton Naples, and Jardinière. Chef McGlamery also created and executed a self-styled apprenticeship at Gordon Ramsey in London and Guy Savoy in Paris. Before joining Luma, he was the chef de cuisine at Bacchanalia in Atlanta, Georgia. Working with local farmers on a daily basis, Chef McGlamery focuses on using the freshest ingredients available in his cuisine. The availability of key fresh ingredients and choice cuts of meat dictate what dishes are offered and when.

Yields 2 duckss

- **2 fresh ducks (gizzards, liver, and neck removed)**
- **2 gallons water**
- **4 cups soy sauce**
- **2 cups pomegranate juice**
- **4 cups fresh orange juice**
- **2 cups local honey**
- **½ cup julienned orange zest (or blood orange zest)**
- **¼ cup pomegranate seeds**
- **2 tablespoons diced jalapeño**
- **2 tablespoons olive oil**

Combine water, soy sauce, juices, and honey in a large pot.

Bring just to a boil and then simmer.

Remove from heat and let cool.

Place both ducks in a large bucket and pour the cooled mixture over them.

Refrigerate and brine for 2 to 4 days.

Remove the ducks, straining all liquid from them, and place on a roasting rack.

Let the ducks come to room temperature. This is very important.

Season with cracked black pepper and very lightly with salt.

Roast in a 200°F oven for 3 hours.

Place brining liquid on the stove and bring to a simmer, skimming as it cooks.

Continue cooking until it reduces to a glaze.

After the duck is in the oven for an hour and a half, begin glazing with a paintbrush using the simmered brining liquid.

Repeat this process every 15 minutes until duck is roasted

Combine orange zest, pomegranate seeds, jalapeño, and olive oil to create a citrus salsa.

Serve with the duck.

Courtesy of Chef Brandon McGlamery of Luma (p. 45).

Farro Salad with Corn, Tomato, Basil, and Goat Cheese Bruschetta

Makes 4 servings

- **4 cups chicken or vegetable broth**
- **2 cups farro**
- **1 large carrot, peeled**
- **1 stalk celery**
- **1 large onion, peeled and halved**
- **2 bay leaves**
- **1 bunch thyme, tied in butcher's twine**
- **2 cups fresh corn**
- **10 cloves sliced garlic (reserve 1 whole clove for baquette)**
- **2 cups cherry tomatoes, halved**
- **½ cup basil, cubed**
- **Extra-virgin olive oil**
- **Great-quality red, white, or balsamic vinegar**
- **4 slices of baguette**
- **1 cup goat cheese**
- **Salt and pepper to taste**

Place chicken broth, farro, carrot, celery, onion, bay leaves, and thyme in a saucepan and simmer slowly until farro is cooked and puffed. When all liquid is absorbed and farro is cooked through, lay out on a baking sheet and season with salt and pepper, and allow to cool.

In a saucepan add corn, olive oil, and sliced garlic; season with salt and pepper. Sauté corn in pan. When the farro has cooled, place in a mixing bowl and add cooked corn, tomatoes, and basil, and season with olive oil and good-quality vinegar.

Grill or toast baguette. When toasted rub with raw garlic clove and spread with goat cheese; place baguette around rims of the bowl for service.

Courtesy of Chef Brandon McGlamery of Prato (p. 46).

The Rio Cocktail

Makes 1 cocktail

1½ ounces Leblon Cachaça
½ ounce lemon verbena–
  infused simple syrup

6 fresh blueberries
3 leaves mint
Squeeze of lemon juice

In a shaker, muddle: mint, 4 blueberries, and lemon juice together. Add lemon verbena simple syrup and cachaça. Shake vigorously and strain over ice into a highball glass. Garnish with 2 fresh blueberries and lemon twist made from saved slice of lemon from juicing.

Courtesy of Jeremy Crittenden of Luma (p. 45).

The Cetriolo Cocktail

Makes 1 cocktail

1 ¼ ounces Crop organic
cucumber vodka

1 ½ ounces white cranberry
juice

½ ounce agave nectar

2 basil leaves

2 peeled cucumber slices

Splash of sour mix

Muddle 1 basil leaf and cucumber with ½ ounce agave nectar.

Next add 1 ¼ ounces Crop organic cucumber vodka, 1 ½ ounces white cranberry juice, and splash of sour mix.

Shake well and strain into martini glass. Garnish with a basil leaf.

Courtesy of David Arnold of Prato (p. 46).

Lake Meadow
Green Goddess-Stuffed Eggs

Chef-Owner Kathleen Blake of The Rusty Spoon and Pine Twenty2 has long been an advocate of local farms and locally sourced food. Her recipes feature uniquely sourced, local, and sustainable produce and proteins. Kathleen was a participating chef for the 2008 James Beard Foundation Awards Gala, recognizing artisanal Florida.

Makes 2¼ cups

12 Lake Meadow eggs

Green Goddess

3 white anchovies
1 clove garlic, minced
¾ cup chopped parsley
½ cup chopped basil
1½ tablespoons chopped oregano

½ cup chopped dill
¾ cup aioli (recipe follows)
lemon juice
3 tablespoons minced scallions
kosher salt and freshly cracked black pepper, to taste

Put all ingredients except aioli, lemon juice, and scallions in a food processor. Pulse to form a paste. Remove to a large bowl. Add aioli, lemon juice, and scallions. Mix to combine.

2 Lake Meadow egg yolks
3 tablespoons lemon juice

½ tablespoon chopped garlic
2 cups mild olive oil

Place 2 yolks, lemon juice, and garlic in food processor. Gradually add oil while processing to emulsify. Season with kosher salt to taste.

Place 12 Lake Meadow eggs in a pot and add just enough cold water to cover. Bring to a boil and then turn off pot. Cover and let eggs sit in hot water for 11 minutes.

Drain water and "shock" the eggs in ice water until shell is cooled. Crack the shells a bit to expedite the cooling process.

Peel and cut all eggs in half. Separate whites from yolks.

Pulse yolks in a food processor or hand chop until fine.

Fold in green goddess. Mix until just combined.

Stuff the whites with the filling and garnish with a crisp piece of pancetta, freshly cracked black pepper, and a few drops of extra-virgin olive oil.

Courtesy of Chef Kathleen Blake of The Rusty Spoon (p. 18) and Pine Twenty2 (p. 17).

Waterkist Meets Lake Meadow Bloody Mary

Makes 1 cocktail

**6 ounces Waterkist farms
  tomato water**
**2½ teaspoons pickled beet
  brine**
dash Worchestershire sauce
1½ ounces your favorite vodka

juice and zest of half a lemon
**freshly grated horseradish root,
  to taste**
3 shakes celery salt
**freshly cracked black pepper,
  to taste**

Combine all ingredients. Serve over ice.

Garnish with skewer of:

half a pickled hard-boiled Lake Meadow chicken egg

pickled Lake Meadow beet cubes

Courtesy of Chef Kathleen Blake of The Rusty Spoon (p. 18) and Pine Twenty2 (p. 17).

Tuna Tataki

Owner-Chef Chau Trinh and Chef Michael V. Gleason head up Sushi Pop Seafood and Chops, located in one of the final frontiers of Orlando: Oviedo. Inspired by Japanese pop culture, Sushi Pop's high-quality sushi takes center stage in a custom-designed atmospheric space that evokes the mood of a modern avant-garde dining room.

Yields 1 serving

6 ounces tuna
1 tablespoon canola oil
1 teaspoon shichimi pepper
4 tablespoon ponzu (recipe follows)
daikon sprouts

toasted garlic
1 tablespoon black sesame seeds
1 tablespoon shaved scallions
1 teaspoon sesame oil

Heat a nonstick sauté pan to medium-high heat. Pour canola oil into the pan. Season tuna with salt, pepper, and shichimi pepper. Sear tuna on all sides for 15 seconds each side. Remove from the pan and slice tuna against the grain into thin slices onto a plate. Pour the ponzu sauce on top and add daikon sprouts, toasted garlic, black sesame seeds, and shaved scallions, and drizzle sesame oil over the tuna.

Ponzu

½ orange, juiced
½ lemon, juiced
1 tablespoon yuzu
1 cup seasoned rice vinegar

¼ cup + 2 tablespoons light soy sauce
1 tablespoon simple syrup
3-inch piece kombu

Mix all the ingredients together and let marinate for 1 day in the refrigerator before using.

Courtesy of Chef Chau Trinh of Sushi Pop Seafood and Chops (p. 203).

Sautéed Garlic Edamame

Yields 2 servings

**1-pound bag of edamame
    soybeans, in pod**
1 ounce canola oil

2 ounces garlic, minced
3 teaspoons kosher salt

Fill a large saucepot with water and bring to a boil.

*While you are waiting on the water to boil, heat a large sauté pan
with canola oil to medium heat. Once the oil is hot, add minced
garlic to pan. Using a wooden spoon or rubber spatula,
move the garlic around the pan until the garlic becomes a
golden brown. Turn off heat and remove from hot surface.
(Do not let the garlic get too brown or burn. If the garlic
gets too dark, start over.)*

*Drop the edamame beans in the boiling water. When the
soybeans are ready, they will begin to float to the top of the
pot. Once the majority of the soybeans have floated to the
top, approximately 2 minutes, strain the soybeans from the
saucepot.*

*Add the cooked soybeans to the pan with the sautéed garlic
and season with kosher salt. Sauté on medium heat until the
edamame is coated with garlic and salt. Serve immediately.*

Courtesy of Chef Chau Trinh of Sushi Pop Seafood and Chops (p. 203).

Quinoa Salad

Collette Haw is a graduate of the Culinary Institute of America in Hyde Park, New York. After graduation she worked at many restaurants here in Orlando before landing a job at The Ravenous Pig in Winter Park. There she learned a lot from the Petrakis family and moved on to become sous chef at Barnie's CoffeeKitchen. She quickly proved her skill and capability there and was promoted to chef de cuisine.

Makes 5 cups

2 cups quinoa
4 cups vegetable stock
1½ cups roasted red peppers
3 tablespoons scallions, sliced
3 tablespoon parsley, chopped
2 fluid ounces extra-virgin olive oil

2 teaspoons lemon zest
2 lemons, juiced
½ cup feta cheese
Salt, to taste
Black peppercorn, to taste

Combine quinoa and stock in small pot and bring to a boil. Reduce to simmer and cover. Cook 15 to 20 minutes or until liquid has been absorbed and quinoa is tender. After the quinoa is cooked, let cool completely.

While the quinoa cools, prepare the vegetables.

In a large mixing bowl, combine the cooled quinoa with the peppers, scallions, parsley, olive oil, lemon zest, lemon juice, and feta. After all are combined, taste and season with salt and pepper.

Courtesy of Chef Collette Haw of Barnie's CoffeeKitchen (p. 52).

Smoked Salmon Tartine

Yields 1 serving

1 slice brioche, sliced long into 5 pieces

1 ounce olive oil

2 teaspoons lemon juice

1 teaspoon lemon zest

⅛ teaspoon garlic, minced

1 sprig dill, fresh

3 tablespoons crème fraîche

3 ounces red watercress

2½ ounces Ducktrap smoked salmon

Salt, to taste

Pepper, to taste

1 ounce cucumber, halved and sliced

1 teaspoon preserved lemon, minced

Toast the brioche until golden brown.

In a small bowl whisk together the oil, lemon juice, lemon zest, and garlic and season with salt and pepper. This will be the vinaigrette to dress the red watercress.

Chop the dill and mix it with the crème fraîche. Also season this with salt and pepper.

Spread dill crème fraîche across one side of brioche slice.

In a small bowl toss the vinaigrette with the red watercress and place on top of the bread.

Slice the salmon into 5 thin slices. Place 1 slice of salmon on each piece of bread.

Garnish with cucumber and preserved lemon.

Courtesy of Chef Collette Haw of Barnie's CoffeeKitchen (p. 52).

4 Rivers Bacon-Wrapped Jalapeños

John Rivers's diverse career experience spans two decades and ranges from managing a billion-dollar pharmaceutical distribution operation to opening one of the fastest-growing new restaurants in the Southeast with his Texas-inspired 4Rivers Smokehouse locations in Winter Park, Winter Garden, and Longwood, Florida. Rivers's business concept immediately garnered recognition with three consecutive Silver Spoon Awards from Orlando Home & Leisure, and "Best Barbecue" acknowledgments by Florida Travel and Life, the Orlando Sentinel, the Orlando Business Journal, Orlando Magazine, and Orlando Weekly, also for three consecutive years. Rivers was invited to present at the 2011 and 2012 Food Network South Beach Wine & Food Festival and to cook at the James Beard House in New York City in 2013.

Yields 10 pieces

10 jalapeños
⅝ cup whipped cream cheese,
   room temperature

10 slices of bacon
4R Signature barbecue sauce,
   optional

Cut the caps and stems off the fresh jalapeños, then split in halves to deseed.

Pipe 1 tablespoon of whipped cream cheese into the center of the jalapeños.

Wrap a half strip of bacon around each jalapeño, ensuring the ends of the bacon meet on the bottom of the pepper.

Place jalapeños on smoker rack and smoke for approximately 70 minutes at 275°F.

Use 4Rivers Signature barbecue sauce for dipping, if desired.

Courtesy of Chef John Rivers of 4Rivers Smokehouse (p. 43).

Cowboy Steak by Cowboy Kitchen

Yields 1 serving

16-ounce rib eye steak
1 onion, sliced
3 cloves garlic, minced

2 sticks butter
4R Coffee Rub

Rub steak liberally with 4R Coffee Rub 1 hour, or up to 24 hours, before grilling. Wrap tightly in plastic wrap to prevent steak from drying out.

Allow steak to sit at room temperature for 45 minutes before grilling.

Preheat oven to 325°F and preheat grill to high heat, at least 350°F.

While grill is heating, in a large pan sauté onion, garlic, and 1 stick of butter.

When the grill has reached high heat, place steak directly over coals and sear for 4 minutes on each side (for steaks less than 1½ inches in thickness, allow less time). Sear until steak is blackened and crispy on the outside.

Remove blackened steak from the grill and place in the sauté pan with the onion, garlic, and melted butter.

Cover with sautéed onions and another stick of butter and place in the oven for 4-7 minutes for medium rare and 7-10 minutes for medium. Flip steak in butter once during the cooking process.

Courtesy of Chef John Rivers of Cowboy Kitchen and 4Rivers Smokehouse (p. 43).

Coca-Cola & Potato Chip Cupcake

Makes 9 cupcakes

2 cups all-purpose flour
1 cup granulated sugar
1 cup salted butter
3 tablespoons cocoa powder
1 cup Coca-Cola
5 cups buttermilk
2 eggs
1 teaspoon baking soda

1 teaspoon pure vanilla extract
1½ cup mini marshmallows
27 tablespoons broken ridged potato chips (1 12-ounce bag)
9 whole ridged potato chips
¼ cup chocolate almond bar

Frosting

½ pound salted butter
4 ounces cream cheese
2 cups powdered sugar

1 tablespoon cocoa powder
3 tablespoons Coca-Cola
1 cup Coca-Cola (to brush on)

Sift together flour and sugar and set aside.

Melt butter, cocoa powder, and Coca-Cola until mixture boils.

Pour over sugar mixture and mix until combined.

Add buttermilk, eggs, baking soda, vanilla extract, and marshmallows.

Scoop mixture into cupcake wrappers and top with 3 tablespoons of broken potato chips for each cupcake.

Bake at 350°F for 28 minutes or until toothpick inserted comes out clean.

Brush on Coca-Cola while cupcakes are still warm.

Frosting

Combine and beat all ingredients until smooth.

Cover extra whole potato chips with melted chocolate almond bar.

Top each cupcake with 1 chocolate-covered potato chip.

Courtesy of Chef John Rivers for The Sweet Shop at 4Rivers Smokehouse (p. 43).

Honey Walnut Shrimp

Imperial Dynasty was established in March 2001 by Owners Tony and Kathy Chen. They have garnered several top foodie awards in Orlando. Previously owning two other acclaimed Chinese restaurants, they opened Imperial Dynasty in Longwood and have won the hearts of many locals. One of the local favorites is their famous Honey Walnut Shrimp. This dish is very popular, especially during the holiday season. The honey walnut sauce brings a burst of flavor from the delicately fried shrimp.

Makes 4 servings

Ingredients A

1 ounce paprika

1 ounce butter

24 ounces mayonnaise

12 ounces sugar

1 teaspoon salt

1 teaspoon garlic powder

8 ounces hot water

Ingredients B

1 pound large shrimp (use 21–25 count size)

about 3 tablespoons vegetable oil

12 ounces walnuts

Honey to taste

On low heat, stir-fry shrimp with vegetable oil till tender and cooked. Bake walnuts in preheated oven at 300 degrees until crispy but not burnt. Mix walnuts with a little bit of honey and set aside. Mix all the ingredients in Ingredients A to create a creamy sauce. Finally, mix the shrimp and sauce together. Toss walnuts on top of shrimp and serve.

Courtesy of Tony and Kathy Chen of Imperial Dynasty (p. 177).

Grilled Blue Cheese—Crusted Filet

The Everglades Restaurant pays homage to the vast expanse of threatened wetlands in south Florida. Owner Harris Rosen, Rosen Hotels Executive Chef Michael Rumplik, and Everglades Chef Fred Vlachos have been providing both visiting and local diners with creative, delicious fare for more than 15 years. Chef Rumplik and his culinary team are known for their creativity and were most recently acknowledged with Meetings and Conventions' prestigious Gold Platter Award, given to select properties throughout the nation that demonstrate creative and culinary excellence.

Yields 1 serving

For the sauce

2 teaspoons olive oil
1 teaspoon shallots
1 teaspoon garlic, chopped

¼ cup Guinness stout
¼ cup demi-glace sauce
Salt and pepper, to taste

For the plate

5 ounce filet mignon
1 ounce crumbled blue cheese
1 baby zucchini, cut in half
1 baby yellow pattypan squash, cut in half

3 fingerling potatoes, cut in half and blanched
Olive oil

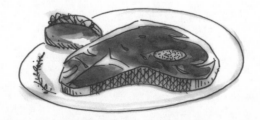

Sauté filet in olive oil to desired temperature. Remove from pan and let rest.

Add shallots and garlic and sauté till golden brown.

Deglaze with Guinness stout.

Add demi-glace and reduce to desired thickness.

Top filet with blue cheese and melt.

Arrange vegetables on plate, place filet, sauce plate, and serve.

Courtesy of Executive Chef Michael Rumplik
of Rosen Center Hotels/A Land Remembered (p. 123).

"A Short Rib by Any Other Name . . . Still Tastes Delicious"

Chef Bryce Balluff, a graduate of the French Culinary Institute who has worked in some of the finest kitchens from New York to south Florida, brings a special reverence for ingredients and a passion for perfection.

Training at Michelin-starred Per Se, Asia De Cuba, and Barbuto, and working locally as the private dining chef at Luma on Park and the chef de cuisine at Puff'n Stuff Catering, Chef Bryce has manned the helm of the kitchens of The Funky Monkey Wine Company and Draft Global Beer Lounge & Grill. Chef Bryce brings over a decade of artistic passion, finesse, and culinary expertise to Fork in the Road.

Chef's note: At Fork in the Road Food Truck, we produce our Angus beef short rib using a variety of modern cooking techniques. Let us begin with the meat. We take boneless beef short rib weighing in at 2–3 pounds per portion and dust them with a mixture of dried sage, smoked Hungarian paprika, garlic powder, onion powder, toasted ground fennel seed, toasted ground black pepper, and sea salt. The ribs are then vacuum-sealed and cooked in a water bath regulated by an immersion circulator (sous vide) for 72 hours at 145°F. For the vegetables, we take red onions and fennel bulb, shave them fine, and vacuum-pickle them. This allows us to pickle in an hour instead of days. For the sauce we make an aioli. This mayonnaise base is blended with chipotle (smoked jalapeño) and the cold smoked and reduced liquid produced by the braised short rib. When ordered, the short rib is heated through and this symphony of flavors is presented between two slices of toasted Tribeca Bakery baguette. We understand that without a vacuum sealer, vacuum canisters, a smoking gun, and a immersion circulator it is not possible to produce the results necessary to make this dish. So we would like to provide you with a version you can make at home.

Makes 2 servings

Braised beef short rib

1 ½ pounds beef short ribs

2 tablespoons chopped fresh
sage

10 turns of fresh peppercorns
from your favorite
peppermill

Sea salt to coat

Safflower oil to coat

5 cleaned cloves fresh garlic,
smashed

1 tablespoon tomato paste

¼ cup red wine (if you wouldn't
drink it, don't cook with it
either)

Preheat the oven to its lowest setting, 170°F.

Clean short rib of any sinew, being careful to leave the bones and fat. This will help insulate the meat while it cooks. Place the short rib whole, bone side down in a roasting pan deep enough to immerse the short rib completely.

Season the meat side liberally with the sage, cracked pepper, and sea salt. Coat the surface of the seasoned short rib section with a thin layer of safflower oil to prevent the ribs from sticking to the pan as well as insulate the meat side while it cooks.

Place 1 cup of water in the pan. Cover the pan with heavy-duty plastic wrap and then tinfoil. It is extremely important to make sure both layers are airtight. Place the pan in the oven and find something to occupy your time for the next 20 hours. For timing purposes I suggest making this dish after finishing dinner the night before, to ensure it is ready for dinner the next night.

When you have reached 20 hours, remove the pan from the oven and peel away the foil and plastic layers. Please resist the urge to begin picking bite-size pieces from the meat—before you know it, there will be nothing left. Delicately remove the short rib section from the pan and place it meat side down on a cutting board. Let the meat rest for 30 minutes. Reserve the liquid from the pan.

Meanwhile, bring the smashed garlic and tomato paste to a slow simmer on the stove in a little safflower oil with a pinch of sea salt. After 30 minutes remove the bones from the short rib section, crack them with the back of a knife, and place them in the sauté of tomato paste and garlic.

Pour the reserved liquid over this mixture and bring to a simmer. Let this simmer for an hour while the ribs continue to cool.

After 1 hour remove the bones, add the wine, and puree the mixture. Reduce this to a nape (when you run your finger through the sauce on the back of a wooden spoon it stays separated). Taste and adjust the seasoning. To finish the dish, cut the rested short ribs into 8-ounce pieces, trimming away some of the remaining fat.

Place a little safflower oil in a very hot sauté pan. Brown the short rib pieces on all sides and coat with the sauce. This can be paired with a starch and vegetable of choice for a complete dish.

If you have the craving and you don't have 20 hours to wait, swing by Fork in the Road for a shortrib-wich.

Courtesy of Chef Bryce Balluff of Fork in the Road Food Truck (p. 230).

Crystallized Ginger Olive Oil Cupcakes with Lime Buttercream, Opal Basil, Mint, and Lime Zest

In 2008 Hollis Wilder opened Sweet! by Good Golly Miss Holly in Orlando, using the same simple formula with cupcakes as she had with the savory foods she had became known for in Los Angeles at her catering business. As winner of the first Cupcake Wars on Food Network, she became known as the creator of the Salmon Cupcake. She recently won her second Cupcake Wars.

Makes 48 mini cupcakes

1½ cups plus ⅛ cup olive oil

2 cups superfine sugar

1½ cups crystallized ginger, run through food processor

8 egg whites

3 cups cake flour

3 teaspoons baking powder

2 tablespoons ground ginger

1 teaspoon salt

1 cup whole milk

3 teaspoons vanilla

Lime Buttercream, recipe follows

Micro opal basil, for garnish

Micro mint, for garnish

Lime zest, for garnish

Preheat the oven to 350°F. Line mini cupcake pans with 48 liners.

In the bowl of a stand mixer with the paddle attachment, mix the oil and sugar on high speed until creamy and fully incorporated. Mix in the crystallized ginger until fully incorporated. Add the egg whites and mix well. Sift together the flour, baking powder, ground ginger, and salt in a large bowl. On medium speed, add the flour mixture alternately with the milk and vanilla mixture until combined.

Do not over-mix. Fill the cupcake liners ¾ of the way and bake for 15 minutes.

To assemble: Using a pastry bag fitted with a small round tip, pipe the top of the cupcakes in a dot pattern with Lime Buttercream, creating 6 dots to cover the tops of the cakes. Snip a small cluster from the stem of each branch of the micro herbs. Place the bunches in the center of the icing. Zest a fresh lime over the cakes to finish off the garnish.

This recipe was provided by professional chefs and has been scaled down from a bulk recipe provided by a restaurant. The Food Network Kitchens chefs have not tested this recipe, in the proportions indicated and therefore cannot make any representation as to the results.

Lime Buttercream

1¼ cups fresh lime juice
2 tablespoons cornstarch
1 pound unsalted butter

1 teaspoon salt
6 cups confectioners' sugar

Place the lime juice and cornstarch in a small pan on the stove. Cook over medium heat, whisking, until the mixture thickens. Transfer the lime curd to a silicone mat and refrigerate until cool, about 5 minutes. In the bowl of a stand mixer with the paddle attachment, cream the butter and salt. Add the cooled lime curd. Add the confectioners' sugar and beat until light and fluffy.

Courtesy of Chef Hollis Wilder of Sweet! by Good Golly Miss Holly (p. 210).

Orange Cream Dream Cupcake

The Yum Yum Cupcake Truck is one of the most popular food trucks in Orlando, owing in no small part to Owners Joey Conicella and Alex Marin's hard work, dedication, and delicious cupcakes. They provide us this wonderful cupcake recipe featuring flavors of oranges reminiscent of the citrus found throughout central Florida.

Makes 12 cupcakes

Cake

4 tablespoons butter, softened

1 cup sugar

1 egg

1 teaspoon orange extract

¼ teaspoon vanilla extract

⅓ teaspoon baking soda

⅔ teaspoon baking powder

¼ teaspoon salt

1 teaspoon orange food coloring, optional

1⅓ cups all-purpose flour

1 cup buttermilk

Filling

8 tablespoons butter

1 cup powdered sugar

Pinch of salt

1 cup marshmallow cream, such as Marshmallow Fluff

1¼ teaspoons vanilla extract

Frosting

⅓ cup butter

1½ teaspoons orange extract

3 cups powdered sugar

For the cake: Preheat the oven to 350°F. Line a cupcake pan with 12 paper liners. Using an electric mixer, beat the butter and sugar until light and fluffy.

Add the egg, orange and vanilla extracts, baking soda, baking powder, salt, and food coloring if using, beating well after each addition. With the mixer on low speed, alternately add the flour and buttermilk in 3 additions. Scrape down the sides of the bowl as needed. Portion the batter evenly in the prepared pan and bake until a toothpick inserted into a cupcake comes out clean, 18 to 20 minutes. Allow the cupcakes to cool before adding the filling and frosting.

For the filling: Using an electric mixer, beat the butter until fluffy. On low speed, add the powdered sugar and salt and mix well before adding the marshmallow cream and vanilla extract.

For the frosting: Using an electric mixer, cream the butter until smooth. Add the orange extract. On low speed, gradually add the powdered sugar. Scrape the sides as needed. Beat on high speed until the frosting is light and fluffy.

To fill the cupcake, add the filling to a pastry bag with a round tip. Insert the tip into the cupcake so that it's a little more than halfway down. While pushing the filling into the cupcake, pull the tip out of the cupcake.

Alternately, you can use a small knife to carve out a small cylinder of cake and fill with the filling. Spread the frosting over the top of the cupcakes.

Courtesy of The Yum Yum Cupcake Truck (p. 233).

Fresh Fruit 'n' Nut Salad
with Citrus Goat Cheese Dressing

Julie Fagan is the author behind the blog Peanut Butter Fingers *(PBfingers .com), which follows her life as she strives to maintain a healthy lifestyle fueled by regular exercise and (mostly) healthy food. With more than 1.5 million monthly page views, her work and her blog have been featured in national magazines, including* Shape, Fitness, Glamour, Women's Day, *and* Women's Health.

Makes approximately 3 (2-tablespoon) servings

Citrus Goat Cheese Dressing

2 ounces goat cheese

1 tablespoon honey

Juice of one clementine, or approximately 2 tablespoons freshly squeezed orange juice

½ teaspoon apple cider vinegar

1 tablespoon olive oil

Combine all ingredients in a food processor and process until a smooth, creamy dressing forms.

Fresh Fruit 'n' Nut Salad

Serves 1

1½ cups arugula

1 cup fresh spinach

1 clementine or tangerine, peeled

5 strawberries, sliced with stems removed

¼ cup fresh blueberries

8 praline pecans

2 tablespoons Citrus Goat Cheese Dressing (recipe above)

Place arugula and spinach on a plate and top with fruit and pecans.

Drizzle dressing on top of the salad and enjoy.

Courtesy of Julie Fagan of PBFingers.com.

Blood Orange Tofu Cheesecake

Kiran and Tarun Srivastava, originally of Malaysia and India, started blogging their journey in America and Orlando in 2007 for their families in their homelands. Their blog is a finalist in the 2012 Best Food Blog Awards of Saveur Magazine *for Best Recipe, Savory or Sweet. Visit their blog at kirantarun.com/food.*

Crust

⅓ cup almonds

12 marigold (any brand) cookies

4 tablespoons butter, melted

Filling

1 (8-ounce) package cream cheese, softened

2 blocks of soft silken tofu, pressed

¾ cup sugar

3 whole eggs

3 blood oranges, juiced

Zest from 2 blood oranges

2 tablespoon Grand Marnier (orange liqueur) or orange extract

Preheat oven to 325°F.

In a food processor, pulse almonds and cookies to form crumbs.

Place crumbs in a bowl and stir in melted butter.

Press crumbs to form a crust in a springform pan or a lightly greased pie pan.

Bake crust for 10 minutes. Allow to cool when done.

In a food processor, blend cream cheese with tofu until silky smooth.

Add sugar and eggs (1 at a time) and pulse just until combined.

Stream in blood orange juice, zest, and Grand Marnier or extract. Pulse until thoroughly combined.

Place cool pie pan/crust on a cookie sheet. Scrape filling onto cool crust.

Gently transfer cheesecake into oven to bake at 325°F for 1 hour.

Turn oven off and leave cheesecake in the oven for 20 more minutes, with the oven door slightly ajar.

Remove cheesecake to completely cool on a cooling rack before refrigerating for a few hours or overnight.

Best served chilled (not room temperature), with orange slices and/or drizzled with any citrus coulis.

Note: Ensure tofu is pressed to remove excess moisture. The cheesecake batter will appear to be too much for the crust, so be careful when transferring it into the oven. Placing it over a cookie sheet definitely helps. Cheesecake will puff a lot while baking. Fear not—it won't overflow.

Courtesy of Kiran and Tarun Srivastava of KiranTarun.com.

Citrusy Champagne Sangria

¼ cup sugar

⅓ cup water

1 lemon, thinly sliced

1 blood orange, thinly sliced

3 clementines, thinly sliced

1 Honey Crisp apple, thinly sliced

½ cup pomegranate arils

4 cups freshly squeezed grapefruit juice

1 cup ginger ale

Pinch of salt

1 bottle chilled Champagne

Prepare simple syrup by stirring sugar and water until sugar completely dissolves. Keep in refrigerator to chill while prepping other ingredients.

In a tall pitcher, add all fruits, grapefruit juice, ginger ale, salt, and simple syrup. Chill in refrigerator for a few hours, preferably overnight.

To serve, add sangria in a fancy-schmancy glass and top it with bubbly Champagne! Toast with your loved ones.

Courtesy of Kiran and Tarun Srivastava of KiranTarun.com.

Florida Seafood Pasta in a White Wine Sauce

Julie Deily is a software engineer and food blogger who grew up in the Orlando area. Julie got her love of cooking and feeding people from her mother, a Vietnamese immigrant. She started the food blog The Little Kitchen *in December 2009 to share recipes with her family and friends. Little did she know that her blog would grow and she would find a wonderful community of food bloggers and make the best friends of her life. She loves trying new things and especially likes to make simple and delicious comfort foods. You can find her recipes at TheLittleKitchen.net.*

Chef's note: *Once your family and friends taste this wonderful pasta dish, they won't believe how easy it is to make! I used Florida littleneck clams and Florida lobster along with white wine made from Florida grapes. Serve with a salad made from locally grown greens and your favorite crusty bread.*

Makes 3–4 servings

- 8 ounces linguine
- 2 tablespoons unsalted butter
- 2 garlic cloves, minced
- ½ cup San Sebastian Reserve white wine
- ¼ cup olive oil
- 12–16 Florida littleneck clams, scrubbed clean
- 1 Florida lobster tail, approximately 3 ounces, chopped
- Salt and pepper
- 2 tablespoons Italian parsley, chopped
- Parmigiano-Reggiano cheese, grated (optional)

Remove lobster from shell by cutting through the bottom of the shell with kitchen shears.

Bring salted water to a boil and prepare linguine according to instructions.

Meanwhile, in a heavy-bottomed pot or Dutch oven, melt butter on medium heat. Add garlic and cook for 2 minutes. Add wine and olive oil and bring to a boil on medium-high to high heat. Add clams and cook for 7–10 minutes or until all clams have opened up. During the last 2 minutes of cooking, add the chopped lobster. Add salt and pepper to taste.

Add the cooked pasta to the seafood pot and mix to allow the clam sauce to coat the pasta. Add parsley and Parmigiano-Reggiano cheese and serve immediately.

Courtesy of Julie Deily of TheLittleKitchen.net.

Strawberry Sangria

Aggie Goodman, of Aggie's Kitchen (aggieskitchen.com), is an active mom of two who's always thinking about the next meal. Her kitchen is her "happy place" where she can relax and do what she loves to do: feed her family and friends. Most of the food she cooks is healthy, but the occasional treat is permitted (and welcomed!). When she's not cooking, she's most likely running after her kids, getting in a good workout, finding peace in a book, or talking food on social media. You can find her on Facebook (facebook.com/pages/Aggies-Kitchen/146611220464) and @aggieskitchen (twitter.com/aggieskitchen) on Twitter.

Chef's note: *The sweetness of Florida strawberries infused into citrus juice makes this chilled and fruity wine drink extra-special. A glass of Strawberry Sangria is a perfect addition to warm spring evenings spent outside in Florida.*

Makes 1 pitcher (8 servings)

- 1 cup fresh strawberries, sliced
- 2 tablespoons sugar
- 1 orange, juiced
- 1 bottle of red wine, chilled (I recommend a non-sweet wine, like Merlot or Cabernet)
- ¼ cup coconut rum
- 1 can berry-flavored sparkling water, chilled (I use LaCroix)
- 1 cup strawberries, sliced and frozen, for serving
- 1 orange, sliced and frozen, for serving

Combine sliced strawberries, sugar, and juice of 1 orange at the bottom of a pitcher. Using a wooden spoon, muddle together berries, juice, and sugar until mashed well. Add wine and rum to strawberry mixture and stir. At this time, you can chill for later use or add your sparkling water if serving immediately. Add frozen strawberry and orange slices to your pitcher and serve.

Courtesy of Aggie Goodman of AggiesKitchen.com.

Grandma's Potato Salad

Says Katie Jasiewicz of KatiesCucina.com, "This was a recipe my grandmother made many years ago. She passed away over 25 years ago and never wrote the recipe down. I remember my mom making this for me as a child—carefully replicating it to the best of her knowledge. One day last year I was in the mood for my grandmother's potato salad—I could taste the flavors of the vinaigrette based potato salad in my mouth. I asked my mom for the main ingredients and went to town re-developing this classic family recipe. My mom says that I make her mom's potato salad better than she did!"

Makes 4 servings

- 6 large red potatoes
- 1 tablespoon salt
- 1 tablespoon minced dried onions
- 1 tablespoon dried parsley
- 1 tablespoon sugar
- ¼ cup canola oil
- 3 tablespoons apple cider vinegar
- Salt and pepper, to taste
- 1 stalk celery, diced

Slice the red potatoes about ¼ inch thick. Add the sliced potatoes to a large pot with enough water to cover the potatoes, and add salt to the pot of water/potatoes. Boil on medium-high heat until soft. Depending on your stovetop, this should take around 25 minutes. Keep a close eye to make sure the potatoes don't get too soft and begin to fall apart.

In a bowl add the minced dried onions, parsley, sugar, canola oil, apple cider vinegar, and salt and pepper. Mix well, then add the diced celery.

Drain the potatoes in a strainer and set aside. In a larger serving bowl add a quarter of the dressing, followed by ⅓ of the potatoes. Pour another quarter of the dressing over the potatoes, followed by more potatoes, and repeat until completed. Gently mix, and chill for as little as an hour. Serve and enjoy.

Courtesy of Katie Jasiewicz of KatiesCucina.com.

Lump Crab-Stuffed Florida Avocado

This is the most popular dish we have ever served on the Big Wheel Food Truck. We love it because it is so fresh and light, and at the same time quick to assemble. It can even be done ahead for a party, and the avocados hold up well. The ingredients are pretty easy to find, especially if you have an Asian market nearby. If not, check the ethnic section of the local grocery store. Buying the seasoned rice wine vinegar is really important, as plain rice wine vinegar just doesn't carry the same flavor. And it's easy to reduce the recipe if needed, but making less than 2 cups of rice is not suggested. The vinaigrette will hold for up to 10 days and goes great on just about anything!

Makes 6 servings

2 cups Japanese sushi rice or other short-grain rice

3 ripe Florida avocados (Haas is an acceptable substitute, but cut the remaining recipe in half)

8 ounces lump crab meat (we use Florida lump crab from Wild Ocean in Titusville)

1 jar nori furikake rice seasoning

For the vinaigrette

¼ cup soy sauce

¼ cup seasoned rice vinegar (bought preseasoned as if for sushi)

1 clove garlic, minced

½-inch knob ginger, minced

1 teaspoon local honey

1 teaspoon Sriracha sauce or minced chiles

For the rice

Cover the rice with 3 cups cold water. Place in a pot that has a tight-fitting lid. Place over low heat, and cook slowly until all the water is absorbed, about 25 minutes. Remove from heat and keep warm, or place on a container and chill to room temperature. (Can be served cold, but we prefer lightly warm or room temperature.)

For the vinaigrette

Add all ingredients together in a bowl. Let sit for at least 15 minutes to marry flavors. Reserve.

To assemble:

Cut each avocado in half from top to bottom. Remove the golf ball–size pit and scoop out any discolored or bruised flesh with a spoon. Fill with approximately the same amount of Japanese rice. Top with crab. Drizzle with vinaigrette and season liberally with nori furikake. Serve.

Courtesy of Chef Tony Adams of the Big Wheel Food Truck (p. 227).

Spinach Empanada

Empanadas first appeared in a Catalan cookbook back in the 1500s and it's believed that they originated in Spain and Portugal. Like the Italian calzone, empanadas are thought to have derived from Arabic meat-filled pies (Samosas). Traditionally empanadas were filled with meat (pork loin or chorizo) or fish (cod, tuna, or sardines) in a tomato-garlic-type sauce and became popular in those medieval days because they made such great portable meals for working people and travelers. The proliferation of empanadas eventually spread to Latin America, where each country has a regionally specific take on them—different dough recipes (made with flour, corn, or yucca) and various traditional fillings.

But the fillings we've been working on are all but traditional: cured ham, cheese, and melon; crab and green tomato salad; vegetarian sausage and peppers; roasted beets and goat cheese; pumpkin pie; s'mores; truffle mac and cheese! Across the sweet-to-savory spectrum, pretty much anything goes, so you can really get creative.

Note: *Makes enough spinach for 4 regular-size empanadas or about 15 mini ones. Find a favorite dough recipe online or look for premade empanada dough at the grocery store. An empanada press is not necessary—the dough edges can be sealed using a fork just as well.*

½ red onion, thinly sliced

1 clove garlic

Salt and pepper, to taste

Drizzle of olive oil and a tad of butter

Squirt of lemon juice

1 bag 10-ounce prewashed spinach

3 ounces small-curd cottage cheese

Light sprinkle of nutmeg

⅛ teaspoon lemon zest

Pinch of red pepper flakes

3 ounces feta, crumbled

1 egg white (for spinach mixture)

1 egg (for pastry egg wash)

Preheat oven to 375°F.

In a large sauté pan, sauté onion and garlic, salt, and black pepper in olive oil and butter over medium heat until onions begin to wilt. Squeeze some lemon juice into the pan. Add as much of your spinach to the pan as will fit and cover so spinach can wilt. Keep adding remaining spinach to the pan in batches as more room becomes available. Uncover once spinach is wilted but still bright green. Pour out any excess water from pan.

Add cottage cheese, nutmeg, lemon zest, a touch more salt, and red pepper flakes, and toss in pan to release steam. Add feta crumbles and remove from heat. Transfer to bowl and fold in egg white while still hot. Toss in bowl to incorporate evenly (the egg white will cook from the heat of the spinach). Set aside and let mixture cool to room temperature to thicken.

If dough is store bought, make sure it is a cool room temperature before you work with it. Pour out any additional moisture that has formed around spinach and add about 2 tablespoons of mixture to center of a dough disk. Moisten rim of dough with water using fingertips. Fold over and seal by pressing prong end of fork all along the edges, creating even imprints. Skip the fork step if using empanada press.

Prepare egg wash in a little bowl by whisking the egg until well blended. Lightly grease a baking sheet. Give each empanada a brush of egg wash on each side. Space evenly on baking sheet and bake until golden crispy (about 15 minutes for full-size and 6 minutes for mini ones).

Courtesy of Chef Gabrielle Arnold of La Empanada Food Truck (p. 231).

Grilled Swordfish
with Heirloom Tomatoes

Dawn Viola is a research and development chef and food editor. She serves on the board of directors as education chair for both Slow Food Orlando and the American Culinary Federation Central Florida Chapter, and works with local and national companies as a healthy recipe consultant with a focus on special diets, food allergies and local, organic and sustainable ingredients.

After an accomplished career as a copywriter, creative director and documentary producer in the advertising industry for over a decade, Dawn switched her writing focus to food and enrolled in culinary school when she discovered she had multiple food allergies. She graduated with honors from the culinary management program at Valencia College, completed her externship at America's Test Kitchen and Cook's Illustrated *magazine in Boston and is currently working towards a dual master's/doctorate degree in holistic nutrition.*

Yields: 4 servings

Prep time: 10 minutes

Cook time: 8 minutes

Allergy info: soy-free, gluten-free, dairy-free

4 (4-oz.) swordfish steaks

¼ cup olive oil, plus more for drizzling

1 garlic clove, minced

2 cups halved organic cherry or grape heirloom tomatoes (if you can't find heirloom, any variety of organic cherry or grape tomato can be used)

¼ cup fresh whole Greek oregano leaves

kosher salt and freshly cracked black pepper

Directions:

Preheat grill pan to medium-high heat; brush olive oil on grates. Using paper towels pat each swordfish steak dry; drizzle each side with olive oil, set aside. In a large bowl combine ¼ cup of the olive oil, garlic, and tomatoes; toss to coat.

Season each side of swordfish with salt and pepper. Place swordfish steaks on grill pan; cook 4 minutes each side, turning ¼ turn halfway through cooking to create crosshatch grill marks.

Meanwhile, place tomato mixture on another section of the grill pan; season with salt and pepper. Cook 3 to 4 minutes, or until lightly charred. Transfer cooked tomatoes to a clean bowl. Fold in oregano leaves and season with salt and pepper to taste; set aside. Spoon tomato mixture over swordfish steaks and drizzle with olive oil; serve warm.

Recipe note: *If using a charcoal grill instead of a grill pan, prepare grill the same way but place a double sheet of aluminum foil over one portion of the grill to prevent tomatoes from falling through the grates. Or, cook tomatoes over the coals in a cast iron pan.*

Courtesy of Chef Dawn Viola.

Appendix A: Orlando Eateries by Cuisine

African

Boma—Flavors of Africa at
Disney's Animal Kingdom
Lodge, 160
Jiko—The cooking place at
Disney's Animal Kingdom
Lodge, 157

American

Bananas Modern American
Diner, 88
Briarpatch Restaurant and Ice
Cream Parlor, 55
Christo's Cafe, 114
Dexter's, 26, 60
Junior's Diner, 118

Technique Restaurant, 223
310 Lakeside, 36
The Town House Restaurant, 211
Treehouse Truck, 232
White Wolf Cafe, 110

Asian

Emeril's Tchoup Chop at Universal
Orlando Resort's Loews Royal
Pacific Resort, 131
Ohana, 164
Roy's, 153

Asian Bakery or Market

Dong A Supermarket, 103
Eastside Asian Market, 212

1st Oriental Supermarket, 198
Phuoc Loc Tho Market, 104
Saigon Market, 104
Sun Pearl Bakery, 196
Tien Hung Complete Oriental
    Foods & Gifts, 104

Asian/Japanese
Bento Cafe, 20
Gokudo, 230

Asian/Malaysian
Hawkers Asian Street Fare, 92

Asian/Mediterranean
Spooky's Black Cat Cafe and Milk
    District Marketplace, 107

Asian/ Mexican
Tako Cheena by Pom Pom, 101

Asian, Modern American
Wolfgang Puck Cafe, 167

Bagels, Jewish
Bagel King, 174

Bakery
Bake Me a Cake, 185
Blue Bird Bake Shop, 117
Charlie's Gourmet Pastries, 82
Donut King, 189
Le Macaron, 64
Sweet! by Good Golly Miss
    Holly, 210
Yalaha Bakery, 39

Barbecue
4Rivers Smokehouse, 43
Harry & Larry's Bar-B-Que, 194
Keller's Real Smoked Bar-B-Q, 64

Brazilian
Nelore Churrascaria, 68
Pao Gostoso Bakery, 134
Texas De Brazil, 126

Breakfast/Brunch
Christo's Cafe, 114
Dexter's, 26, 60
Junior's Diner, 118
The Town House Restaurant, 211
White Wolf Cafe, 110

Burgers
The Crooked Spoon, 229
Graffiti Junktion, 28
Hamburger Mary's Bar & Grille, 29
Johnny's Fillin' Station and
   Johnny's Other Side, 83
Oblivion Taproom, 84
Pine Twenty2 17
Tap Room at Dubsdread, 113
Teak Neighborhood Grill, 139

Cajun
The Big Easy, 192
Emeril's Orlando, 130
King Cajun Crawfish, 93
Tibby's New Orleans Kitchen, 72

Caribbean
Caribbean Sunshine Bakery, 193
Caribbean Supercenter Grocery, 198
Norman's, 214
Singh's Roti Shop and Bar, 195

Chinese or Dim Sum
Eastern Pearl, 218
Golden Lotus Chinese, 219
Imperial Dynasty Chinese
   Restaurant and Lounge, 177

Magic Wok, 132
Ming Court Wok & Grille, 133
Ming's Bistro, 95
Tasty Wok BBQ & Noodle
   House, 101
Teriyaki House, 197
Trey Yuen Chinese Restaurant, 140

Coffeehouse
Austin's Coffee, 52
Barnie's CoffeeKitchen, 52
Drunken Monkey Coffee Bar, 106
Stardust Video & Coffee, 120

Continental European
Cafe Rouge, 174
Chatham's Place, 144
Citricos at Disney's Grand Floridian
   Resort & Spa, 161
The Venetian Room, 58

Cuban/Latin
Black Bean Deli, 55
Cuban Sandwiches on the Run, 175
Padrino's Cuban Bistro, 215
Rincon Cubano Cafeteria, 70
Rolando's Cuban Restaurant, 183
Yaya's Cuban Cafe and Bakery, 85

Deli, Sandwiches
C & S Brisket Bus, 228

Desserts
The Batter Bowl Truck, 227
Beard Papa's Fresh'n Natural Cream
    Puffs, 173
The Dessert Lady, 25
Jeremiah's Italian Ice, 208
Peterbrooke Chocolatier, 77
Rainbow Sno-Cones, 118
The Yum Yum Cupcake Truck, 233

Ethiopian
Nile Ethiopian Restaurant, 133

French
The Bistro on Park Avenue, 54
Cafe Rouge Express, 229
Chez Vincent, 57
Croissant Gourmet, 58
Le Cafe de Paris, 150
Le Coq au Vin, 80
Les Chefs de France at Disney's
    Epcot, 163
Les Petits Pleasures, 112
Paris Bistro, 68

Gastropub
David's Club Bar & Grill, 130
The Rusty Spoon, 18

German
Hollerbach's Magnolia Square
    Market, 185
Hollerbach's Willow Tree Cafe, 170
The Ravenous Pig, 47

Greek
Cypriana Restaurant, 175
The Greek Corner, 109
Olympia Restaurant, 209
Taverna Opa, 138
Zorba's Greek Taverna, 142

Hot Dogs
Hot Dog Heaven, 82

Indian
Aashirwad Indian Cuisine, 126
Anmol Indian Cuisine, 205
Bombay Cafe, 217
Kohinoor Indian Cuisine, 178
Passage to India, 135
Saffron Indian Cuisine, 153

Irish

Fiddler's Green Irish Pub and
Eatery, 63

The Harp and Celt Restaurant and
Irish Pub, 30

Raglan Road Irish Pub and
Restaurant, 164

Italian

All Italian Market & Deli, 224

Antonio's La Fiamma Ristorante and
Antonio's Market and Cafe, 50

Cafe Trastevere, 21

Cala Bella, 129

Cavallari Gourmet, 212

Christini's Ristorante Italiano, 148

Enzo's Restaurant on the Lake, 176

Gino's Pizza Italian Restaurant, 207

Il Pescatore, 83

Juliana's, 114

La Luce By Donna Scala at the
Hilton Bonnet Creek, 158

Nick's Italian Kitchen, 33

Prato, 46

Primo by Melissa Kelly, 216

Ravalia's Pasta Bar & Italian
Rotisserie, 182

Stefano's Trattoria, 183

Terramia Wine Bar and
Restaurant, 184

Japanese

Amura, 20

Bayridge Sushi and
Steakhouse, 206

California Grill, 161

Dragonfly, 149

Funky Monkey Wine Company,
91, 155

Hanamizuki Japanese, 124

Japan Food Aki Restaurant, 131

Kobé Japanese Steakhouse
& Sushi Bar, 177

Mikado Japanese Cuisine, 220

Nagoya Sushi, 151

RanGetsu Restaurant & Orchid
Lounge, 182

Seito Sushi, 119

Shari Sushi Lounge, 35

Shìn Japanese Cuisine, 100

Sushi Lola's, 121

Sushi Pop Seafood and
Chops, 203

Sushi Tomi, 222

Jewish/Bagels
Bagel King, 174

Korean
Bee Won Korean Cuisine, 147
Korea House Restaurant, 179
Korean BBQ Taco Box, 231
Shin Jung Korean Restaurant, 100
Woo Sung Oriental Food Mart, 115

Latin
Arepas El Cacao, 227
Fortuna Bakery & Cafe, 209
Guavate Puerto Rican Eatery &
   Bistro, 202
La Empanada Food Truck, 231
Mi Viejo San Juan, 202
Pio Pio Restaurant, 136
Q'Kenan Venezuelan
   Restaurante, 136

Mediterranean
Aladdin's Cafe, 172
Cedar's Restaurant of
   Orlando, 147
Maxine's on Shine, 107
Mediterranean Blue, 32
Mediterranean Deli, 65

Middle East Market, 220
Tony's Deli, 102

Mexican
Agave Azul, 127
Beto's Mexican, 217
Border Grill, 128
Paxia Alta Cocina Mexicana, 115

Modern American
Big Wheel Food Truck, 227
The Boheme, 16
Chef's Table at the Edgewater
   Hotel, 189
Citrus Restaurant, 23
Cress Restaurant, 168
5 Gastronomy, 229
Fork in the Road, 230
Funky Monkey Wine Company,
   91, 155
Hillstone, 44
Hue Restaurant, 31
K Restaurant, 112
Luma on Park, 45
Napa at The Peabody, 125
The Ravenous Pig, 47
Seasons 52 Fresh Grill, 154
The Table, 145

The Tasting Room at the
Chef's Table at the
Edgewater, 190
Victoria and Albert's at Disney's
Grand Floridian Resort &
Spa, 159
Vines Grille & Wine Bar, 155
Vitale Spa Cafe, 223
Wolfgang Puck Cafe, 167

Organic
Hoover's Market and Sunflower
Cafe, 186

Pizza
Armando's Cucina Italiana &
Pizzeria, 51
Gino's Pizza & Brew, 28
Goodfella's Pizzeria, 207
Lazy Moon Pizza, 208
Pizzeria Del-Dio, 84
Pizzeria Valdiano, 69
Terramia Brick Oven Pizza, 184

Polish
Anna's Polish Restaurant, 49
Polonia Polish Restaurant, 181

Pub Food
Downtown PourHouse, 27
Nona Tap Room, 222
Shipyard Brew Pub, 71

Russian
Lacomka Russian Bakery & Deli, 76

Sandwiches
Beefy King, 106
Bikes, Beans & Bordeaux, 117
Brianto's Original Hoagies, 201
Dylan's Deli, 60
Earl of Sandwich, 162
Green Lemon Cafe, 63
Italian Beefstro, 37
LaSpada's Original Philly Cheese
Steaks & Hoagies, 180
903 Mills Market, 86
Perrotti's NY Deli, 195
Pom Pom's Teahouse and
Sandwicheria, 98
Press 101 Sandwich & Wine
Bar, 152
That Deli!, 172
Virgin Olive Market, 37
Yellow Dog Eats Cafe, 191

Seafood

Big Fin Seafood Kitchen, 143
Cityfish Restaurant, 24
Flying Fish Cafe, 163
Fresh on the Fly, 169
Lee & Rick's Oyster Bar, 194
MoonFish, 150
The Oceanaire Seafood Room, 152
Todd English's bluezoo, 166
Winter Park Fish Company, 72

Soul Food

Angel's Soulfood and BBQ, 173

Steak House

A Land Remembered, 123
Bull & Bear Steakhouse at Waldorf
   Astoria, 156
Fleming's Steakhouse & Wine
   Bar, 149
Kres Chophouse, 17
Linda's La Cantina, 81
Shula's Steak House, 165
Spencer's for Steaks and
   Chops, 137
Stonewood Grill & Tavern, 137
Vito's Chop House, 141

Sushi/Japanese

Amura, 20
Bayridge Sushi and
   Steakhouse, 206
California Grill, 161
Dragonfly, 149
Funky Monkey Wine Company,
   91, 155
Hanamizuki Japanese, 124
Japan Food Aki Restaurant, 131
Kobé Japanese Steakhouse & Sushi
   Bar, 177
Mikado Japanese Cuisine, 220
Nagoya Sushi, 151
RanGetsu Restaurant & Orchid
   Lounge, 181
Seito Sushi, 119
Shari Sushi Lounge, 35
Shìn Japanese Cuisine, 19
Sushi Lola's, 121
Sushi Pop Seafood and Chops, 203
Sushi Tomi, 222

Tapas/Spanish

Cafe Tu Tu Tango, 128
Ceviche Tapas Bar & Restaurant, 23
El Bodegon, 61

mi Tomatina Paella Bar, 66

Tex-Mex
Cocina 214 Restaurant & Bar, 58
Gringos Locos, 29
Prickly Pear Steakhouse, 34

Thai
Napasorn Thai, 33
NaraDeva Thai Restaurant, 221
Royal Thai, 210
SEA Thai Restaurant, 99
Thai Basil, 205
Thai Blossom, 197

Turkish
Anatolia Orlando, 146
Bosphorous Turkish Cuisine, 42

Vegetarian
Artichoke Red Vegan Market, 108
Bombay Cafe, 217
Cafe 118 Degrees Living Cuisine
   Cafe & Juice Bar, 56
Dandelion Communitea Cafe, 90
Ethos Vegan Kitchen, 62

Garden Cafe, 91
Raphsodic Bakery Urban Pastry Art
   House, 99

Vietnamese
Ánh Hông, 88
Banh Mi Nha Trang, 89
Boston Bakery & Cafe, 89
Lac Viet Bistro, 94
Pho 88, 96
Pho Hoa Noodle Soup
   Restaurant, 97
Pho Vinh Restaurant, 97
Yum-Mì Sandwiches, 102

Wine Bar
Eola Wine Company, 27
Press 101 Sandwich & Wine
   Bar, 152
Tim's Wine Market, 110
The Wine Room on Park
   Avenue, 73

Wings
Flyers Wings & Grill, 193

Appendix B: Food Events

January

Vietnamese Lunar New Year Festival, facebook.com/miss vietnamflorida, asiatrendmagazine.com/AT_events.html. This Vietnamese cultural new year festival, hosted by the vibrant Vietnamese American community of central Florida, features children's games, an illustrious pageant contest for Miss Vietnam Florida, cultural performances, music, and booths with Vietnamese ethnic street food, such as *banh mi* sub sandwiches, rice porridge congee, grilled beef on a stick, sugarcane juice, and more. The food is as close to Vietnam as you can get. Check *Asia Trend Magazine*'s calendar of events for the exact date, as it varies each year.

February

SeaWorld Bands Brew and BBQ, seaworldparks.com/en/sea world-orlando/Events/Bands-Brew-and-BBQ. Throughout February and March, SeaWorld theme park puts on this event featuring local Orlando barbecue vendors, nearly 50 craft beers, grilled food, and rock and country music. The music and food are both included in the price of general admission.

Orlando Chili Cook-Off, eventsforchangeinc.org/events/orlando-chili-cook-off. The Orlando Chili Cook-Off at Blue Jacket Park in Baldwin Park is a chili lover's delight; thousands attend each year. With dozens of competing teams, the event charges an entry fee that includes all the chili you can sample, live music, a kids' zone, and the chance to vote for your favorite chili in the People's Choice Award. Make sure to get there early, as the chili does run out in the late afternoon. A portion of the proceeds benefits Special Olympics Florida, the Wounded Warrior Project, A Gift for Teaching, and the Lone Sailor Memorial.

March

Florida Strawberry Festival, flstrawberryfestival.com. Started in 1930, this popular festival running throughout March features strawberries from Plant City, Florida, at season's peak. At the festival you will find delicious strawberry short-cakes, a beauty pageant for the Florida Strawberry Festival Queen, carnival rides, fresh strawberries, jams and preserves, entertainment, music, and more. Drop by the Parkesdale Farm Market nearby to pick up some fresh fruit and try their world-famous shortcake.

Downtown Food and Wine Festival, downtownfoodandwine
fest.cbslocal.com. The Downtown Orlando Food and Wine Festival,
produced in conjunction with the Florida Restaurant and Lodging
Association, is a hugely popular event at Orlando landmark Lake
Eola that features over 30 of Orlando's best restaurants with over
100 menu items, wine stations, live cooking demonstrations featuring local and national chefs, a specialty drinks
station, a dessert station, and a portable sports bar.

Food and Wine Festival at Baldwin Park, cff.org/
Chapters/Orlando. This event, hosted by the Orlando
chapter of the Cystic Fibrosis Foundation, helps to raise
funds to find a cure for the disease. Dozens of fine-dining
and local restaurants as well as the Orlando mayor participate in
this worthwhile event in scenic downtown Baldwin Park.

April

**Celebration Exotic Car Festival's Portofino Food and Wine
Party,** celebrationexoticcars.com. The Portofino Food and Wine
Party at Loews Portofino Bay Hotel, Universal Orlando, is a part of
the Celebration Exotic Car Festival, which benefits children's charities including Make-a-Wish, Special Olympics, and Arnold Palmer
Children's Hospital. In the past nationally celebrated chefs such as
Thomas Keller and Paul Bocuse, and chefs from the Bravo television
show *Top Chef* were at the event preparing beautiful dishes for the
upscale crowds. Highlighting the evening, along the waterfront

setting modeled after the famous Italian seaside town, is a display of Ferraris, Lamborghinis, Nissan GT-Rs, and other exotic cars, live music, performance artists, silent and live auctions, and much more.

Taste of Winter Park, winterpark.org/content/taste-winter-park. The Winter Park Chamber of Commerce hosts this evening event of culinary excellence at the Winter Park Farmers' Market. Taste creations from the area's top chefs, bakers, caterers, brewers and more from 40 different purveyors. Awards are given out for Best Dessert, Best Booth, Best Entree, Best Side Dish and Best Healthy Dish.

Florida Film Festival, floridafilmfestival.com. Every year the Florida Film Festival premieres the best in current independent and foreign cinema. For several years, the festival has celebrated special food-centric events, bringing together a love of film and food. Their opening-night party features some of the best local chefs in the area and their creative, delicious dishes, all to live music. During the festival, a foodie-related panel discussion takes place and the film schedule lineup often includes a few foodie-themed films.

Taste of College Park, collegeparkrotary.org/programs/taste-of-college-park. The Rotary Club of College Park hosts this event featuring over 15 different tasting stations providing food, desserts, wine, and beer. At the gorgeous historic Dubsdread Golf Course in College Park, patrons at the event not only sample some great local food and drinks, but also help to raise funds for organizations, such as the Ronald McDonald House, that impact the College Park community.

Cattle Barons' Ball for the American Cancer Society at Rosen Shingle Creek Resort, cattlebaronsballorlando.com. The Cattle Barons' Ball, the signature gala supporting the American Cancer Society–Central Florida Unit, features an evening of western-themed fund-raising in the ongoing pursuit of a cure for cancer. Guests taste-test culinary creations from local restaurants including Jack's Place, A Land Remembered, Everglades, Cala Bella, B. B. King's, K Restaurant and Wine Bar, Cress–Deland, and more. The event also features local brewery Orlando Brewing Co. and live music.

Taste of Pointe Orlando, pointeorlando.com/taste. The Taste of Pointe Orlando to benefit Florida Hospital's Esophageal Cancer Research Program features unlimited food samplings from some of the venue's award-winning restaurants. Some of the participating restaurants include B. B. King's Blues Club, Ben & Jerry's, Copper Canyon Grill, Cuba Libre Restaurant & Rum Bar, Funky Monkey Wine Company, Maggiano's Little Italy, Pizzeria Valdiano, Taverna Opa, The Pub Orlando, and Tommy Bahama's Restaurant & Bar.

Bacchus Bash, bacchusbash.org. This charitable street-party event produced by the Central Florida Hotel and Lodging Association Foundation benefits local hospitality education and features 60-plus food and beverage vendors, 4 continuous entertainment stages, and a silent auction of 200 items.

American Pie Council's Great American Pie Festival, piecouncil.org. This popular, free-admission festival hosted in downtown Celebration has all the activities that have made it a family favorite, including demonstrations, children's activities, and pie-eating contests. The highlight of the festival is the Never Ending Pie Buffet, featuring pies from all over the country as well as a few of the champion pies from the festival.

Festival of Chocolate, FestivalofChocolate.com. The Festival of Chocolate includes the area's best chocolate and confection companies selling everything chocolate from truffles, cakes, crepes, and cupcakes to cookies, brownies, and gelato. Chocolate savory items including mocha chili, chocolate barbecue sauce, seasonings, coffee, and meat rubs are also featured. Throughout the weekend, award-winning pastry chefs and chocolatiers host interactive demonstrations sharing techniques and tricks of the trade while live competitions give breathtaking artistic chocolate sculptures a tasty twist.

A Taste of Compassion, atasteofcompassion.org. This gala street party supports two of the biggest organizations in downtown Orlando whose only purpose is to help and support the area's homeless population: Central Care Mission and Compassion Corner. The event is a collaboration of the two ministries and some of Orlando's best chefs and restaurants, including members of the Central Florida chapter of the American Culinary Federation. There are also street performances, musicians, stilt walkers, jugglers, and mimes to entertain during the event.

May

Winter Garden Harvest Festival, wintergardenharvestfestival
.com. This local event features a local, producer-only farmers'
market adjacent to the city's existing Saturday market and offers
an assortment of local food, craft vendors, farm- and food-related
demonstrations, family-friendly activities, and live entertainment.
Neighbors and visitors alike have the opportunity to interact with
local food purveyors, gardeners, and food experts throughout the
day. *Edible Orlando Magazine* also hosts "Sips and Skylines," a
rooftop garden tour of Green Sky Growers and a cocktail tasting
and mixology demo in Winter Garden's new restaurant, Al Fresco.
Following the daytime festivities, a farm-to-table dining event is
held inside Winter Garden's beautiful downtown pavilion, highlighting West Orange County chefs' local, seasonal farm-fresh ingredients, as well as some of central Florida's best microbrews.

Orlando Weekly's **Orlando Restaurant Week,** orlandorestau
rantweek.com. Prepare to dine on some wonderful signature dishes
around Orlando and at a great price. Pace yourself. During this
week, local restaurants feature 2- and 3-course prix-fixe meals for
lunch and dinner at discounted prices.

Zellwood Sweet Corn Festival, zellwoodcornfestival.com/index
.html. This festival north of Orlando in Apopka celebrates with all
things corn including sweet corn on the cob, corn dogs, kettle corn,
and more. Music performances, carnival rides, and other entertainment are also available, all benefiting local area projects.

Chef's Gala Benefiting Heart of Florida United Way, chefs gala.org. This event hosted at Walt Disney World's Epcot World Showplace features mouthwatering cuisine from more than 20 of central Florida's top chefs. It also includes thoughtfully paired wines, a sparkling wine and martini bar reception, fabulous desserts, live music, and an elegant silent auction. Proceeds from Chef's Gala support United Way programs that provide shelter, food, and other basic necessities to central Floridians in desperate need.

June

Wine Quest, questinc.org/events.html#. Hosted at the JW Marriott Orlando, Grande Lakes, and prepared by the wonderful culinary team there, Wine Quest is an event where guests can sample and sip on nearly 200 wines from around the world accompanied by a gourmet assortment of street food–inspired bites. At the grand tasting and auction, savor an urban chic 5-course wine dinner at the Premier Dining Experience, and partici-pate in exciting live and silent auctions. All proceeds go to benefit Quest Inc., a nonprofit that works to transform the lives of thousands of individuals with disabilities, enabling them to become more indepen-dent and to achieve their dreams.

LakeRidge Winery & Vineyards's Annual Harvest Festival, lakeridgewinery.com/Events. LakeRidge Winery's flagship festival has the ever-popular annual stomping of the grapes and is loads of fun for the entire family. All ages are welcome to participate. Over 80 local artists' and crafters' displays and live music can be enjoyed during the entire weekend. LakeRidge wine, beer, soft drinks, and a variety of food is available for purchase, along with complimentary winery tours and tastings.

August

Share Our Strength's Taste of the Nation Orlando, ce.strength .org/events/taste-nation-orlando. This is one of my favorite culinary events of the year, where guests sample delectable specialties and creative culinary sensations prepared by chefs from central Florida's leading restaurants, including The Ravenous Pig, K Restaurant and Wine Bar, Rosen Shingle Creek's A Land Remembered, and more. Don't miss Chef Jean-Louis of the Royal Plaza's bananas Foster dessert. All ticket sales go toward ending childhood hunger.

September

Long & Scott Farms' Fall Corn Maze Adventures, longand scottfarms.com/fall_maze.html. This local farm, which also provides the sweet corn for the Zellwood Corn Festival, is bio-friendly, with no use of synthetic fertilizers or pesticides for their crops. Open each fall, this maze adventure includes 6 acres of corn mazes, a

60-foot super slide, hayrides, and play areas for the family. Check out Scott's Country Market and Cafe while you are there and pick up some corn to take home. The Maze Adventures usually last from mid-Sept to mid-Dec.

Visit Orlando's Magical Dining Month, visit orlando.com/magicaldining. Visit Orlando, the area's official tourism and convention bureau, hosts this annual monthly event where the finest restaurants all over Orlando feature 3-course prix-fixe meals for just $30, oftentimes a terrific deal, with $1 going toward charity. This event is of great value especially since a few of the entrees would merit over $30 alone on a regular night. Look for participating restaurants on the list, and when you dine, ask your server for the Magical Dining Month menu and enjoy.

Epcot International Food and Wine Festival, disneyworld .disney.go.com/parks/epcot/special-events/epcot-international-food-and-wine-festival. Running for 45 days from late September to mid-November, the Epcot International Food and Wine Festival at Walt Disney World serves up international cuisine, culture, and live entertainment from 6 continents, with more than 25 international marketplaces featuring tapas-size portions paired with beer, wine, and inventive cocktails. A craft beers marketplace serves up 8 select brews for sampling. The festival requires Epcot admission, and some experiences during the festival require advance reservations. Every Saturday evening during the festival, World Showplace opens its doors to Party for the Senses, a food- and wine-tasting extravaganza that continues to grow in popularity and reputation.

October

A Taste of Thornton Park, thorntonpark.org/A_Taste_of_ Thornton_Park.html. This event, put on by the Thornton Park Neighborhood Association, features over 40 local food and drink vendors including samples and sips from restaurants Hue, Dexter's, Cityfish, Shari Sushi Lounge, and newcomers Nick's Italian Kitchen, Prickly Pear, and much more. Proceeds go to benefit Outreach Love Inc., an organization that tutors and mentors at-risk children in the Parramore area in downtown Orlando.

Latin Food and Wine Festival, latinfoodandwine.com. The Hispanic Chamber of Commerce of Metro Orlando hosts this culinary event during Hispanic Heritage Month, drawing an audience of 5,000 to 7,000 wine and food lovers. The Latin Food and Wine Festival is a 2-day, premier wine and culinary festival with a Latin twist where patrons can enjoy live entertainment, a silent auction, and dishes prepared by local restaurants bringing out the best of Latin cuisine in Orlando.

Swan and Dolphin Food and Wine Classic, swandolphin foodandwineclassic.com. Set to coincide with the Epcot International Food and Wine Festival, the Swan and Dolphin Food and Wine Classic features beverage seminars, food tastings, and live entertainment. At the tasting booths, you can stroll the causeway on Crescent Lake to immerse yourself in a culinary festival with live music and tastings from Swan and Dolphin's restaurants, including Shula's Steak House, Il Mulino New York Trattoria, and Todd English's bluezoo. Beverage seminar topics include wine blending, modern mixology, beer, and sake.

November

Slow Food Orlando's Eat Local Week, eatlocalweek .com. This weeklong event features everything you can dream about eating local in Orlando: Select restaurants that feature local ingredients offer their prix-fixe menus highlighting these items during the week, and Slow Food Orlando organizes farm and bakery tours to connect local consumers with local farmers and producers. The week is meant to emphasize that eating local in central Florida not only is possible, it's also delicious—and helps local restaurants, farmers, and artisans develop lasting, mutually beneficial relationships and build consumer awareness of local food and farmers while promoting reconnection with family and friends around the dinner table.

Winter Park Harvest Festival, winterparkharvestfestival.com. This hugely popular event produced by A Local Folkus features a "producer-only" farmers' market from local farmers, gardeners, and artisan producers; seminars, workshops, and roundtables focused on the local food system; cooking demonstrations; DIY gardening and Urban Ag sessions; a mobile community garden; youth-focused sessions; crafts; bluegrass and folk music; and much more. There is also a farm-to-table dinner consisting of locally sourced foods prepared by some of Winter Park's most talented chefs, and countless artisan-produced local food items available at the market

Orlando Greek Fest, orlandogreekfest.com. Hosted by the Holy Trinity Greek Orthodox in Maitland, this Greek festival showcases fun for the whole family, featuring authentic Greek foods, dancing, live music, church tours, iconography presentations, and much more. Try their baklava, *arni psito*, a Greek-style sliced boneless leg of lamb baked in an oven, moussaka, and other authentic Greek delights.

Orlando Japan Festival, orlandojapanfestival.com. This festival, put on by the local Orlando Japanese community, features not only taiko drumming, Japanese dance performances, arts, and crafts, but also delicious street food offerings from local Japanese restaurants. Proceeds are donated to Orlando Hoshuko (formerly Japanese Language School of Orlando).

Battle of the Parks, facebook.com/battleoftheparks. This annual event pits chefs from the College Park, Winter Park, and Thornton Park neighborhoods in an *Iron Chef*–like battle where each chef has 40 minutes to transform a secret ingredient into a plated entree for a panel of celebrity judges. The event's proceeds go to charities sponsored by each of the neighborhood restaurants. In the past, K Restaurant and Wine Bar represented College Park, The Ravenous Pig represented Winter Park, and Hue restaurant represented Thornton Park.

Index

A

Aashirwad Indian Cuisine, 126

Agave Azul, 127

Aladdin's Cafe, 172

A Land Remembered, 123, 265

All Italian Market & Deli, 224

American Pie Council's Great
   American Pie Festival, 302

Amura, 20

Anatolia Orlando, 146

Ancient Olive, The, 75

Angel's Soulfood and BBQ, 173

Ánh Hông, 88

Anmol Indian Cuisine, 205

Anna's Polish Restaurant, 49

Antonio's La Fiamma
   Ristorante, 50

Antonio's Market and Cafe, 50

Arepas El Cacao, 227

Armando's Cucina Italiana &
   Pizzeria, 51

Artichoke Red Vegan
   Market, 108

Audubon Park Community
   Market, 9

Austin's Coffee, 52

B

Bacchus Bash, 302

Bagel King, 174

Bake Me a Cake, 185

Bananas Modern American
   Diner, 88

Banh Mi Nha Trang, 89

Barnie's CoffeeKitchen, 52,
   258, 259

Batter Bowl Truck, The, 227

Battle of the Parks, 311

Bayridge Sushi and
   Steakhouse, 206

Beard Papa's Fresh'n Natural
   Cream Puffs, 173

Beck Brother's Blueberries, 12

Beefy King, 106

Bee Won Korean Cuisine, 147

Bento Cafe, 20

Beto's Mexican, 217

Big Easy, The, 192

Big Fin Seafood Kitchen, 143

Big Wheel Food Truck, 227, 283

Bikes, Beans & Bordeaux, 117

Bistro on Park Avenue, The, 54

Black Bean Deli, 55

Blue Bird Bake Shop, 117

Boheme, The, 16

Boma—Flavors of Africa at
    Disney's Animal Kingdom
    Lodge, 160

Bombay Cafe, 217

Border Grill, 128

Bosphorous Turkish Cuisine, 42

Boston Bakery & Cafe, 89

Brianto's Original Hoagies, 201

Briarpatch Restaurant and Ice
    Cream Parlor, 55

bubble tea, 92

Bull & Bear Steakhouse at Waldorf
    Astoria, 156

C

Cafe 118 Degrees Living Cuisine
    Cafe & Juice Bar, 56

Cafe Rouge, 174

Cafe Rouge Express, 229

Cafe Trastevere, 21

Cafe Tu Tu Tango, 128

Cala Bella, 129

California Grill, 161

Caribbean Sunshine Bakery, 193

Caribbean Supercenter
    Grocery, 198

Cattle Barons' Ball for the
    American Cancer Society, 302

Cavallari Gourmet, 212

Cedar's Restaurant of
    Orlando, 147

Celebration Exotic Car Festival's
    Portofino Food and Wine
    Party, 300

Ceviche Tapas Bar &
    Restaurant, 23

Charlie's Gourmet Pastries, 82

Chatham's Place, 144

Chef's Gala Benefiting Heart of
    Florida United Way, 305

Chef's Table at the Edgewater
    Hotel, 189

Chewy Boba Company, 92

Chez Vincent, 57

Chowhound.com, 8

Christini's Ristorante
  Italiano, 148
Christo's Cafe, 114
Citricos at Disney's Grand Floridian
  Resort & Spa, 161
Citrus Restaurant, 23
Cityfish Restaurant, 24
City of Maitland Farmers'
  Market, 11
Cocina 214 Restaurant & Bar, 58
College Park Farmers' Market, 9
cooking classes, 95
Cress Restaurant, 168, 246
Croissant Gourmet, 59
Crooked Spoon, The, 229
C & S Brisket Bus, 228
Cuban Sandwiches on the
  Run, 175
Cypriana Restaurant, 175

D

Dandelion Communitea Cafe, 90
date night itineraries, 22
David's Club Bar & Grill, 130
Dessert Lady, The, 25
Dexter's, 26, 60
Dong A Supermarket, 103

Donut King, 189
Downtown Food and Wine
  Festival, 300
Downtown Orlando Farmers'
  Market, 11
Downtown PourHouse, 27
Dragonfly, 149
Droolius.com, 7
Drunken Monkey Coffee Bar, 106
Dylan's Deli, 60

E

Earl of Sandwich, 162
Eastern Pearl, 218
Eastside Asian Market, 212
EatLocalOrlando.com, 7
Eat More Produce, 75
Edible Orlando, 5
El Bodegon, 61
Emeril's Orlando, 130
Emeril's Tchoup Chop, 131
Enzo's Restaurant on the
  Lake, 176
Eola Wine Company, 27
Epcot International Food and
  Wine Festival, 307
Ethos Vegan Kitchen, 62

F

Festival of Chocolate, 303

Fiddler's Green Irish Pub and
  Eatery, 63

1st Oriental Supermarket, 198

5 Gastronomy, 229

Fleming's Steakhouse & Wine
  Bar, 149

Florida Film Festival, 301

Florida Strawberry Festival, 299

Fluker, Anjali, 6

Flyer's Wings & Grill, 193

Flying Fish Cafe, 163

Food and Wine Festival at
  Baldwin Park, 300

Forkful.net, 7

Fork in the Road, 230, 267

Fortuna Bakery & Cafe, 219

4Rivers Smokehouse, 43, 260,
  261, 262

Freshfields Farm, 85

Fresh on the Fly, 169

Funky Monkey Wine Company,
  91, 155

G

Garden Cafe, 91

Gindin, Rona, 6

Gino's Pizza & Brew, 28

Gino's Pizza Italian
  Restaurant, 207

Gokudo, 230

Golden Lotus Chinese, 219

Goodfella's Pizzeria, 207

Graffiti Junktion, 28

Greek Corner, The, 109

Green Lemon Cafe, 63

Gringos Locos, 29

Guavate Puerto Rican Eatery
  & Bistro, 202

H

Hamburger Mary's Bar &
  Grille, 29

Hanamizuki Japanese, 124

Harp and Celt Restaurant and
  Irish Pub, 30

Harry & Larry's Bar-B-Que, 194

Hawkers Asian Street Fare, 92

Hayes, Joseph, 5

Hillstone, 44

Hollerbach's Magnolia Square
  Market, 185

Hollerbach's Willow Tree Cafe, 170

Homegrown Local Food
   Cooperative, 11
Hoover's Market & Sunflower
   Cafe, 186
Hot Dog Heaven, 82
Hue Restaurant, 31

I

Il Pescatore, 83
Imperial Dynasty Chinese
   Restaurant and Lounge,
   177, 264
International Food Club
   Specialty Food Market
   & Cafe, 225
Italian Beefstro, 37

J

Japan Food Aki Restaurant, 131
Jeremiah's Italian Ice, 208
Jiko, 157
Johnny's Fillin' Station, 83
Johnny's Other Side, 83
Joseph, Scott, 5
Juliana's, 114
Junior's Diner, 118

K

Kapher, Holly, 5
Kara, Faiyaz, 5
Keller's Real Smoked Bar-B-Q, 64
King Cajun Crawfish, 93
Kobé Japanese Steakhouse
   & Sushi Bar, 177
Kohinoor Indian Cuisine, 178
Korea House Restaurant, 179
Korean BBQ Taco Box, 231
Kres Chophouse, 17
K Restaurant, 112

L

Lacomka Russian Bakery
   & Deli, 76
Lac Viet Bistro, 94
La Empanada Food Truck,
   231, 285
LakeRidge Winery & Vineyards's
   Annual Harvest Festival, 306
La Luce by Donna Scala at the
   Hilton Bonnet Creek, 158
LaSpada's Original Philly Cheese
   Steaks & Hoagies, 180
Latin Food and Wine
   Festival, 308

Lazy Moon Pizza, 208
Le Cafe de Paris, 150
Le Coq au Vin, 80, 238
Lee & Rick's Oyster Bar, 194
Le Macaron, 64
Les Chefs de France at Disney's
    Epcot, 163
Les Petits Pleasures, 112
Linda's La Cantina, 81
Lombardi's Seafood Market, 76
Long & Scott Farms' Fall Corn
    Maze Adventures, 306
Luma on Park, 45, 248, 251

M

Magic Wok, 132
Maxine's on Shine, 107
Meat House Neighborhood Butcher
    & Grocer, The, 77
Mediterranean Blue, 32
Mediterranean Deli, 65
MegaYummo.com, 6
Middle East Market, 220
Mikado Japanese Cuisine, 220
Ming Court Wok & Grille, 133
Ming's Bistro, 95
mi Tomatina Paella Bar, 66

Mi Viejo San Juan, 202
MoonFish, 150

N

Nagoya Sushi, 151
Napa at The Peabody, 125
Napasorn Thai, 33
NaraDeva Thai Restaurant, 221
Nelore Churrascaria, 68
Nick's Italian Kitchen, 33
Nile Ethiopian Restaurant, 133
903 Mills Market, 86
Nona Tap Room, 222
Norman's, 214

O

Oblivion Taproom, 84
Oceanaire Seafood Room, The, 152
Ohana, 164
Olympia Restaurant, 209
organic craft beers, 31
Orlando Brewing, 31
Orlando Business Journal, 6
Orlando Chili Cook-Off, 299
Orlando Greek Fest, 310
Orlando Japan Festival, 310
Orlando magazine, 5

Orlando Sentinel, 4
Orlando Weekly, 5

P

Padrino's Cuban Bistro, 215
Pao Gostoso Bakery, 134
Pappy's Patch U-Pick
 Strawberries, 12
Paris Bistro, 68
Passage to India, 135
Paxia Alta Cocina Mexicana, 115
Penzey's Spice, 77
Perrotti's NY Deli, 195
Peterbrooke Chocolatier, 77
Petty's Meat Market, 186
Pho 88, 96
Pho Hoa Noodle Soup
 Restaurant, 97
Pho Vinh Restaurant, 97
Phuoc Loc Tho Market, 104
Pine Twenty2, 17, 253, 255
Pio Pio Restaurant, 136
Pizzeria Del-Dio, 84
Pizzeria Valdiano, 69
Polonia Polish Restaurant, 181
Pom Pom's Teahouse and
 Sandwicheria, 98

Prato, 46, 250, 252
Press 101 Sandwich & Wine
 Bar, 152
Prickly Pear Steakhouse, 34
Primo by Melissa Kelly, 216

Q

Q'Kenan Venezuelan
 Restaurante, 136

R

Raglan Road Irish Pub and
 Restaurant, 164
Rainbow Sno-Cones, 118
RanGetsu Restaurant & Orchid
 Lounge, 181
Raphsodic Bakery Urban Pastry
 Art House, 99
Ravalia's Pasta Bar & Italian
 Rotisserie, 182
Ravenous Pig, The, 47, 240,
 242, 244, 245
Redlight Redlight, 119
Rincon Cubano Cafeteria, 70
Rolando's Cuban Restaurant, 183
Royal Thai, 210
Roy's, 153

Rusty Spoon, The, 18, 253, 255

S

Saffron Indian Cuisine, 153

Saigon Market, 104

Scott Joseph's Orlando Restaurant
    Guide, 5

Seasons 52 Fresh Grill, 154

SEA Thai Restaurant, 99

SeaWorld Bands Brew and
    BBQ, 298

Seito Sushi, 119

Share Our Strength's Taste of the
    Nation Orlando, 306

Shari Sushi Lounge, 35

Shìn Japanese Cuisine, 19

Shin Jung Korean Restaurant, 100

Shipyard Brew Pub, 71

Shula's Steak House, 165

Singh's Roti Shop and Bar, 195

Slow Food Orlando, 8

Slow Food Orlando's Eat Local
    Week, 309

Soggy Acres Pomelo Grove, 12

Spencer's for Steaks and
    Chops, 137

Spice & Tea Exchange, The, 78

Spooky's Black Cat Cafe and Milk
    District Marketplace, 107

Stardust Video & Coffee, 120

Stefano's Trattoria, 183

Stonewood Grill & Tavern, 137

Sundew Gardens, 12

Sunflower Cafe, 186

Sun Pearl Bakery, 196

Sushi Lola's, 121

Sushi Pop Seafood and Chops,
    203, 257

Sushi Tomi, 222

Swan and Dolphin Food and Wine
    Classic, 308

Sweet! by Good Golly Miss Holly,
    210, 270

T

Table, The, 145

Tako Cheena by Pom Pom, 101

Tap Room at Dubsdread, 113

Taste of College Park, 301

Taste of Compassion, A, 303

Taste of Pointe Orlando, 302

Taste of Thornton Park,
    A, 308

Taste of Winter Park, 301

Tasting Room at the Chef's Table at the Edgewater, The, 190

TastyChomps.com, 7

Tasty Tuesdays at the Milk District, 232

Tasty Wok BBQ & Noodle House, 101

Taverna Opa, 138

Teak Neighborhood Grill, 139

Technique Restaurant, 223

Teriyaki House, 197

Terramia Brick Oven Pizza, 184

Terramia Wine Bar and Restaurant, 184

Texas De Brazil, 126

Thai Basil, 205

Thai Blossom, 197

That Deli!, 172

310 Lakeside, 36

Tibby's New Orleans Kitchen, 72

Tien Hung Complete Oriental Foods & Gifts, 104

Tim's Wine Market, 110

Todd English's bluezoo, 166

Tony's Deli, 102

Town House Restaurant, The, 211

Treehouse Truck, 232

Trey Yuen Chinese Restaurant, 140

Truffles and Trifles, 95

U

U-Pick Blackberries, 12

Urbanspoon.com, 9

V

Venetian Room, The, 158

Victoria & Albert's at Disney's Grand Floridian Resort & Spa, 159

Vietnamese Lunar New Year Festival, 298

Vines Grille & Wine Bar, 155

Virgin Olive Market, 37

Visit Orlando's Magical Dining Month, 307

Vitale Spa Cafe, 223

Vito's Chop House, 141

W

White Wolf Cafe, 110

Whole Foods Market, 78, 142

Wine Quest, 305

Wine Room on Park Avenue, The, 73

Winter Garden Farmers' Market, 10
Winter Garden Harvest
   Festival, 304
Winter Park Farmers' Market, 10
Winter Park Fish Company, 72
Winter Park Food Truck Stop, 233
Winter Park Harvest Festival, 310
Wolfgang Puck Cafe, 167
Woo Sung Oriental Food Mart, 115

Y
Yalaha Bakery, 39

Yaya's Cuban Cafe and Bakery, 85
Yellow Dog Eats Cafe, 191
Yelp.com, 8
Young, Jessica Bryce, 5
Yum-Mì Sandwiches, 102
Yum Yum Cupcake Truck, The,
   233, 272

Z
Zellwood Sweet Corn Festival, 304
Zorba's Greek Taverna, 142

Regional Travel at Its Best